The HEALTHY HOUSEPLANT Book

Coen Gelein

The HEALTHY HOUSEPLANT Book

Coen Gelein

GUILD PUBLISHING LONDON

A QUINTET BOOK

This edition published 1987 by
Book Club Associates
by arrangement with Quintet Publishing Ltd

Originally printed as
Elseviers Groot Kamerplanten Boek
Elsevier Boeken BV © 1981

This book was designed and produced by
Quintet Publishing Limited
6 Blundell Street
London N7

Translated from the Dutch and typeset in Great Britain by
Moody Graphic International, London
Manufactured in Hong Kong by Regent Publishing Services Limited

Printed in Hong Kong by Leefung-Asco Printers Limited

CONTENTS

Abutilon

Flowers throughout the summer

The Abutilon is a bushy plant which will brighten up your home with magnificent deep-red, orange or yellow-ochre flowers throughout the summer till late into the autumn (fall). The plant belongs to the genus *Malva* of the mallow family and many of the mallows have been known as herbs for medicinal purposes for a very long time. Like the Abutilon, they have beautiful, delicate flowers and leaves which can be eaten as a vegetable.

Easy to grow

The Abutilon is an easy-to-grow plant which is at its best in the summer provided that the temperature and humidity are not too extreme. In the winter the plants have to rest. Place them to one side in the dry at a lower temperature.
The Abutilon is also an easy plant to take cuttings from. The best time to do this is from late winter to mid-spring. First bring the plant into strong overall growth by giving it more heat and water for a month beforehand (see page 169 cuttings). Stand the stem cuttings or intermediate cuttings for two to three weeks in a pot filled with peat compost under plastic foil or mist (see page 169). Sufficient roots will have grown by then for the cuttings to be grown in a normal pot.
After a single topping (see page 173 topping) pot them off, when they are again growing strongly, in a final pot containing ordinary potting compost. After four to six months you will have sturdy plants which will give magnificent flowers the following year.

Flowering and pruning

In winter keep them on short rations: little water and no fertilizer. In the growing season, however, they are very thirsty and need a small quantity of fertilizer once a week.
Although the plants should always be placed in full light, from early spring onwards you must shield them against very fierce sunlight. The Abutilon is a semi-shrub which flowers on the young shoots. In order to get plants of the right shape and to give them a rich bloom, spray the shoots once with growth inhibitor when they are about 2 in/5 cm long (see page 170 growth inhibitors).
The concentration of the latter depends on the strength with which the shoots are growing. Repeat the treatment after 14 days if they are still coming through. Move the plants into the full light in this condition in the spring.
Then prune them down to the old wood, paying close attention to the shape. If you treat an Abutilon like this, you can count on it giving you magnificent blooms throughout the summer.

Abutilon "Golden Fleece"

'Golden Fleece'

A splendid Abutilon with yellow flowers.

'Fire-bell'

A noted Abutilon with fiery red flowers. The cultivated Abutilons are crosses of wild species such as the Abutilon darwinii and the Abutilon striatum.

'Gold Prince'

"Gold" refers not to the flowers, which are red, but to the leaves.
Multi-coloured leaves on Abutilons are due to the presence of a naturally occurring, harmless virus. Abutilon striatum "Thompsonii" is an example of one of these variegated hybrids.

Belgian flag

This plant owes its name to the three different colours of the flowers. The Abutilon megapotamicum "Variegatum", to give the Belgian flag its official name, is found mainly as a flowering hanging plant. It is also sometimes grown as a graft onto the stem of an Abutilon striatum.

Abutilon "Fire-bell"

Treatment table

	cutting	growth	rest
pot	3 in/7 cm	4-4½ in 10-11 cm	—
soil	peat compost	RHP	—
feeding	none	1tsp compound fertilizer per pt water/ 3g per litre	none
watering	frequently	frequently	infrequently
temperature	68-72°F 20-22°C	64-68°F/18-20°C max. 77°F/25°C	50°F/10°C
rel. humidity	95%	70-80%	70%
light	plenty	plenty	plenty
flowers	—	early spring- early autumn (fall) Cyclocel	—

special instructions shield against excessively fierce sun

Abutilon "Belgian Flag"

Acalypha hispida

Acalypha hispida
This red-flowering Acalypha has a long inflorescence or catkin, to which it owes its common name, "cat's tail". The stinging nettle-type leaf can be clearly seen, from which the name Acalypha unjustly comes.

Acalypha wilkesiana "Musaica"

Acalypha wilkesiana 'Musaica'
This species is grown mainly for its leaves.
The name reflects this: the leaf is a mosaic of brown-red, orange, pink and green.

Acalypha wilkesiana 'Hamiltoniana'
A variety cultivated by Hamilton selected particularly for its pretty dark-red leaves. The leaf edges of this variety are strongly indented. Acalypha species that are grown for their leaves have small and unsightly catkins of no decorative value.

Acalypha hispida in the wild in Java

A noted family
The Acalypha hispida is a member of the Spurge family, which includes many noted members , such as Christ's Thorn and Euphorbia pseudocactus, which, as the name implies, closely resembles a cactus. The poinsettia, or Christmas Star, is also a spurge.
The name Acalypha comes from the Greek kalephe, which means stinging nettle. Although the plant has no effect of this kind, its leaves certainly bear some resemblance to those of a stinging nettle. Hispida means rough-haired, shaggy, bristly and refers to the inflorescence.

A difficult guest
Acalypha comes originally from New Guinea where it flourishes in the hot, humid climate. This means that it must be kept in a light, sunny and warm room. It also likes high humidity and is therefore difficult to keep in a centrally-heated room. If the air is too dry, the leaves shrivel. The lower leaves fall off and the plant can catch all kinds of diseases such as red-spider mite (see page 174 red-spider mite). When you are taking cuttings remember the importance of humidity. Take cuttings from stock plants in late winter to early spring (see page 169 cuttings). Place the cuttings under plastic foil in a pot or tray filled with a mixture of peat compost and sharp sand. After three weeks the cuttings will have sufficient roots to be planted in a final pot. Place two cuttings in a 4 in/9 cm pot containing a nutritious and substantial potting compost. A month later, if all goes well, the plant will flower with two or more "catkins".
To get a beautiful branching plant, you must top the young shoots (see page 173 topping). You will then get much shorter catkins than with untopped plants. You know yourself which you find more beautiful: many short catkins or a few long ones. The flowers fall of their own accord when they are finished.

Light and humid
The Acalypha can bloom year after year, from early spring to late summer. But it needs careful treatment if it is to do so. This means lots of light, warmth and humidity, particularly in the growing period. In intense sunlight it is very difficult to keep the degree of humidity at the required level, and the plant should therefore be shielded in the summer against the fiercest sun.
In the autumn (fall) and winter the plant takes a rest. Keep the soil moderately moist at this time.
During the growing period give the plant some fertilizer every week. In the autumn (fall) reduce the amount gradually.
If you want to have a compact and not too lanky plant, spray it once before it flowers with growth inhibitor (see page 170 growth inhibitor).

Treatment table

	cutting	growth	rest
pot	3½ in/9 cm	4½ in/11 cm	—
soil	¾peat compost ¼sharp sand	¾RHP ¼sharp sand	—
feeding	none	¼tsp compound fertilizer per pt water 2g per litre	none
watering	frequently	frequently	moderate
temperature	72°F/22°C	68°F/20°C	64°F/18°C
rel. humidity	80%	80%	>70%
light	full	full	full
blooms	—	early spring-late autumn (fall)	—
growth inhibitor	—	0.5% Cyclocel	—

special instructions shield against fierce sun.

Achimenes longiflora 'Paul Arnold'
This variety of Achimenes is recognizable by its large purple flowers.

Achimenes coccinea 'Tango'
Coccinea means 'chocolate red', but the Tango is more pink than red. Most Achimenes varieties are mutants which have been produced by irradiation.

Achimenes

Achimenes coccinea

Variegated plants
Achimenes longiflora belongs to the Gesneria family (Gesneriaceae). These plants are named after the Swiss doctor and botanist, Conrad Gesner, who lived in the 16th century.

Gesneriaceae form a variegated family with many well-known members such as African Violet, Gloxinia and Rechtseineria. Most plants of this family live in tropical countries in the humus-rich leaf mould beneath the trees.

Achimenes longiflora, which comes originally from Central America and Mexico, was first cultivated in England in 1841. The word *achimenes* comes from Greek and means 'no storm or cold'. There is normally no danger of this inside a house. *Longiflora* means 'with long flowers' in Latin.

If taken good care of, they will give an excellent crop throughout the summer.

Long tubers
Achimenes is a tuberous plant with longish, caterpillar-shaped tubers, known as rhizomes.

In the autumn the part of the plant above ground dies. When this happens, leave the tubers undisturbed in the soil and place the plant to one side in a not-too-warm room.

If you want to have young plants in the following year, take cuttings. You can also, however, divide the old tubers, after placing them for some time in moist peat dust. This can take place from mid-winter to mid-spring, depending on the desired flowering time.

When a tuber has formed side-shoots with four to six leaves, cut off one of the shoots.

Place 3 to 5 cuttings in a 3½-in/9-cm pot or 5 to 7 cuttings in a 4½-in/11-cm pot filled with RHP potting soil.

The earliest flowering time for Achimenes is mid-spring. By letting the tubers sprout at different times or by taking cuttings at different times, you can stagger the flowering times.

Most plants produce their most luxuriant flowers in the summer. Flowering ends in the autumn through want of light. If there is a beautiful autumn with lots of sunlight, flowering may well last until nearly the end of the season. But a drizzly autumn sometimes puts the plant to sleep very early. Dead-head the plants regularly.

Combined light and shade
Although in nature the plant grows under trees, there is far more light in its native habitat, Mexico, than in many other countries. The plant must therefore have plenty of light, though it should never be exposed to the full glare of the midday sun in the spring or summer.

Plants which come into flower early have long, weak, soft stems as a result. To prevent this, spray the shoots with an inhibitor when they are about 3-4 in/8-10 cm long. You will then get a fine, compact plant which sets many flowers. During the growing season, keep the soil fairly moist. Water the plant preferably in the morning, taking care not to pour water on to the leaves and making sure that the water is not too cold. Cold water produces rings of dead tissue in the leaves which are neither healthy nor pleasing to the eye.

Treatment table

	cutting	growth	rest
pot	3½-4½ in/ 9-11 cm	3½-4½ in/ 9-11 cm	—
soil	peat dust (tuber)	RHP	—
feeding	none	1-1½tsp compound fertilizer per pt water/2-3g per litre	none
watering	moist	moist	none
temperature	72° F/22° C	64° F/18° C	59° F/15° C
rel. humidity	95%	70%	70
light	—	light but no sunlight	—
flowers	—	mid-spring to mid-autumn	
inhibitor	—	B9, ½ fl oz per pt water/25 ml per litre	—

special features No fertilizer for the first three to four weeks. Discontinue fertilizer when the plant is fully in flower.
The temperature for renewed growth of the tubers is 64-68° F/18-20° C with a relative humidity of 75%.

Achimenes longiflora 'Paul Arnold'

Acorus (Sweet sedge)

A useful plant

Acorus gramineus is a member of the arum family. Aros is greek for useful, refers in this case to the healing properties of the roots. Acorus gramineus is closely related to Acorus calamus, better known as sweet sedge. Calamus means stalk, and gramineus grass-like. This illustrates the difference between them. The leaves of Acorus gramineus are far more delicate and pointed than those of the sweet sedge. The sweet smelling roots of these water-side plants are an important component of various beverages which are drunk before meals. The root contains the active ingredient choline, which is an aid to digestion. The sweet sedge was "discovered" by a Viennese botanist, Carolus Clusius, who imported it in the 16th century as a medicinal plant from Turkey and planted it in his botanical garden.

Not really a house plant

Acorus gramineus is naturally very elegant as a foliage plant and it can be used to good decorative effect in many rooms. But it is really a plant for a cool place and does not care very much for efficient central heating systems. In mild winters the plant can therefore quite easily winter outside. It makes a fine bank plant at the edges of ponds. Because of the strong, attractive leaves, which remain fresh for quite a long time, the plant is very suitable for floral decoration, for example in the making of corsages. Acorus spreads quickly by propagating itself through root-stock division. You can take advantage of this fact for cultivation purposes. In the spring and summer, take a cutting of the full-grown shoots, complete with a piece of root-stock from the stock plant (see page 169 cuttings). If you put these shoots in a plastic pot filled with humus-rich soil, which can contain a great deal of moisture, and place it in a cool, light, spot, your efforts are sure to succeed.

Lots of water

Acorus is a genuine shallow-water plant, growng almost in the water. You must therefore give the plant a great deal of water during the growing period; the potting soil must be permanently wet. In the darker winter months keep the soil slightly drier. During the growing period apply fertilizer weekly. The plant requires a good light and a high degree of humidity, otherwise dead spots appear on the leaves.

Treatment table

	cutting	growth	rest
pot	3 in/8 cm	large	—
soil	RHP	RHP	—
feeding	—	¼ tsp compound fertilizer per pint water/3 g per litre	—
watering	frequently	very frequently	infrequently
temperature	50-59°F/ 10-15°C	68°F/20°C (in the sun)	41°F/5°C
rel. humidity	75-80%	75-80%	75-80%
light	full	full	—
flowers	—	rarely	—

special instructions: give full light for good growth and a beautiful colour, but avoid full sun.

Acorus gramineus "Aureovariegatus"

Acorus gramineus 'Aureovariegatus'
A coarse-grownig variety with gold-coloured stripes (aureo). It is this variety which is cultivated in the main.

Acorus gramineus 'Argenteostriatus'
This finer-growing variety, in which the black-with-white-spots markings are more pronounced, is found to a limited extent. Argenteo means silver-coloured.

Adiantum cuneatum

Capillus-veneris means literally hair of Venus. One of the common names for this lovely plant, Venus Hair, comes from this.

The Adiantum is a fern with a magnificent covering of light-green leaves, which are, curiously, water-repellent. The Greek word a-dianten means "not to be made wet".

Most of the Adiantums, which are grown as houseplants for the decorative value of their leaves, came originally from tropical America.

Spores and divisions

Adiantum is a fern and it can be propagated by sowing the spores in a humus-rich mixture (see propagating by spores page 168). The soil must be clean and not too acid, otherwise the spores will not germinate.

After about seven weeks the so-called prothallium or "pre-germinator" develops. This is a green moss-like layer in which the fertilization takes place. After about three months, plant out individual pieces of the prothallium, from which the fern plantlets will grow. When they are clearly distinguishable as plants, plant them in a small tray containing frozen peat as potting soil and after two to three months transfer the plants into a pot for cuttings. Six to seven months later the ferns will have grown into beautiful plants. Like many ferns, Adiantum has a root-stock. It is therefore simpler to propagate the plant by dividing it. But a great deal of care is required in order to get fine new plants again with a pure "head of hair".

A difficult guest

As a houseplant, the Adiantum is not so easy to maintain in a healthy condition becuase the relative humidity of the air must be comparatively high and, above all, constant and this is rarely possible in a room. A greenhouse or conservatory in which temperature and humidity can be controlled, is really the best place for growing these ferns. Place your Adiantum in a shaded spot and if you want to keep it in perfect condition, repot it each year.

Water it regularly, but make sure that the soil never gets water logged.

Give it some fertilizer once a week. The concentration of the latter must not be too high and the pot should therefore be immersed in a bucket of water once a week and left to drain afterwards.

Adiantum does very well in a tray with other plants which do not have such high reuirements with regard to humidity.

Adiantum tenerum "Scutum Roseum"

Adiantum tenerum

Tenerum means tender. This lovely plant comes from tropical America. The commonest variety is "Scutum Roseum" In Roman times a scutum was a wooden shield with a leather covering. The name refers to the young leaves which resemble pink-red shields.

Adiantum hispidulum

Hispidulum means "with small bristles" This Adiantum comes not from America but from Australia and New Zealand.

Adiantum cuneatum

This fern comes originally from Brazil. Cuneatum means wedge-shaped and refers to the shape of the leaves. The following varieties of the fern are cultivated:
"Gold Else"
"Fritz Luthi"
"Matador" and "Brilliant Else". This variety cannot be propagated by means of spores; it has to be divided.

Adiantum hispidulum

Treatment table

	young plant	growth	rest
pot	3-4 in/8-10 cm		—
soil	RHP	ditto	ditto
feeding	½ tsp compound fertilizer per pt water/ 1 g per litre	ditto	ditto
watering	frequently	frequently	frequently
temperature	68°F/ 20°C	68°F-86°F/ 20°-30°C	59°F/ 15°C
rel. humidity	80%	80%	80%
light	low	low	full

special instructions the relative humidity must remain constant and must not be more than 80% or less than 60%.

Aechmea

Aechmea is a Bromeliad (see Bromeliaceae, page 36). The name comes from the Greek word *aechmea* and means 'point of a lance'. The name refers to the thorny, pointed tip of the outermost sepal. The plant came originally from eastern Brazil, where most species grow epiphytically, ie, not in the ground, but on the bark of a tree. The leaves form a kind of gully which collects water and conveys it into a sheath where it remains. The plant was introduced to Europe via England in 1826. It is grown for the decorative quality of its flowers and leaves.

The flower keeps its brilliant colours for months on end. When the plant has finished flowering, the terminal buds die off and the plant continues to grow via its side-shoots.

Light germinators

The plant is propagated commercially from seed. As soon as the pollen is mature, it is applied to each open floweret. The seeds ripen after about six months and one seed plant can produce some 6,000 seeds.

Aechmea is sown in a very humus-rich mixture. The seeds are never covered. They germinate in the light. After six months the seedlings are graded by size and planted out at a distance of ½ in/1 cm. Six months later they are planted out once again, this time 1¼ in/3 cm apart, and after another six months, 2 in/5 cm apart. After another half-year the plants are placed in a pot for cuttings and six months on again in a 5-in/12-cm final pot.

With the aid of growth regulators the plants flower six to eight months after being placed in the final pot.

Cuttings may be taken from the plant, by removing the side-shoots which have formed during flowering from the mother plant. The side-shoots should be fully grown. If they are removed earlier they remain small and do not flower in the first year. The shoots can be potted on immediately.

Sturdy

Aechmea is a sturdy houseplant. But you must bear a few points in mind if you want to get beautiful flowering plants. A very humus-rich, light soil is an absolute necessity. Keep this soil moderately moist, and ensure that the leaf-sheath has plenty of water at all times.

During the growing season feed weekly with a nitrogen-potassium compound fertilizer in the ideal proportion 1:2. In the wild the plant grows beneath the shelter of its host, a tree. Aechmea will not therefore tolerate strong sunlight, though in the winter it is very greedy for light. By replacing the plants regularly after flowering with fine young shoots, Aechmeas will give you pleasure for many years.

Aechmea fasciata 'Variegata'

Aechmea fasciata
This is the most widely distributed Aechmea, with white, felt-like leaf markings, *fasciata* meaning 'banded' in Latin. Varieties with short, broad leaves and a bright-coloured inflorescence are commonly grown.

Aechmea fulgens 'Discolor'

Aechmea fulgens 'Discolor'
Fulgens means 'brilliant' and *discolor* is Latin for 'varying in colour'. These properties are found in these Aechmeas with a long, red and blue tinted inflorescence.

Aechmea miniata 'Discolor'
Also varying in colour, this variety has a short inflorescence which is red-lead (*miniata*) and blue in colour.

Aechmea miniata 'Discolor'

Aechmea chantinii

Aechmea aquilega in the wild

Aechmea victoriana in the wild.

Aechmea chantinii
A beautiful Aechmea with a yellow and red inflorescence.

Treatment table

	cutting	growth	rest winter
pot	5 in/12 cm	5 in/12 cm	—
soil	very humus-rich	very humus-rich	—
feeding	compound fertilizer 10:5:20 1 tsp per pt water/ 2 g per litre	compound fertilizer 10:5:20 1 tsp per pt water/ 2 g per litre	compound fertilizer 10:5:20 1 tsp per pt water/ 2 g per litre
watering	moderately moist	moderately moist	moderately moist
temperature	68-77° F/ 20-25° C	68-77° F/ 20-25° C	64° F/18° C
rel. humidity	75-80%	75-80%	75-80%
light	moderate	moderate	light
flowers		after two years	
regulators		min. temp. before flowering 68° F/20° C	

special features Sow at 77° F/25° C. Large plants require 3½ fl oz/100 ml compound fertilizer solution per pot.

Aeschynanthus speciosus

Aeschynanthus speciosus

This is a beautiful houseplant which flowers for long periods with splendid, large, red flowers. For good flowering it is best to grow new plants each year. Old plants produce shoots of unequal length and the plant shape is also less pleasing.

Aeschynanthus lobbianus

Aeschynanthus lobbianus

In contrast to the other species, this fine hanging plant is always more beautiful as an old plant. You must therefore ensure that it continues to grow properly. This requires careful and devoted treatment.

Aesachynanthus speciosus

Two species

Aeschynanthus is a Gesneria. Two of the most popular species are Aeschynanthus speciosus (meaning 'beautiful'), a large-flowered Danish variety and Aeschynanthus lobbianus, a brilliant hanging plant with fiery-red flowers.

Treat well

Both species of Aeschynanthus are profusely-flowering houseplants which last for years if treated well. Treatment for both species includes a special temperature and dryness regime. Both species may be propagated by taking cuttings. Take an intermediate cutting from A. lobbianus with one leaf pair A. speciosus with two leaf pairs. (See page 169 for cuttings).
This can be done from mid-winter until mid-summer.
Tip cuttings may also be taken from already-rooted cuttings. To propagate from the hanging plant, take cuttings from the long tendrils and place four of them in a 4-in/10-cm pot filled with frozen peat as potting compost. From the other species, plant three cuttings in a 3½-in/9-cm pot. Under plastic foil the cuttings will grow roots after three weeks. At the end of the winter you can top the cuttings (see page 173 for topping). Do not leave until later, or the shoots will have insufficient growing time before flower formation.

Temperature and dryness regime

This regime varies somewhat for the two specimens. Keep the hanging plants dry and cool (60° F/15° C) when the tendrils are 6-8 in/15-20 cm long. After two to three months give them slightly more water; add more fertilizer and increase the temperature to 68° F/20° C. (In sunlight this may mean a temperature of 86° F/30° C). In the latter part of the summer the plants will then produce splendid bunches of fiery-red flowers.
Treat the other species differently. When the new shoots have formed three or four leaves, wash the soil (see page 167 for washing) to avoid salt damage. Then allow the soil to dry out for as long as possible.
Water sparingly, making sure that the plant does not dry up. The plant will by now have reached its full height and flower buds will form. When this happens, moisten the soil and increase the temperature. Feed the plant weekly. The total period from cutting to flowering is five to six months. Shield the plants against strong sunlight.

Treatment table

	cutting	growth	rest
pot	4 in/9-10 cm	4 in/9-10 cm	—
soil	frozen peat potting compost	RHP	—
feeding	none 1 litre water	3 tsp/g compound fertilizer	—
watering	normal	see regime	—
temperature	68-72° F/ 20-22° C	see regime	—
rel. humidity	95%	70% see special features	—
light	plenty	plenty	—
flowers	—	mid-spring to early winter	—
growth hormone	Rhizopon AT 0.5% Rhizopon BY 0.1%	(A. speciosus) (A. lobbianus)	

special features The cuttings grow at 68° F/20° C with a relative humidity of 80%.
During dryness regime, the temperature is 64° F/18° C with a relative humidity of 60%.

Aglaonema

Not a difficult plant

Aglaonema is unjustly known as a difficult plant. It is true that it does not do well on a sunny window-sill, but placed out of direct sunlight on a small table or bookcase, it can have a very decorative effect as a single plant.

Even so, the plant is at its best in a flower basket under the shelter of larger, more leafy plants. It is best to place the basket in a sunny position, but it must be kept fairly moist. Aglaonema comes from south-east Asia. Most species were cultivated in Europe in the 19th century. In recent years some crosses of originally wild species, the so-called hybrids, have come from America.

The plant belongs to the large Araceae or arum family. The name Aglaonema comes from the Greek *aglao* and *nema,* and means 'shining tissue'. The name refers to the beautifully coloured and decorated leaves of the various species.

Linguistic confusion

The genus Aglaonema contains numerous species with different leaf-shapes and colours.

There is some confusion among experts regarding the nomenclature.

The most important species are:
Aglaonema brevispathum f. hospitum or Aglaonema hospitum
Aglaonema commutatum var. Maculatum or Aglaonema marantifolium
Aglaonema commutatum var. Robustum
Aglaonema commutatum 'Pseudobracteatum' or Aglaonema pseudobracteatum
Aglaonema commutatum 'Treubii' or Aglaonema treubii
Aglaonema costatum
Aglaonema crispum or Aglaonema roebelinii
Aglaonema nitidum or Aglaonema oblongifolium
Aglaonema pictum

The meanings of these names are:
brevispathum: 'with short bracts'
hospitum: 'host-free'
commutatum: 'changeable'
maculatum: 'spotted'
pseudobracteatum: 'with apparent bracts'
costatum: 'with ribbed thickened mid-rib'
crispum: 'curly'
nitidum: 'shining'
pictum: 'painted' or 'decorative'
oblongifolium: 'with oblong leaves'
treubii: named after M. Treub
roebelinii: named after the Swiss Roebelin
marantifolium: with maranta leaf

Cuttings

The taking of cuttings from an Aglaonema is very simple and can be done at any time of the year.

You can take a shoot cutting or a stem cutting (see page 169 for cuttings). In a pot filled with potting compost for cuttings, under double glass or plastic foil, the cuttings will form roots within three weeks. Then plant the cuttings in a 4-in/10-cm pot with a humus-rich RHP potting soil, taking care not to press down too firmly. The cuttings must be treated generously with growth hormone (see page 170 for growth hormone).

Aglaonema roebelinii 'Silver Queen'

Aglaonema commutatum Treubii

This plant is named after M. Treub, the Director of the Royal Botanical Gardens at Buizenzorg in the former Dutch East Indies from 1880 to 1890.

Aglaonema crispum or Aglaonema roebelinii 'Golden Fleece'

This crossed Aglaonema is named after its discoverer, the 19th-century Swiss plant researcher, Roebelin.

Aglaonema pseudobracteatum

Aglaonema roebelinii

Aglaonema marantifolium

Treatment table

	cutting	growth	rest
pot	—	4 in/10 cm	—
soil	peat-based compost for cuttings	RHP	—
feeding	—	1 tsp compound fertilizer per pt water/ 2 g per litre	none
watering	moist	moist	moderate
temperature	68° F/20° C	64-68° F/ 18-20° C	up to 64° F/18° C
rel. humidity	80%	80%	80%
light	no sunlight	approx. 1,100 mW per yd²/m²	—
growth hormone	Rhizopon B, 0.1%		

special features Water, if possible, with rainwater. A full-grown plant also needs a lower relative humidity.

Moist and shady

The Aglaonema species are long-lasting foliage plants which, in spite of their tropical origin, are highly suitable as houseplants.

They are at their best in flower baskets, where it is somewhat shady and sufficiently moist.

They are also suitable for hydroculture (see page 171 for hydroculture). The decorative value of the leaves is negligible. Some species bear beautiful, orange-red berries. The plants grow quickly, last well and become quite large. Five to six months after taking cuttings you will have a sizeable plant. In the spring and summer they grow at a great pace. Feed them then regularly with water, preferably soft rainwater, because the plants are salt-sensitive. In the resting season during the darker winter months keep the soil moderately moist.

During the growing season add some fertilizer weekly.

A full-grown Aglaonema is content with the temperature and humidity of a normal room. If you pot it on each year in mid- to late-spring, you will enjoy it for many years.

Not a true houseplant

Although the plant is called 'house creeper', many people do not consider it a true houseplant, because it sheds its leaves in the winter.

Nor does Ampelopsis come from tropical regions. The plant is a native of north-east Asia and was first described in Russia in 1870, though the variegated variety, 'Variegata', was known in western Europe by the early 19th century.

Ampelopsis nevertheless does exceptionally well inside the house, although it is most suitable for a sheltered balcony, as a hanging plant in a flower basket, for example. In the winter, when there are no more flowers in the basket, allow the plant to rest in a frost-free place. Ampelopsis is a vine-type plant, but though it looks like a creeper, it is not a true one. *Ampelos* means 'creeper' in Greek, and *opsis* means 'apparent'. The Brevipedunculata variety takes its name from its short-stalked inflorescence. It is related to the wild creeper which often grows as a climber in gardens and resembles it closely, except that the tendrils of Ampelopsis, unlike those of the wild creeper, have no suckers.

Take cuttings in August

Ampelopsis is a splendid shrub with long climbing tendrils and variegated leaves.

The plant is easy to take intermediate cuttings from (see page 169 for cuttings). Do this in late summer. Place the cuttings in a mixture of peat dust and sand. Under double glass the cuttings will form roots in three to four weeks. You must then add some growth hormone (see page 171 for growth hormone).

Frost-free wintering

When the cuttings have rooted, plant them in a 3-in/7-cm pot. Winter them thereafter in a frost-free place, for example in a cold frame.

The following year pot the plants into a bigger pot and in late spring place the pots in outdoor beds.

In the autumn, when they have lost their leaves, prune the cuttings back to the stem if the plants have grown too big. You will then get strong young twigs with beautifully coloured leaves in the spring. You can bring the plants on in late winter by placing them in the light with a slightly higher temperature and degree of humidity than usual.

The plant grows in any good potting soil. During growth, when the plant is making leaves, water frequently. In late summer water less often, and in winter hardly at all.

During the sprouting period the plant is fed weekly. When the shoots are fully grown, feed every two weeks and discontinue at the beginning of autumn.

Treatment table

	cutting	growth	rest
pot	3 in/7 cm	4-5 in/10-12 cm	—
soil	2/3 peat dust 1/3 sand	RHP	—
feeding	—	1½ tsp compound fertilizer per pt water/3g per litre	—
watering	moist	frequently	moderate
temperature	61° F/16° C	64-68° F/ 18-20° C	32-41° F/ 0-5° C
rel. humidity	60%	60%	60%
light	normal	2.000 mW per yd²/m²	—
growth hormone	Rhizopon B 0.2.%		

special features When the plant is coming into leaf, the relative humidity must be approximately 80%.

Ampelopsis brevipedunculata 'Variegata'

Ampelopsis brevipedunculata 'Variegata'

This shrub has long climbing tendrils and irregularly decorated leaves in green, white and pink.

Ananas comosus

Ananas comosus
The well-known pineapple plant with the sharply dentate green leaves, which grow too long for a house plant.

Ananas comosus 'Aureovariegatus'
This variety with variegated leaves is suitable as a houseplant.
The colourful young shoots are also used by the horticulturist in floral decoration.

Ananas comosus 'Aureovariegatus'

Ananas photographed in the wild

Pseudo-fruit
If you buy a pineapple or Ananas fruit in the shops with a good crown, you can grow a houseplant from it. Although it will be difficult to get it to flower, the leaves have good decorative value. The plants grow very high and the leaves have sharp edges. Ananas is a Bromeliad (see Bromeliaceae) and comes from Brazil. The name is a Portuguese corruption of an Indian word.
Ananas was introduced as a houseplant in England in 1690, and has since spread to all regions around the equator. In Africa it even occurs in the wild. The plant is not useful for producing fruit, though in the Philippines a very fine fabric is made from the fibres of the leaves.
In fact, the Ananas which we know is not a real fruit at all, but a pseudo-fruit. It has a fleshy thickening of the stem at the place where berries are formed from the hundreds of tiny flowers, and this pseudo-fruit is topped by a crest of leaves, from which Ananas gets its generic name, *comosus*, which means 'hairy' or 'crested' in Latin.

Flowering treatment
Commercial growers place the young plant in a 5-in/12-cm pot filled with a very humus-rich mixture and they do apply a flowering treatment after six months. (In winter the lack of light makes it very difficult to get the plant to flower.) Without a flowering treatment the plant rarely flowers even after years. This treatment is described in detail under Bromeliaceae.
The plant is treated three to four times a week. Plants with a light leaf-colour react best to acetylene treatment. The plants flower three to four months after the treatment and the young shoots continue to grow after the flowering.

Free-growing plant
Ananas is a strong, free-growing plant, especially if it is not encouraged to flower. Above all it needs a good humus-rich potting soil and a light position.
Give it some fertilizer once a week during the growing season and keep the soil moist by ensuring that there is always water in the vase.

Treatment table

	cutting shoot	growth	rest growth
pot	5 in/12-13 cm	5 in/12-13 cm	5 in/12-13 cm
soil	very humus-rich	very humus-rich	very humus-rich
feeding	—	compound fertilizer 10:5:20 1 tsp per pt water/2 g per litre	compound fertilizer 10:5:20 1 tsp per pt water/2 g per litre
watering	moderately moist	moderately moist	moderately moist
temperature	68-86° F/ 20-30° C	68-86° F/ 20-30° C	> 68° F/ 20° C
rel. humidity	75-80%	75-80%	75-80%
light	strong	strong	strong
flowers	—	after 1 year	—
regulators	—	after 6-10 months	—

special features Leaf vase with water.

A flower with a tail

Who does not know these colourful plants with their twisting flower spathes which make one immediately think of a flamingo? But the namer of this plant was thinking of another part of the body. The Flamingo plant should really have been called the Tail plant. For *anthos* is 'flower' in Greek, and *oura* means 'tail'.

Anthurium is a real tropical plant from Central and South America. In the house it therefore needs plenty of warmth, humidity and light, although since it is a forest plant it must not be exposed to the full sun.

Anthurium belongs to the Arum family and has a flower spike or spathe on which a spadix grows.

Suckers, tissue-growing and sowing

Anthurium andreanum may easily be propagated by taking cuttings from suckers.

It is also possible to propagate Anthuriums by tissue culturing of leaves (see page 169 for tissue culturing), which is widely practised with Anthurium andreanum. A piece of leaf or stem is placed on an artificial nutrient medium in a test-tube. Wound tissue, the so-called callus, then forms on the tissue. The addition of growth regulators produces shoots and roots from the callus.

A successful propagating method, and the one most widely used, is sowing. It is wise to pay careful attention to the 'mother plant' from which the seed is taken, selecting it for flower-shape, colour, size, richness of bloom and the shape, colour and size of the leaves.

Good pollination is also very important. If the spadices are shining and sticky, then the pistils are mature. As soon as the stamina are also mature, brush dusting preparation on to the pistils a few times each week with a camel-hair brush. The dusting preparation must come from another plant for there to be cross-pollination.

When the berries of A. scherzerianum, which grow on the spadix, are ripe, the spadix will hang down. This may well take six months to a year. Sowing can now begin. Remove the germination-inhibiting fruit flesh and lay the seeds ½ in/1 ½ cm apart in a fibrous peat dust with 2 tsp Dolokal per pt of peat litter/4 g per litre. Plant out the seedlings after four to six months. To get a fine compact plant, place two plants together. After five to six months transplant them into a 3-in/7-cm plastic pot. (In an earthenware pot the roots stick :ogether.) After six months pot them off into a 5-in/12-cm final pot.

Cold regime

Anthuriums make excellent houseplants, which have a long life and flower freely throughout the year, provided that a certain number of rules are kept carefully. For good renewed growth it is important that the plant be repotted each year in the spring. Anthurium grows best in a fibrous, light and humus-rich potting soil.

A mixture specially for Anthuriums, based on coarse-fibred peat litter, is available commercially.

During the growing season water the plant generously in the summer, but take good care that the soil does not get too wet. This causes root rot through oxygen deficiency. Keep the soil moderately moist in the winter. In the growing season add extra fertilizer weekly, from mid-autumn to the end of winter once every two weeks.

In order to get rich flowers from A. scherzerianum, give the plant a cold treatment in the winter by keeping the plant at 60° F/15° C for at least six weeks. If after six weeks you keep them for a good month at 68-77° F/20-25° C, you can count on early profuse flowering. Anthurium creates no problems as a greenhouse or hothouse plant, but you must observe its special requirements.

Anthurium scandens

This is a climbing plant which is also not grown for its flowers. This *anthurium* grows white mother-of-pearl berries.

Anthurium crystallinum

This *anthurium* is grown not for the decorative value of its flowers but for its foliage. The leaves are then distinguished by a beautiful silver-coloured pattern.

Anthurium x cultorum

A recently cultivated small-flowered *Anthurium*.

Anthurium andreanum

Anthurium scherzerianum

Anthurium andreanum

Anthurium scherzerianum
This species is also known as Anthurium hortulanorum. It is a genuine flamingo plant with long curling spadices. The flower spathe is mostly red, sometimes red-and-white speckled, salmon-pink or creamy white. The plant was discovered by Karl von Scherzer in 1857 and brought to Europe.

Anthurium andreanum
Also called Anthurium cultorum, 'Painter's Palette' Anthurium is widely grown for cut flowers. The plant was discovered by E André in Colombia in 1867 and introduced into Europe. The flower spathe is sometimes partially green and the spadices all have tints of red, salmon-pink and white.

Treatment table

	seed	growth	rest
pot	3 in/7 cm plastic	4-5 in/10-12 cm	—
soil	peat dust	special mixture	—
feeding	—	1½ tsp compound fertilizer per pt water/ 3 g per litre	—
watering	—	generous	moderate
temperature	72° F/22° C	64-68° F/ 18-20° C	59° F/ 15° C
rel. humidity	95%	70-80%	70%
light	—	light but avoid strong sunlight	—
flowers	—	all year	—
growth hormone	2 g Dolokal per pt of peat dust/4g per litre	—	—
special features	Grow seedlings at 68° F/20° C and a relative humidity of 90%. In the sun the temperature may rise to 91° F/33° C; the relative humidity may then not exceed 80% at night; otherwise grey leaf patches will be obtained as growth damage.		

Aphelandra

Decorative plant

Aphelandra is a beautifully coloured and even more finely decorated plant which obtains its full decorative effect in a flower basket.

The plant belongs to the Acanthus family and is a native of Brazil. The original species is not cultivated.

In Greek *apheles* means 'without decoration' or 'simple', while *andros* is the Greek word for 'man'. But there is nothing particularly masculine about this plant and it is certainly not simple. The name refers exclusively to the male reproductive organs, the anthers, which are indeed simple.

Squarrosa is Latin and means 'stiff'. This refers to the inflorescences which are on the stiff side.

Take cuttings in the winter

Because it requires a great deal of sunlight, it is not easy to get — or to keep — a fine, richly-flowering Aphelandra. For spring flowers, start to take cuttings in the autumn; continue taking them into the spring for summer and autumn flowers. Take cuttings from young mother plants (see page 169 for cuttings). One plant gives one head cutting and eight to ten eye cuttings.

The eye cuttings are obtained by cutting the stem between the two leaves. Each eye cutting thus has half a piece of stem with a bud and a leaf. Place the cuttings in a 3-in/7-cm pot filled with peat-based potting compost. Under plastic foil or mist they will have roots after four weeks. One month later pot them off into the final pot. If you want flowers in late spring, pot off in mid-autumn.

Light is the most important factor in the growing time. A head cutting can come into flower in a clear winter after about nine months, whereas an eye cutting may well need a year in a gloomy winter.

Salt-free diet

Aphelandra requires a nutritious RHP frozen peat potting soil with a low salt concentration.

Aphelandra is very salt-sensitive and with too high a concentration the leaves start to drop. Water the plant constantly, but do not allow the soil to get too wet. When the plant has been one month in its final pot, add fertilizer weekly and discontinue when the plant flowers. The plant requires lots of light, but must be well shielded against the full glare of the sun.

If you want to keep Aphelandra strong and compact, spray it about three weeks after repotting with inhibitor (see page 171 for inhibitor) and repeat the spraying every 10 days until the bud appears.

Prune a plant which you wish to enjoy for a long time and repot it regularly once a year, paying close attention to ensure that the salt concentration does not get too high.

Aphelandra squarrosa 'Danica'

Aphelandra squarrosa 'Danica'

Aphelandra squarrosa 'Uniflora Beauty' is a variety with profuse, silver-white leaf decoration.

Aphelandra squarrosa 'Leopoldii'

This variety dates from 1855.

Aphelandra squarrosa 'Louisae'

This variety was first grown in 1860.

Aphelandra squarrosa 'Fritz Prinsler'

This variety originated from a cross of two previous varieties.

Treatment table

	cutting	growth	rest
pot	3 in/7 cm	5 in/12-13 cm	—
soil	peat-based potting compost	RHP frozen peat	—
feeding	—	1 tsp compound fertilizer per pt water/ 2 g per litre	—
watering	frequently	frequently (rainwater)	frequently
temperature	72-75° F/ 22-24° C	75-77° F/ 22-23° C	
rel. humidity	95%	80%	80%
light	strong	avoid direct sunlight	—
flowers	—	spring and summer	
growth hormone	Rhizopon BTO, 1%	—	—
inhibitor	—	1/16 fl oz of Cycocel/1/32 wetter per pt. 3.4ml and 2ml per litre	—
special features	In sunlight the temperature may rise to 86° F/30° C. The night temperature must be 64-68° F/18-20° C. At a low winter temperature (approximately 64° F/18° C) the plant sets flowers and makes side-shoots. On long summer days at a temperature of 77° F/25° C flowers quickly appear, but no side-shoots.		

Araucaria heterophylla 'Gracilis'

Araucaria bidwillii

Araucaria angustifolia
This auracaria has needles more leaf-like in shape than most varieties.

Araucaria bidwillii
This variety has sharp, leaf-shaped needles.

Araucaria heterophylla 'Gracilis'
This small ornamental tree is grown by means of cuttings.
Heterophylla means 'with different leaves'. This refers to the varying lengths of the needles.

Araucaria heterophylla 'Glauca'
This variety has blue-green needles.

A house tree

Arauco, a province in southern Chile, is the home of the Indian tribe, the Araucani. Araucaria imbricata, also called Araucaria araucana, grows there. The plant is therefore named after the Indian tribe.

Araucaria heterophylla, which we know as a houseplant, is also called Araucaria excelsa.

Excelsa means 'high' in Latin, and this variety is a high tree which grows on the Norfolk Islands. In the natural state it can reach 200 ft/60 m in height, with a circumference of 20-30 ft/6-9 m.

Indoors it remains a dwarf which grows no higher than 5 ft/ 1.5 m, and then only after many years. The room temperature must not be allowed to rise above 65° F/18° C. Araucaria belongs to the spruce family. It was first cultivated in France in 1793.

Sowing and cuttings

Cuttings from an Araucaria can be taken only from the top of the plant. The side-shoots do not give the desired regularity of shape, which is also so important with that other well-known 'spruce', the Christmas tree. Place the cutting in a pot containing a sandy mixture in late autumn or early winter. Keep it well out of the sun and it will root within three to four months. The plant must remain cool in the winter.

Indoors the pine never becomes full-grown, because it forms no cones or seed.

To grow the Indoor pine from seed, the seed must be collected from the wild. Sow in a sandy mixture mixed with a bit of soil from a pot where an indoor pine is already growing. The plant cannot survive except in a symbiotic relationship with its own particular soil mould which is active the whole time.

Short rations

If you are somewhat forgetful by nature, the Indoor pine is an ideal plant for you. Coolness and dryness are the most important requirements for optimum growth. The Indoor pine needs a sandy, porous soil.

The best soil is a mixture of RHP potting compost, clay and river sand. During the growing season keep the soil fairly dry, though never, of course, completely dry. In the summer give the plant some fertilizer once every three weeks.

The Indoor pine requires very little light and holds its own in places where no other plant would survive.

If you place the plant outside in the summer, choose a shady spot. Slight shade is best for good rapid growth.

Treatment table

	cutting	growth	rest
pot	3 in/8 cm	4-5 in/10-12 cm	—
soil	¼ RHP, ¼ clay, ½ river sand	¼ RHP, ¼ clay, ½ river sand	¼ RHP, ¼ clay, ½ river sand
feeding	1 tsp compound fertilizer per pt of water/ 2 g per litre		
watering	moderately	moderately	dry
temperature	68° F/20° C	64° F/18° C	41-50° F/ 5-10° C
rel. humidity	70-80%	60%	50-60%
light	moderate	shade	—
special features	Young plants grow best with a very high atmospheric humidity. In winter a temperature of 41° F/5° C is ideal.		

Two generations of berries

Ardisia crenata belongs to the family, Myrsinaceae. The genus Ardisia includes some 200 species which are native to tropical Asia.

The name Ardisia refers to the shape of the anthers, which come to a point. *Ardis* in Greek means 'arrow-head'. Ardisia crenata is a proud evergreen shrub which is particularly prized for its beautiful red berries. If you treat the plant well and keep it neither too dry nor too warm, the berries will remain on the plant for a long time. You will always have new berries, while the best from the previous year will still stay bright on the stalks.

Seed from good berries

In the wild Ardisia grows in shady tropical forests. This means that the plant needs a great deal of humidity during the growing season and must not be exposed to excessive sunlight. Water liberally, therefore, but when the berries are ripe reduce the watering slightly until flowering. You can sow Ardisia easily yourself. Take seeds from plants with a good crop of berries. Remove the fruit flesh and sow in a low-acid, humus-rich mixture. The seeds germinate after three to four weeks. After 10 to 12 weeks separate the young plants. You can also take cuttings from the plant. Take the tips of young plants in order to get a good-branching plant. Place the cuttings in a peat-based compost under double glass (see page 169 for cuttings). About two weeks after pricking out, top the young plants (see page 173 for topping), making sure that each of them still has three or four good leaves left. After about seven months place the plant in a 3½-in/8-cm pot and six to nine months later (depending on the time of year) in a larger pot up to 5-in/13-cm.

Increases in beauty

Ardisia is a houseplant which lasts for years and if you treat it well its beauty increases.

It flowers in spring with bunches of small white flowers. For good fruit formation it requires lots of light (see page 171 for light).

When the berries ripen, the shoots start to come through; they will flower and bear fruit the following year.

The berries are in colour in the autumn. Cease feeding at this time. Add some fertilizer weekly during the growing season. Ardisia is sensitive to many pesticides, particularly those in aerosol form. On the underside of the leaves there are small thickenings where bacteria required by the plant live. In order to keep the bacteria alive during insect control, use mild agents such as methylated spirit, nicotine or soap and water.

Ardisia crenata

Ardisia crenata

This proud and free-growing houseplant, with dark green leaves, a mass of small, white flowers and magnificent red berries, can be just as beautiful after more than a year.

Ardisia polycephala

A quick-growing Ardisia with black berries, this plant is cultivated to only a limited extent. *Polycephala* means 'many-headed' in Greek and refers to the large number of shoots.

The berries are non-poisonous.

Treatment table

	pot	growth	rest
pot	3 in/8 cm	4-5 in/10-12 cm	—
soil	peat-based potting compost	RHP frozen peat based	—
feeding	—	1 tsp compound fertilizer per pt of water/2 g per litre	none
watering	normal	liberally	moderately
temperature	68-72° F/ 20-22° C	64-77° F/ 18-25° C	> 60° F/ 15° C
rel. humidity	95%	75-80%	> 60%
light	—	avoid strong sunlight	avoid strong sunlight
flowers	—	early to mid-spring	—

special features Sow in humus-rich mixture containing river sand at a temperature of 68-72° F/20-22° C.

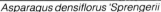
Asparagus densiflorus 'Sprengerii'

Asparagus densiflorus 'Sprengerii'
Densiflorus means 'with thick inflorescence'. The flowers are not large and they stand close together. The plant is named after K. L. Sprenger (1846-1917), an Italian flower-grower who introduced many new houseplants into Europe.

Asparagus secateus (Asparagus plumosus)
This is the famous green sprig. *Secateus* means 'brush-shaped' and *plumosus* means 'feather-shaped'. When it grows well it forms climbing tendrils 3 ft/1m long, which you can train along a wire. If this is not possible, cut the tendrils back to a length of about 20 in/50 cm.

Asparagus densiflorus 'Myriocladus'
Myriocladus means 'with many twigs'. This many-twigged variety, with rosettes of fine small leaves, is making headway as a houseplant.

Asparagus densiflorus 'Meyers'

Asparagus densiflorus 'Meyers'
This plant is named after E. H. F. Meyer (1791-1858), Director of the Botanical Gardens in Königsberg.

Asparagus falcatus

Asparagus falcatus
Falcatus means 'sickle-shaped' and refers to the leaves. This species has broad leaves and is a strong grower.

Vegetable and greenery
Perhaps even better known than Asparagus as a vegetable is Asparagus as a sprig of greenery between cut flowers.

In ancient Greece the plant was already called Asparagos and probably had something to do with the old Greek word, *aspartos*, which means 'unsown'.

Asparagus, in fact, does not need to be sown, because it has very strong rhizomes which are able to make new plants. As a vegetable the suckers grow so thick that they are fibrous and tasty.

The Asparagus belongs to the lily family. It also has many family members in the wild.

The Asparagus species which we know as houseplants came originally from South Africa.

Slow germinators
You can propagate Asparagus from seed, but you must sow quickly, because the seed soon loses its germinating power. The seed must first pre-germinate in moist river sand at a temperature of 77° F/25° C. When it has pre-germinated, sow it out in fresh river sand to prevent the roots being attacked by the mould, Rhizoctonia.

One gram of seed gives eight to ten plants. You can sow the seeds fairly close together. Cover the moist seed-bed with plastic foil.

After this you must be patient. Germination occurs irregularly and may well take up to three weeks.

When the first leaves are a good dark green, place them in pairs in a 3½in/8cm pot. Select only good undamaged plants and pot with at least ¾ in/2 cm of soil above the root crown. After three to four months pot off into a 4-in/10-cm pot, which may be increased in size each year.

You can divide the plants, but it then becomes difficult to get beautiful, compact plants.

Sturdy houseplants
All Asparagus species are sturdy houseplants which have a life expectancy of ten years or more.

Remove old stems with yellow leaves and repot every year. Large plants require a spacious pot because the root system develops gradually. In summer keep the soil well moistened and add some fertilizer weekly. In winter the water and fertilizer requirements are less. The plants cannot tolerate strong sunlight, which scorches the leaves and turns them light green.

Treatment table

	young	growth	rest
pot	3in/8cm	up to?	—
soil	RHP and sand 3:1	RHP and sand 3:1	—
feeding	weekly 1 tsp compound fertilizer per pt water/ 2 g per litre	weekly	less
watering	moist	moist	infrequently
temperature	64-68° F/ 18-20° C	68-77° F/ 18-25° C	> 60° F/ 15° C
rel. humidity	normal	normal	normal
light	approximately 100mW per yd²/m²	approximately 100mW per yd²/m²	full

special features Shield from strong sunlight.

Aspidistra

Plant without a stem

The Aspidistra, which belongs to the lily family, came originally from China and was cultivated in England in 1842. It has rhizome and the peculiar feature is that the leaves and the non-dropping purple flowers grow directly from it. The plant therefore has no stem.

The name comes from the Greek word, *aspis*, the name for a circular shield in antiquity. The broad stigma in the flower of the Aspidistra resembles a shield.

Outside

The Aspidistra, like almost all plants with suckers, can be divided at a rhizome. This can be done from mid-summer to early autumn. Simply divide the plant, with its roots, into the number of new plants you wish to get. The young shoots grow best placed together in twos or threes in a 4½-in/11-cm pot. Pot on older plants into a bigger pot. If you want lots of young plants, grow a number of Aspidistras outside in the greenhouse. The rhizome will thrive there and growth will therefore be much stronger than in pots.

Old-fashioned

The Aspidistra is an old-fashioned plant with an iron constitution which is valued particularly for its beautiful bright green, lancet-shaped leaves and its single purple flowers. It does excellently in RHP soil.

During the growing season in the summer months keep the potting soil fairly moist. For the rest of the year, adjust the amount of water to the requirements of the plant. This depends on the temperature and the amount of light which the plant gets.

During the growing season add some fertilizer every two weeks. Cease feeding in the period when the plant shows little or no growth.

The plant grows excellently at room temperature and can also tolerate low temperatures (a temperature of 46-50° F/8-10° C is ideal in the winter, provided there is no frost).

It makes few demands as to relative humidity.

The Aspidistra is a beautiful, evergreen plant which can last for several decades. Repot the plant every year and cut off old or damaged leaves at soil level.

Treatment table

	shoots	growth	rest
pot	4½ in/11 cm (2-3)larger		—
soil	RHP	RHP	—
feeding	1 tsp compound fertilizer per pt water/2 g per litre	1 tsp compound fertilizer per pt water/2 g per litre	none
watering	moist	moist	seldom
temperature	60-68° F/ 15-20° C	60-68° F/ 15-20° C	46-50° F/ 8-10° C
rel. humidity	60-70%	60-70%	—
light	avoid sunlight	avoid sunlight	—
special features	Avoid temperatures below freezing point. 'Variegata variety': avoid temperatures below freezing point. This variety must have more light or the variegated leaves will turn solid green.		

Aspidistra elatior

Aspidistra elatior
Elatior means 'higher' or 'more exalted'. This is the well-known, original greenleaved species.

Aspidistra elatior 'Variegata'

Aspidistra elatior 'Variegata'
This variegated variety will not tolerate temperatures below 60° F/16° C.

Asplenium nidus

Asplenium bulbiferum

Asplenium nidus

Nidus means 'nest'. This refers to the way in which the leaves are intertwined. A sort of heart-shaped nest is created, hence the popular name of 'nest fern'.

Asplenium bulbiferum

Bulbiferum means 'bulb-bearing'. The young plants grow on full-grown leaves from the bulbs.

No spleen

Asplenium is a Fern, most species of which have broad, light-green leaves.
The name comes from the Greek word *splen*, which means 'spleen'. The plant was previously used in medicine against diseases of the spleen. *A-splen* means 'without spleen', ie the patient is devoid of spleen when the medicine has taken effect. The Fern is a native of tropical Asia, East Africa and Polynesia. It sometimes grows there epiphytically, ie on the bark of a tree, which means that it has no defence against dryness or excessive water. It must have a reasonable amount of warmth, but does not require excessive sunlight.

Plants on the leaf

With Asplenium bulbiferum, new plantlets grow on the older leaves. These plants are therefore also called 'brood ferns'. If you wait until these small plants have roots, you can plant them in a humus-rich mixture with some river sand. It takes a long time for them to 'strike', but if you then pot them off into a humus-rich RHP potting soil, you will get splendid new Ferns. The propagation of Asplenium nidus takes place by means of spores (see page 168 for propagation by spores).
Sow the spores out in a humus-rich soil. The soil must be pure and not too acid for the spores to germinate.
After about seven weeks, a mossy layer will appear. This layer is called the prothallium and germination takes place in it. After about three months, plant out individual pieces of the prothallium. When the little Ferns which emerge from this are more or less separate plants, prick them out a few times in frozen peat soil until each plant stands on its own. Five to six months later, transplant them into a pot for cuttings. About six months later you will have beautiful new Ferns.

Less sturdy

Asplenium is one of the less sturdy plants, but it is still good to keep in the house. If you devote attention to it, it will grow quite large and last many years.
Although it originates from a humid region, it is nevertheless satisfied with a slightly less humid environment. Place the plant in slight shade; in the growing season it needs a certain amount of light, but no direct sunlight. Add fertilizer weekly at this time. Keep the potting soil moderately moist and ensure that the soil never becomes dry. Asplenium is particularly salt-sensitive and must be repotted annually.

Treatment table

	young plants	growth	rest
pot	3 in/7 cm	4-5 in/10-12 cm	—
soil	mixture with river sand	RHP	—
feeding	—	1 tsp compound fertilizer per pt water/2 g per litre	none
watering	moist	moist	moist
temperature	64-72° F/ 18-22° C	64-72° F/ 18-22° C	64-72° F/ 18-22° C
rel. humidity	70-80%	70-80%	60-70%
light	moderate	slight shade	slight shade

Leaves, flowers, large and small

The Begonia named after Michel Bégon, a Frenchman who lived from 1683 to 1710 and was, among other things, governor of Canada and a patron of botanical science.

The most important characteristic of the Begoniaceae family is that most species have asymmetrical eye or heart-shaped leaves. There are Begonias which are grown specially for their leaves and there are Begonias with magnificent, long-lasting flowers. Some species flower throughout the year.

The ancestors of the leaf Begonias came from Asia. The perpetually flowering Begonias with small flowers came originally from Africa and Begonias with large flowers have been obtained through crosses with tuberous Begonias from South America.

Begonia bowerii was cultivated in Mexico in 1950. It is the ancestor of many green-leaved hybrids.

Leaf cuttings

Many Begonias have the property of forming new buds on plant sections which have been cut off. Use is made of this property in the taking of cuttings in the form of a leaf or part of a leaf, so-called leaf cuttings.

Choose a good, undamaged specimen for leaf cuttings and remove young, immature leaves.

With numerous winter-flowering Begonias you place the leaves in a 2½-in/6-cm pot filled with peat-based compost, ie peat litter with a pH of 5.1 (see page 168 for acid level). The cuttings develop roots under double glass, plastic foil or mist (see page 169 for cuttings).

After two to three weeks roots appear on the leaf stalk and four weeks later sprouting begins. After a total of three months the cutting is sufficiently developed to be placed in a final pot.

You can take Begonia leaf cuttings throughout the year. With a leaf Begonia, the period is from mid-summer to mid-autumn. Cut the leaves into four-sided or triangular (Iron Cross Begonia) pieces approximately ½ in/1.5 cm long. Lay these pieces out on a mixture of three parts peat and one part river sand. Lay three to four pieces every 3 in²/20 cm² Roots will first appear at the edge of the pieces and the young plants will emerge later from the veins. About three months after taking cuttings, plant the young plants out at intervals of 1¼ in/3 cm. After two to three months place the plants in a pot for cuttings.

Pot on bigger plants after three months into a 5-in/12-cm pot. Pot the plants on again in mid-spring.

The growing period from cutting to mature plant is about nine months.

When growing leaf cuttings, the temperature must not rise above 68° F/20° C, or the cuttings will make too few suckers. The relative humidity during the rooting of the cutting must be about 90%. The ideal temperature for a good crop of suckers is 65° F/18° C. After potting on this becomes 68° F/20° C. Continue growing them thereafter at 65-68° F/18-20° C.

Leaf-cutting is the most suitable method of propagating Begonias.

Begonia Rieger hybrid 'Swabia'

Begonia Eliator hybrids

These large-flowered, winter-flowering Begonias were introduced into England at the end of the last century, when Veitch crossed Begonia socotrana with tuberous Begonias from South America, as well as the red Begonia veitchii, the yellow Begonia pearcei and the orange Begonia boliviensis. Due to mildew and bud-dropping, among other things, cultivation declined in the 1930s.

Begonia Rieger hybrid

Begonia Rieger hybrid

Begonia gigantea in the wild in Nepal

Begonia Semperflorens hybrid

Begonia boweri (and hybrids)

This species, named after Bower, was cultivated in America from Mexico in 1950. It is the ancestor of some green-leaved hybrids which are cultivated in the Laboratory for Horticultural Plant Breeding of the Agricultural College in Wageningen.

They are beautiful foliage plants with a leaf pattern in shades of green.

Begonia Semperflorens hybrids

Semperflorens means flowering the whole time. These hybrids are crosses of the South American species *Begonia semperflorens*, *Begonia gracilis* and *Begonia schmidtiana*.

They are profusely-flowering pot plants which are also widely grown for planting in the garden. There are white, red, pink and salmon-coloured varieties in many shades. Some are green-leaved, others are dark-leaved with a bronze-like tint. A well-known double-flowered variety is "Gustav Lind" with pink flowers. "Ingrid" is a white mutant and "Catharine" and "Remco" are red mutants of "Gustav Lind"; these are propagated from cuttings.

Shoot cuttings

You can propagate the winter-flowering Begonias by taking cuttings of young shoots from healthy, undamaged plants. In order to get plants which will themselves provide cuttings later — so-called 'mother plants' — take cuttings in mid-summer. You can take cuttings from these 'mother plants' from mid-winter to mid-summer.

Use a clean knife disinfected with methylated spirit to take the cutting. If you do not do this, you run the risk of infecting the cutting with bacterial pests such as Xanthomanus begoniae. The cuttings should be 4-5 in/10-12 cm long. Treat the wound tissue with Rhizopon BTO 0.1% growth hormone for a good rooting of the cutting.

Place the cuttings in peat-based compost with a pH of 5.1 (see page 168 for acid level). They root under double glass, plastic foil or mist (see page 169 for cuttings). The first cuttings have no leaf buds in the leaf axils and are called 'flower cuttings'. Plants from them are grown in a 3½-in/9-cm pot.

Place the rooted cuttings of perpetually flowering species in the pot in the winter months. In the spring and summer, pot them on into a 4-in/10-cm pot. If you have a leaf cutting with three suckers, you will get a beautiful, large plant without topping.

You can also place a single cutting with a single sucker in a pot. In this case top the latter about three weeks after potting, so that four leaves remain, after which the plant will branch out.

The growing time from cutting to flowering plant is about three months in winter and nine to ten weeks in summer. The cuttings root at a temperature of 65° F/18° C. Thereafter keep the temperature as for leaf cuttings. The relative humidity during the taking of cuttings should be 90% with the perpetually flowering species up to 95%. The cutting temperature for Rex hybrids, boweri and Iron Cross Begonia should be 68-77° F/20-25° C.

Sowing

The Begonia Semperflorens hybrids are propagated from seed. The seed is extremely fine-grained: some 70,000 seeds make up 1 tsp/g. The seed is usually sold in bags containing about 1,000 seeds. A certain amount of skill is required to sow these seeds evenly, so that they are not too close together and the young plants can develop freely.

Sow in a humus-rich seed-bed with a pH of 5.3 or even higher (see page 168 for acid level).

After six to eight weeks plant out the seedlings at intervals of ¾ in/2 cm. Six weeks later, plant them out 2 in/5 cm apart. A month later, pot the plants on into an 3½-in/8-cm pot. The growing period from sowing to the first flowering is about five months.

If you want a large plant, pot on two months after the initial potting into a 4½-in/11-cm pot.

The sowing temperature is 68-72° F/20-22° C with a relative humidity of 90-95%.

Long days

Winter-flowering Begonias, to grow well, need long days of 14 to 15 hours. If the days are too short, lengthen them by lighting with lamps. The wattage for bulbs is 7 Watt per yd²/m² and for TL 33, 3 Watt per yd²/m².

For best results, provide the lighting as a nightly interruption from 11 pm onwards, in the period from early autumn to mid-spring.

Begonia

Short days

The winter-flowering Begonia is a short-day plant which flowers more profusely and more regularly after a short-day period.

When the cuttings are 2½ in/6 cm long in summer and 4-5 in/10-12 cm in winter, the Begonia needs a short day for good flowering. A short day lasts 9 to 10 hours and the short-day period lasts twelve to fourteen days, depending on temperature and variety.

If later on you wish to spread the flowering over the whole year, apply a long- and a short-day treatment alternately. During flowering a temperature of 60° F/16° C is ideal. High temperatures above 77° F/25° C have an adverse effect on the flowers, giving them a 'shrunken' appearance. Moreover, full-grown leaf Begonias also flower profusely in the summer, with a mass of light-pink flowers on a long stem.

Bud-dropping and mildew

Bud-dropping and mildew are two problems in the growing and keeping of winter-flowering Begonias. You can help preserve the buds by preventing too many changes of climate from occurring in the room. Double-flowering varieties such as 'Aphrodite' are especially sensitive, particularly in the autumn and winter. Mildew occurs when the relative humidity falls below 65%. By regular spraying and sulphur vaporization or atomizing, you can prevent mildew from attacking Begonias. Sulphur must not be used on open blooms, or they will scorch.

Inhibiting and growing

For a beautiful, sturdy plant, spray it with an inhibitor when the flower bud has formed. Depending on the requirement, repeat the treatment after eight to ten days.

A requirement for all Begonias is that the soil must always remain fairly moist.

Flowering Begonias require a light position away from direct sunlight. The light requirement for a long day is normally 200 mW per yd²/m²; perpetually flowering specimens require more light (6000 mW per yd²/m²) and again no direct sunlight. Leaf Begonias need far less light and even strong, indirect daylight in the summer can be harmful. These plants give a good account of themselves in a room with slight shade. During the growing season, give the plant some fertilizer weekly.

Feed flowering Begonias once every two weeks.

Begonia rex hybrid

Begonia Rex hybrids

These leaf Begonias were obtained from the crossing of the Begonia rex from Assam with the Begonia diadema from Borneo. They are perennial plants of which there are a large number of varieties with various leaf colours and shapes.

Begonia Rieger hybrids

In the 1950s the German, Otto Rieger, crossed Begonia socotrana with modern tuberous Begonia hybrids, called B. bertinii hybrids. He produced new hybrids with good resistance to bud-dropping and mildew. This group includes the most widely grown variety, 'Swabia' (red), with a few orange, yellow and white mutants. The variety 'Krefeld', with dark red stems and leaves, was also produced, as were varieties with small flowers such as the red 'Anita', from which mutants were again obtained. The double-flowering pink variety, 'Aphrodite', and the white mutant, 'Marco', are prone to bud-dropping in the winter.

Begonia socotrana has been crossed with tuberous Begonia hybrids to produce a number of outstanding hybrids, such as the varieties 'Trudy' (red), 'Tacora' (carmine), 'Toran' (orange) and many others.

Treatment table Begonia Rex hybrids

	cutting	growth	rest
pot	2½ in/6 cm	4-5 in/10-12 cm	—
soil	peat dust and river sand 3:1	RHP	—
feeding	—	1 tsp compound fertilizer per pt water/2 g per litre	—
temperature	68-77° F/ 20-25° C	64-68° F/ 18-20° C	—
rel. humidity	90-95%	75%	
light	—	slight shade 300-1,100 mW per yd²/m²	—
flowers	—	summer	—

special features   The temperature of pricked-out plants during growing should be 68°F/20°C with a relative humidity of 70-80%.
The temperature should never be more than 77° F/25° C.

Begonia rieger hybrid 'Krefeld'

Begonia rieger hybrid 'Aphrodite'

Begonia masoniana

This leaf Begonia is also known as Iron Cross Begonia. The plant is named after the 20th-century American botanist Herbert L. Mason.
The plant was introduced to the West as a novelty from Singapore in 1945.

Begonia masoniana 'Iron Cross'

Begonia maculata 'Picta'

Treatment table   Begonia Elatior hybrids

	cutting	growth	rest
pot	1½-2½ in/ 4-6 cm	4-5¾ in/ 10-14 cm	—
soil	peat-based compost	RHP	RHP
feeding	—	1 tsp compound fertilizer per pt water/2 g per litre	—
watering	moist	moist	—
temperature	< 68° F/ 20° C (leaf) 64-68° F/ 18-20° C (shoot)	64-68°F/ 18-20° C	60-62°F/ 16-17°C
rel. humidity	90%	65-70%	65-70%
light	strong	200 mWp per yd²/m²	200 mW per yd²/m²
inhibitor	—	¹/₆ -¹/₃ fl oz CCC and ¹/₁₆ fl oz wetter per pt water/5-10 and 2 ml per litre	—
growth hormone	Rhizopon BTO 0.1%	—	—

special features   No growth hormone should be used with leaf cuttings. The ideal temperature during flowering is 60° F/16° C.

Treatment table Begonia Semperflorens hybrids

seed	cutting	growth	rest
pot seed	3 in/7 cm	4-5 in/10-12 cm	—
soil seed	peat-based compost	RHP	—
feeding	—	1 tsp compound fertilizer per pt water/2 g per litre	
temperature	64-68° F/ 18-20° C	68-77° F/ 18-25° C (sun)	—
rel. humidity	95%	70-80%	—
light	strong	6,000 mW per yd²/m²	—
flowers	—	all year	—
inhibitor	—	¹/₆-¹/₃ fl oz CCC and ¹/₁₆ fl oz wetter per pt water/ 5-10 ml and 2 ml per litre ('Gustav Lind')	—

special features   The temperature in the flowering season should be 64° F/18° C.
The sowing temperature should be 68-72° F/20-22° C with a relative humidity of 90-95%.

Begonia maculata
A Begonia with speckled leaves.

Begonia fuchsioides
These Begonias have bunches of orange-red flowers.

Begonia serratipetala
This is a small-leaved variety with a bronze-coloured leaf which is speckled red.

Begonia hydrocotylefolia
This Begonia has fibrous, round, dark-green leaves.

Begonia heracleifolia
This species has large, deeply-indented leaves.

Begonia hispida 'Cucullifera'
This is a green-leaved species with small plants on the leaf.

Begonia incana
This succulent-type Begonia has grey, felty leaves.

Begonia Lorraine hybrids
These are small-flowered, winter-flowering Begonias which were obtained by crossing Begonia socotrana with Begonia dregei. By mutation and further inbreeding of Begonia socotrana, varieties such as 'Marina' (pink), 'Regent' (pink) and the white 'Snowprincess' were obtained. A particular variety has a darker, reddish leaf colour.

Beloperone/Shrimp plant

Sharp and pointed

The name Beloperone comes from the Greek *belos* and *perone*. *Belos* means 'spear' and *perone* means 'long needle'. The description, sharp and pointed, refers to the shape of the connective.

Beloperone, which belongs to the Acanthaceae family, comes originally from Mexico. It was cultivated in England in 1934.

Beloperone is a free-flowering pot plant with herbaceous stems. It flowers from late winter to mid-summer.

Undamaged plants

When taking cuttings of Beloperone, select a healthy, undamaged plant. The plant is sensitive to root rot and can be attacked by root knob nematode, a disease which can be recognized by knob-type thickenings of the roots. It is preferable not to use a specimen affected in this way for taking cuttings.

You can start taking cuttings in mid-summer and continue up to late winter, provided that the shoots have not formed buds. Place five to seven cuttings in a 3½-in/9-cm pot filled with frozen peat potting soil, or nine to eleven cuttings in a 4½-in/11-cm pot. A single cutting can also be placed in a 2-in/5-cm pot and transferred to its final pot after five to six weeks. Cover the cuttings with plastic foil or place them under mist (see page 169 for cuttings). They will be well-rooted after four weeks. If you want large plants, top them once. The growing period is three to seven months, depending on the desired plant size and whether topping has taken place or not.

When the shoots are 3-4 in/8-10 cm long, spray them with an inhibitor in order to check the upward growth. In warm weather the plant sometimes grows too luxuriantly, in which case spraying with half the concentration of inhibitor should be repeated after 10 days.

Light and moist

Beloperone needs lots of light. It is a long-day plant which needs shielding against strong sunlight in the spring and summer. During the growing season water it frequently; the potting soil must be fairly moist at all times. Apply fertilizer weekly some six weeks after taking cuttings. Discontinue when the plant flowers.

Beloperone guttata

Beloperone guttata 'Norgaards Favorite'

Beloperone guttata

The best variety is 'Norgaards Favorite'. *Gutta* means 'drop' in Latin, and *guttata* means 'speckled with drops' or 'drop-like spots'. The flowers of this Beloperone have dark-coloured dots.

Beloperone is sometimes called the shrimp plant and the hanging inflorescences certainly resemble a shrimp. The bracts of the flowers also have the orange-pink colour of shrimp. The flowerets themselves are white and soon drop. But the decorative and colourful cover can still be enjoyed for a long time.

Treatment table

	cutting	growth	rest
pot	4 in/9 cm	4-5 in/10-12 cm	—
soil	frozen peat potting soil	RHP	—
feeding	—	1 tsp compound fertilizer per pt water/2 g per litre	none
watering	copiously	frequently	moderately
temperature	72° F/22° C	60-62° F/ 15-16° C	—
rel. humidity	> 95%	70-80%	—
light	light	strong	—
flowers	—	late winter to mid-summer	—
inhibitor	1¾ fl oz B9 per pt water/50 ml per litre	⅞ fl oz B9 per pt per water/25 ml per litre	—

special features Use a potassium-rich mixture as fertilizer. Maintain the temperature at 60-62°F/15-16°C to avoid luxuriant growth. Shield against strong sunlight.

Billbergia x windii

Billbergia x windii

This plant, which is the variety most commonly found, is a cross between Billbergia decora (ornamental) and Billbergia nutans.

Billbergia nutans

Another Bromeliad

Billbergia is named after G. J. Billberg, the Swedish author of a book on the flora of Scandinavia.

Billbergia is a Bromeliad (see Bromelaceae), but this easy-to-grow houseplant differs in certain respects from most other Bromeliads. To begin with, it grows in the wild on the ground and not epiphytically.

Secondly, Billbergia is much easier to get to flower, without the need for any flowering treatment with acetylene gas. The suckers from the mother plant flower together in a single pot. Most species of the genus Billbergia are natives of Brazil, there being about thirty in all. You will not meet them very often in floriculture. They are true plants for the enthusiast, with Billbergia x windii being the favourite. This is a cross of Billbergia decora and Billbergia nutans. *Decora* is Latin for 'ornamental' and *nutans* means 'waving'.

Straight into a final pot

Suckers used to propagate Billbergia should be allowed to reach their full length on the mother plant. They can then be placed straight into a 4½-in/11-cm final pot.

Repot in the early summer

Billbergia is a strong and simple houseplant. It poses few problems for persons who pay little attention to their houseplants. If you allow the suckers to remain on the mother plant, they will flower in a year's time without any treatment. In that case repot the plants in late spring or early summer. In this way you will get a large plant with numerous peduncles in the summer.

The plant should not be repotted after its autumn flowering, since repotting then inhibits the growth of young shoots. Billbergia requires a humus-rich, light soil which must be kept moist at all times. Keep the leaf sheath part-filled with water. During the growing season, feed weekly with a nitrogen-potassium mixture in the proportions of 1:2.

Treatment table

	suckers	growth	rest
pot	5 in/11 cm	6 in/12 cm	—
soil	very humus-rich	very humus-rich	
feeding	compound fertilizer 10:5:20 1 tsp per pt water/2 g per litre	compound fertilizer 10:5:20 1 tsp per pt water/2 g per litre	—
temperature	64-77°F/ 18-25°C	64-77°F/ 18-25°C	> 60°F/ 15°C
rel. humidity	75-80%	75-80%	60-70%
light	moderate	plenty, but avoid strong sunlight	plenty

special features The minimum night temperature is 60°F/15°C.

Blechnum

Fern

Blechnum is an old Greek word for 'fern'. The plant is indeed clearly a Fern and many members of its family are not easy to keep as a houseplant (see Pteridaceae). Blechnum belongs to the family Blechnaceae.

Blechnum gibbum came originally from the New Caledonia Islands in the Pacific Ocean. Other Blechnum species which are grown as houseplants occur in the wild in tropical America. Blechnum is a Fern which in the course of time acquires a tree-like stem.

Spores

Blechnum, like all Ferns, is propagated directly from spores. These are not seeds, because they are not yet fertilized and by themselves can never grow into full-grown plants. Fertilization takes place after the spores have pre-germinated. They form then a mossy layer, called the prothallium.

To allow the seeds to pre-germinate, sow the spores in a pure, not too acidic, humus-rich mixture. Soil which is too acid impedes the pre-germination.

First plant out individual pieces of the prothallium, and when little Ferns can clearly be seen emerging, plant them out in a frame containing frozen peat potting soil. After two or three months, place them in a pot for cuttings and about six months later you will have some handsome ferns. (see page 168 for propagation by spores).

High relative humidity

Blechnum insists on a moist, light, shady environment. The relative humidity must therefore be high, and the potting soil should be kept moderately moist. Repot the plant every year. Although this is a splendid Fern with beautiful, shining leaves, it is usually difficult to keep in the home. If you keep it in a hothouse or greenhouse and give it the attention it needs, you can nevertheless enjoy it for many years.

Treatment table

	growth	rest
pot	5 in/12 cm	—
soil	humus-rich RHP	—
feeding	1 tsp compound fertilizer per pt water/2 g per litre	none
watering	fairly moist	infrequently
temperature	64-77° F/ 18-25° C	> 54° F/ 12° C
rel. humidity	70-80%	70-80%
light	slight shade	light

special features   The plant cannot tolerate too low a relative humidity in any circumstances.

Blechnum gibbum

Blechnum gibbum

Gibbum means 'vaulted' and refers to the shape of the leathery leaves. This is the most common species.

Blechnum occidentale as a tree Fern

Blechnum occidentale

The leaves of this Blechnum are somewhat sickle-shaped and do not stand so close together on the stem.

Blechnum brasiliense

This Blechnum has somewhat leathery leaves which sit close together in rosettes and partly cover each other.

Bougainvillea spectabilis (Bougainvillea glabra) 'Alexandra'

Spectabilis means 'amiable' or 'loveable' and *glabra* means 'smooth, hairless'. 'Alexandra' is the most widely grown variety. It has deep violet bracts and the flowers, which quickly wilt, are flute-shaped and creamy-white.

Bougainvillea spectabilis 'Amethyst'

This variety, with its purple-violet bracts, is usually found with its branches trained along a wire.

Bougainvillea peruviana 'Variegata'

This variegated variety is only occasionally encountered and almost never flowers.

Bougainvillea spectabilis 'Gruss aus Bodenweiler'

This is the best of a group of Bougainvilleas with large flowers in the colours red, orange, yellow and pink. This pink variety is the only one which flowers well in a pot. The others flower well outside in the greenhouse.

South American family

This plant makes one think of the south of France rather than Brazil, from where it originally came. It is named after a famous French seafarer, L.A. Bougainville (1729-1811). He accompanied the botanist, Commerson, who during his expeditions collected more than 25,000 plants, including Bougainvillea, from all over the world.

Bougainvillea is a member of the family Nyctaginaceae, which occurs in the wild exclusively in South America.

Light and sun

Take an intermediate cutting of Bougainvillea with three or four pairs of leaves. Cut the cutting from well-developed twigs. You can take cuttings throughout the year, but summer is the best time.

Place the cuttings in a mixture of two parts peat dust and three parts river sand, after first treating them with growth hormone. The cuttings grow roots under plastic foil or under mist (see page 169 for cuttings).

After five to six weeks they will have rooted and you can place them in a 4-5 in/10-12 cm pot, depending on the size of plant desired. For a good compact plant, place two cuttings in a single pot. Top them twice and then let the plants overwinter. If they get lots of light and sun in the spring, cut them back and the young shoots will flower in the summer.

Dry treatment

You can get the plant to flower if the pot ball shows good root penetration. Cut back all branches, allowing a small piece of each stem to remain. When new shoots have formed on the latter, set the plant in a light and sunny position for six weeks for the formation of flower buds on the young shoots. During this period give the plant just enough water to prevent the young shoots from drying up. The day temperature may be up to 95° F/35° C, though the night temperature must then drop considerably. Too high a night temperature has an adverse effect on the formation of flower buds. When the flower buds appear, after about six weeks, water liberally. In the growing season give extra feed each week. Starve the plant during the dry treatment and renew weekly feed thereafter (with a lower concentration of fertilizer). When the plant is flowering well, plunge it in growth hormone. Then allow it to dry quickly to prevent the dropping of new flower buds.

Bougainvillea is a sturdy plant, but it grows and flowers well only if it gets lots of sunlight. You will rarely get a Bougainvillea to flower in the spring because of the lack of light.

It is a woody plant which lasts a long time and its magnificent colours can be enjoyed for many years in a hothouse or greenhouse, but only if it is allowed to overwinter frost-free.

Bougainvillea spectabilis 'Alexandra'

Treatment table

	cutting	growth	rest
pot	4-5 in/10-12 cm	4-5 in/10-12 cm	—
soil	peat dust/ river sand 2:3	RHP	—
feeding	—	1½ tsp compound fertilizer per pt water/3 g per litre	—
watering	moist	frequently	seldom
temperature	72-77° F/ 22-25° C	68-95° F/ 20-35° C	> 10° F/ 50° C
rel. humidity	> 95%	60-70%	60-70%
light	strong	abundant	abundant
flowers	—	late spring to mid-autumn	—
growth hormone	Rhizopon AK 0.5%	Rhizopon B 10 mg/1 l water (tablets)	—

special features   During the flowering treatment, water infrequently with no feed. Thereafter use 1 tsp of compound fertilizer per pt water/2 g per litre. Treat cuttings with growth hormone. During the dry treatment the temperature is 64°-95° F/18-35° C, at night 64-68° F/18-20° C, with a relative humidity of 80%.

Bromeliaceae/Bromeliads

Tropical South America

The Bromeliaceae form a plant family which has a large turnover in the pot-plant trade.

They are sturdy and easy-to-maintain plants whose beautifully decorated leaves, once the plants have flowered, retain their ornamental effect for a long time.

Bromeliads are plants with a short stem from which the leaves form a sort of gully leading into a water-tight sheath. The water which the plant takes up via the base of the leaves collects there. These leaves are lancet-shaped and mostly hard and leathery.

The Bromeliaceae include 60 genera, all of which originate from South America. Some species, such as Ananas, have as a result of human cultivation also run wild in other regions, most notably Africa.

They grow only in tropical and sub-tropical regions between 38° N and 24° S. They very often grow on the bark of trees and tree trunks, ie epiphytically, but since they do not use the trees as a source of food, they are not parasites. The leaves form spiral-shaped rosettes and the longitudinal growth ends in a flower bud. After flowering, the plant continues to grow via its side-buds, which grow out to form new plants.

Growth regulators

Depending on the genus and the circumstances, Bromeliads normally flower four to seven years after they have emerged from seed. Moreover, they flower at a certain time of the year, though with growth regulators they can be brought to flower both much earlier and also over the whole year. Commercial growers use various methods to achieve this. For example, they cover the plants for 24 hours with plastic foil and gas them with acetylene gas from cylinders at a pressure of 0.2 atmospheres. Alternatively, they bubble acetylene gas from a cylinder into the water contained in the leaf sheath at a pressure of 0.2 atmospheres. After a week the water is poured out of the sheath. Another method is to bubble acetylene gas for 10 minutes in 20 pt/10 l of water at a pressure of 0.2 atmospheres, and then pour ½ fl oz/15 ml of the solution into the sheath. The solution is poured out again a week later.

There is also a special agent on the market: BOH (Brombloei). You should pour 8 fl oz/250 ml of this into a plastic bucket containing 6 pt/3 l of water, and again pour ½ fl oz/15 ml of the solution into the sheath and leave for a week. BOH is the most reliable agent with the best results on young plants and in the hard winter months. It is obtainable in packs of 8 fl oz/250 ml and the solution must be used immediately after preparation. The undiluted agent can be kept indefinitely.

There is also a solvent, Ethrel-Brom, with spreader which has to be sprayed over the plant. Use 4 pt/2 l of sprayed liquid per yd²/m². The dosage varies from ½-2 fl oz per pt of water/25-110 ml per litre, depending on the genus and the time of year.

A plant must be large enough for the treatment and no longer in the growing stage. The temperature during the treatment must not be less than 68° F/20° C. The results are better in the summer than in months with reduced light. The plant will flower two to four months after the treatment.

Guzmania 'Minor Orange'

Aechemea in the wild in Colombia

Browallia speciosa 'Major'

Browallia speciosa 'Major'

Speciosa means 'delicate beauty' and major means 'big'.
Browallia is one of the few flowering pot plants with blue flowers. It is an attractive summer-flowerer with lustrous leaves which, if you treat the plant well, will give you pleasure for several years.

Blue flowers

Browallia is named after the Finnish professor of physics, Johan Browallius (1707-1755), who collaborated with the famous Swedish scientist, Linnaeus.
Browallia is a member of the family Solanaceae, the nightshades. The nightshade family is of great interest to man because some of its members, such as the tomato, the Spanish pepper, the paprika and the potato, are an important source of food. Browallia, a native of Colombia, is one of the few flowering pot plants with a beautiful blue colour. The plant was cultivated in England in 1846.

Very small seeds

You can take cuttings from the plant from late winter to mid-summer. Select herbaceous shoots and allow them to root in so-called calceolaria soil under mist or plastic foil (see page 169 for cuttings).
You can also grow the plant from seed in late winter. The seeds are very small: one gram contains 4,200 seeds and gives about 3,000 plants. Sow in calceolaria soil and six weeks after sowing plant the seedlings in a 3½-in/9-cm pot. Or set them out separately after four weeks, planting three plantlets in a 3½-in/9-cm pot after a further four weeks. Remove the tops three to four weeks later.
About ten weeks after topping, the plants are ready to flower. If you do not top them, you can also set five or six plants in a 3½-in/9-cm pot. The growing period is then a month shorter.

Calceolaria soil

Browallia grows best in calceolaria soil. Extra iron is added to this soil to prevent the leaf turning yellow through lack of chlorophyll.
Keep the soil moist during the growing season, dry during the winter. Feed weekly during the growing season. The plant will flower once every two weeks except during the winter.
Browallia needs plenty of light but cannot tolerate strong sunlight in the spring or summer.
To prevent the shoots which are to flower coming through too far and becoming weak, treat them when they are about 1½ in/4 cm long with inhibitor. Repeat the spraying after ten days and continue the treatment until the plant flowers. A well-cared-for Browallia can grow to be a large plant.
Adequate light is required for profuse flowering. It is a long-day plant and therefore flowers only in the summer.
After the winter cut the plant back and young shoots will then appear on which the plant will flower.

Treatment table

	cutting	growth	rest
pot	3¾ in/9 cm	4-5 in/10-12 cm	—
soil	calceolaria	calceolaria	—
feeding	—	1½ tsp compound fertilizer per pt water/3 g per litre	—
watering	frequently	moist	dry
temperature	72° F/22° C	64-74° F/ 18-23° C	50-60° F/ 10-15° C
rel. humidity	> 95%	70%	60-70%
light	strong	strong	strong
flowers	—	summer	—
inhibitor	—	²/₃ fl oz B9 per pt water/ 20 ml per litre	—

special features Overwinter in cool and airy conditions. Avoid strong sunlight in spring and summer.

Brunfelsia

A shadow in the night

Brunfelsia, like Browallia, is a member of the family
Solanaceae, the nightshades. Although there are some very
useful nightshades, such as the tomato, the paprika and the
potato, other members of this family are highly poisonous.
The word 'nightshade' comes from 'night shadow' and the
plant was at one time associated with evil spirits in the night.
Brunfelsia is named after Otto Brunfels (1489-1534), a
theologian who became chaplain to Martin Luther.
It is a shrub with large pink flowers and a native of Brazil. It
was first cultivated in England in 1850.

Keep leaves intact

If you want to take cuttings of the plant, select a strong,
undamaged plant and take either the top or parts of shoots
(intermediate cutting).
Do not shorten the leaves, because this will permanently
damage the plant's appearance. Take cuttings in high
summer and treat them with Rhizopon BT for good rooting.
Place the cuttings in a 3-in/7-cm pot filled with RHP potting
soil. To produce compact plants set three cuttings in a single
pot. Under double glass or plastic foil they will have rooted
after six to seven weeks.
Each plant can be placed in a 4-5-in/10-12-cm final pot after
about 10 weeks.

Cold treatment

To get the plants flowering well, give them a cold treatment
lasting for six to nine weeks from mid-autumn. Give them a
good feed with nitrogen beforehand. This gives more flowers
and prevents the leaves from turning yellow. During the
treatment the temperature should be 48-54° F/ 9-12° C at six
weeks and 54-59° F/12-15° C at nine weeks. During the cold
treatment keep the soil fairly moist, but when the buds
become visible water generously. The plant is normally fed
weekly, but four weeks before the cold regime give it some
extra nitrogen-rich fertilizer, such as urea. Feed once every
two weeks thereafter up to flowering.
The plant does not require much light and can certainly not
tolerate strong sunlight. Give it as much light as possible in
autumn and winter. After topping, the herbaceous shoots
form few branches or none at all. You must therefore prune
back to the wood. Brunfelsia can become a large, sturdy
shrub, flowering abundantly every year, if you give it a cold
treatment plus a good feed.

Brunfelsia calycina

Brunfelsia calycina (Brunfelsia)

A profusely flowering shrub with large
pink flowers.
Calycina means 'with large persistent
calix'. The magnificent profusion of this
free-flowering houseplant will give you
pleasure for many years. It is difficult both
to produce and to keep sufficient foliage
on the plant. The feeding plays an
important role here.

Treatment table

	cutting	growth	rest
pot	3 in/7 cm	4-5 in/10-12 cm	—
soil	RHP	RHP	—
feeding	—	1 tsp compound fertilizer per pt water/2 g per litre	—
watering	liberally	moist	moderate
temperature	77-86° F/ 25-30° C	64-77° F/ 18-25° C	about 50° F/ 10° C
rel. humidity	> 90%	80%	60-70%
light		slight shade	light
flowers	—	spring and summer	—
growth hormone	Rhizopon BT, 0.2%	—	—
special features	Shield well against strong sunlight. Give it a nitrogen-rich feed before the cold regime in solution of 1 tsp urea per pt water/2 g per litre. Cold regime: 48-54°F/9-12°C or 54-60°F/12-15°C, and thereafter 68°F/20° C with a relative humidity of 70-80%. Water a budding plant generously.		

Various grafted cactaceae

Living water tank

Cacti are desert plants with thick fleshy stems which are pillar-, disc- or ball-shaped. The name Cactus is a Latin form of the old Greek name, *kaktos*, by which is meant a thorny plant (not a Cactus). The first Cacti became known after the discovery of America in 1492. Originally they were indigenous to America, but since then they have spread throughout the world to all hot, dry regions.

Cacti are capable of absorbing large amounts of water in a short time and retaining it over long periods.

In most cases they have no leaves, but prickly thorns with which to ward off thirsty animals in the desert.

Cacti are ideal houseplants for many people. They can stand in the sun and require little attention. Temperature fluctuations do not do any harm; on the contrary, they will flower better as a result. Central heating, the great enemy of most houseplants, does not harm them, unless it remains on at night.

Certain flowering Cacti, such as Zygocactus, Rhipsalidopsis, Epiphyllum and Chamaecereus, are dealt with individually in this book.

Cuttings, seed and grafting

Take cuttings in the rest period from full-grown shoots. Allow the wound to dry up. For good root formation, this drying must take place vertically; otherwise you will get roots only on one side of the cutting wound. Place the cuttings in equal parts of river sand and peat dust. All Cacti species can also be grown from seed. The seeds germinate very quickly in a lime-rich, highly porous mixture. The soil and the seed must never get dry. For a better growth, many Cactus species can be grafted on to a rootstock. Rootstocks often used are Pereskia, Pereskiopsis and Trichocereus. You sometimes see in the shops Cacti which have been incorrectly grafted for a longer life. The well-known red Gymnocalcium mihanovichii 'Friedrichii', which requires little water and a low temperature in the winter, is very often grafted on to Myrtillocactus geometrizans, which needs frequent watering and lots of heat. The grower has had rapid growth in mind, but the life of the cactus has been reduced.

Hot and cold

You must give Cacti a life as similar to that of the desert as possible. They like hot days with strong sunlight, followed by cold nights. In the wild the day temperature may well rise to 122° F/50° C, and the night temperature drop to freezing point. Water generously once a week during the growing period.

In the winter allow the plants to rest and keep the temperature and relative humidity low. Most Cacti absorb practically no water at this time. Feed sparingly, except in the growing period.

Cacti do not like an acid soil. Grow them in a mixture of three parts RHP peat dust potting compost, two parts heavy clay and one part river sand. If the mixture is too acid, add 2½ tsp of Dolokal per pint of the mixture/5 g per litre in order to increase the pH.

Treatment table

	cutting	growth	rest
pot	dependent on size	dependent on size	—
soil	sand-peat 1:1	RHP-clay-sand 3:2:1	—
feeding	—	lime-rich mixture ½ tsp compound fertilizer per pt/1 g per litre	none
watering	one generous watering	one generous watering	seldom
temperature	up to 105° F/ 40° C	up to 120° F/ 50° C (cool at night)	40-60° F/ 5-15° C
rel. humidity	low	low	low
light	as much as possible	as much as possible	as much as possible

special features Water generously once a week.
Feed sparingly with a relative humidity of less than 50%.
They can flower the whole year if given a short-day treatment.

Caladium

Edible tubers

The name Caladium is a Latin corruption of the Malay word, Keladi, better known as Taro. Caladium, like many other members of the Arum family (Araceae), has tasty, edible roots. The Caladium species which we know as houseplants are crosses of Caladium bicolor, Caladium humboldtii and Caladium schomburghii. These species are natives of tropical South America.

A large amount of cross-breeding of these species has taken place in the United States, where 30 or more named species are grown.

Tubers which keep

The leaves of Caladium die in the autumn and the plant then overwinters as a tuber. In addition to one large tuber, a number of small, immature tubers are produced each year. These grow into full-sized tubers in the subsequent growing season. From the end of winter to mid-summer place the dry tubers in a 4-5-in/10-12-cm pot. The soil must be warm to produce good leaf formation.

You can also lay the tubers out first in a tray with peat dust in order to germinate. If suckers appear, pot them up. This method takes up less space.

The growing time from laying out to mature plant is four to five months.

Caladium can also be propagated from seed. Obtaining and growing the seedlings is done in the same way as with Anthurium (see Anthurium). Commercial growers usually grow the plants from tubers cultivated in America.

Beautiful plants with a short life

This splendid foliage plant, with its delicate colours, is not often grown, perhaps because it is beautiful only in the summer months. When the days begin to get shorter, the plant starts to die. For many people this short life is a drawback. For the genuine enthusiast, however, the Caladium is a splendid plant. It makes high demands on temperature and relative humidity and requires a long day for its growth. When the daylight becomes less than 12 hours, the leaves die and the tuber starts to grow. Discontinue watering at this stage.

During the growing season keep the soil fairly moist and place the plant in a light position. Shield it against strong sunlight. If the tuber has sprouted, give it a weekly feed. Keep the dry tubers in dry peat dust at a temperature of 59-64° F/15-18° C. You can keep it in this state for up to seven months and can stagger the potting.

Caladium bicolor hybrid

Caladium bicolor hybridum

This is one of the many beautiful end-products of crosses which have been made in the United States with Caladium bicolor, Caladium humboldtii and Caladium schomburghii.

Caladium bicolor hybrid

Treatment table

	tuber	growth	rest
pot	tray	4-5 in/10-12 cm	tray
soil	peat dust	humus-rich RHP	peat dust
feeding	none	1 tsp compound fertilizer per pt water/2 g per litre	none
watering	moist	moderate	dry
temperature	72-77° F/ 22-25° C	64-68° F/ 18-20° C up to 86° F/ 30° C in the sun	60-68° F/ 15-18° C
rel. humidity	80%	80-85%	50-60%
light	light	light	—

special features   Shield against strong sun. Harden the plant off at 64° F/18° C, with a relative humidity of 70-80%.

Caladium 'Candidum' hybrid

Calathea lancifolia

Calathea makoyana

Calathea crocata

Calathea makoyana

This species is a native of Brazil. The leaves of this beautifully decorated plant are frequently used in artificial flower arrangement.

Calathea lancifolia

Lancifolia means 'lancet-shaped leaves'. These leaves are often cut off and used for embellishing floral arrangements.

Calathea ornata 'Roseolineata'

This is also a plant which is used for decorative purposes, ornata meaning 'decorative'. The leaves have pink lines.

Calathea ornata 'Albolineata'

A plant with white (albo) lines on the leaf.

Calathea ornata 'Sanderiana'

This variety has a broader leaf with fine pink, later white, leaf decoration. Calathea picturata, Calathea mediopicta, Calathea roseopicta and Calathea zebrina are cultivated to only a limited extent.

Calathea insignis

Insignis means 'attracting attention in a decorative fashion'. The splendid leaves of this plant certainly do this.

Calathea crocata

Crocata means 'saffron-coloured'. This splendid Calathea is grown for its leaves.

Not Maranta

This plant is, incorrectly, also called Maranta, although with its very finely decorated leaves it certainly resembles the well-known Ten Commandment Plant.

Although they belong to the Maranta family, Marantaceae, Calatheas develop wings and grow higher than the little Maranta. In addition, the ovary of Calathea consists of three parts (triangular), whereas Maranta is unicellular.

The name Calathea comes from the Greek kalathos, which means 'wicker-basket'. The inflorescence of Calathea somewhat resembles a basket. The Calathea species are natives of South America and the Indians there used at one time to weave baskets from the long leaves of these plants.

Division

Calathea is a plant which can be propagated by division. To do this, plant it outside. When the plant is fully grown, it forms a mass of young shoots in the autumn. Remove the plant from the ground in mid- to late autumn and pull out the young shoots with pieces of root individually. Each shoot must have at least three leaves. Plant each of these shoots in a pot containing a fibrous, porous, humus-rich soil. The so-called Bromelia soil is excellent for this purpose.

The plant will now form new roots and in the spring you will again have magnificent new plants.

Leaves and flowers

Most Calathea species are grown for their foliage. The leaves are so beautifully decorated and they keep so long when cut, that they are widely used to embellish flower arrangements. Calathea crocata is grown for its magnificent orange inflorescence and darker metal-coloured leaf. A Calathea needs lots of water during the growing season, but the underside must not get so wet that you can squeeze the water from it. Feed weekly during the growing season, once a month in the darker winter months. Calathea is by origin a forest plant; so plant it in slight shade. With excessive light the temperature may rise too high (above 77° F/25° C) or the relative humidity fall too low (below 80%).

Calatheas are some of the most beautiful foliage plants, but they are difficult houseplants because they need such a high relative humidity and are so salt-sensitive. The quality of many plants leaves much to be desired, because they often stand too low in the pot and have insufficient new roots to make good growth.

They are ideal plants for growing in the greenhouse and are particularly suited to planting out in a greenhouse border.

Treatment table

	cutting	growth	rest
pot	dependent on size	6-7 in/15-18 cm (plastic)	—
soil	Bromeliad soil	—	—
feeding	—	1 tsp compound fertilizer per pt water/2 g per litre	1 tsp compound fertilizer per pt water/2 g per litre
watering	moist	generously	moderately
temperature	72° F/22° C	68-72° F/20-22° C	64-68° F/18-20° C
rel. humidity	95%	> 80%	> 80%
light	moderate	shade	light no sunlight

special features In sunlight, the maximum temperature is 77° F/25° C, with a minimum relative humidity of 80%.

Many relatives in our country

Although most Calceolaria species are descended from wild plants in Chile and Peru, they have many relatives in the West. They belong to the Scrophulariaceae, or bent grass/herb family.

The name Calceolaria comes from the Latin *calceolus* for 'half-boot'. But the wide, puffed-up lower lip of the flower is more like a small slipper. It is therefore sometimes called the Slipper plant. The present-day hybrids are crosses of Calceolaria arachnoidea, Calceolaria corymbosa and Calceolaria crenatiflora.

Cold regime and long day

Calceolaria is an annual which cannot be overwintered, but has to be resown each year. If you select a handsome seed plant and pollinate it artificially with a brush, the seed will be ripe two months after pollination and you will have about 30,000 little seeds. In order to prevent damping off, disinfect the seed with a fungicide. Sow the seed throughout the summer, depending on the desired flowering time.

After eight weeks you will have some sturdy plantlets for pricking out, which after another six to eight weeks can be placed in a 3-4-in/8-9-cm final pot. The plant should then be watered generously. For good flowering the plants must stand in a cool spot, preferably at a temperature of 46-50° F/8-10°C. After four to six weeks the flower buds will appear, at which time the flowering may be advanced by a long-day treatment, using light as a nightly interruption to extend the day up to 16 hours. A TL 33 provides 1,000 mW per yd^2/m^2. If you start the treatment in late autumn, the plants will flower in six weeks. Shorten this period by a week as the months progress. If you start in mid-winter, the plant will flower after as little as four weeks.

Cool and moist

Calceolaria is by origin a mountain plant which likes cool, humid air. A house is not so suitable a place for it. The plant can also be attacked by aphids.

On a window-sill you must shield it against the sun. The plants normally flower in mid- to late spring, but the flowering can be advanced artificially as described above.

The plant is grown in special Calceolaria soil (RHP). Extra iron is added to this soil to prevent a shortage of chlorophyll, which turns the leaves yellow. Keep the potting soil fairly moist without letting it become waterlogged. Feeding is not necessary during the growing season, but when flowering begins give the plant some fertilizer once every two weeks.

Calceolaria Herbeo hybrid 'Multiflora'

Calceolaria Herbeo hybrid 'Multiflora'

Calceolaria Herbeo hybrid 'Multiflora'

This is the collective name of small-flowered varieties which were obtained by the crossing of Calceolaria arachnoidea (spider-type), Calceolaria corymbosa (berry-type) and Calceolaria crenatiflora (with curled leaf).

Multiflora means 'with many leaves'. The natural habitat of th Calceolaria species is the forests and mountains of Peru and Chile; they were cultivated in England in 1830 and much work has since taken place to provide new varieties which require practically no cold period. Flowering can, as a result, be staggered considerably.

Calceolaria Herbeo hybrid 'Grandiflora'

Grandiflora means 'with big flowers'. The colour range of these Calceolaria is very wide with very many beautiful and individual colours. Large-flowered Calceolarias must be placed in 4-5 in/10-12 cm pots and have a longer growing season.

Calceolaria Herbeo hybrid 'Multiflora'

Treatment table

	sowing	growth
pot	—	3-4 in/8-10 cm
soil	RHP calceolaria soil	
feeding	none	1 tsp compound fertilizer per pt water/2 g per litre
watering	moist	moist
temperature	54-60° F/12-15° C	50-60° F/10-15° C
rel. humidity	95%	80%
light	plenty	plenty
flowers	—	mid- to late spring
special features	Shield against sunlight. Initiate flowering by cold treatment. Lengthen the day for premature flower-ing (see text). Feed once every two weeks when flowering begins with a solution of 1 tsp compound fertilizer per pt water/2 g per litre.	

Camellia japonica 'Chandleri Elegans'

Camellia japonica 'Chandleri Elegans'

One of the many hundreds of varieties of this magnificent houseplant which flowers in the winter, this variety originates in America, where it was developed as early as 1931.
In arboriculture, red, white and pink varieties are also grown, as well as single and double-flowered ones which are fairly hardy.

A very old variety

The tea-plant, Thea sinensis, which provides us with cups of tea, and the Camellia belong to the family Theaceae. The Camellia is named after the Austrian missionary, Georg Joseph Kamel (in Latin Camellus), who lived from 1661 to 1706. The plant is a native of China, Japan and Sri Lanka. Many varieties of the plant were already being grown there before it was introduced in England in 1739. Associations of Camellia enthusiasts exist in England and America, where hundreds of varieties of this brilliant houseplant are grown.

From pot to greenhouse

The plant can be propagated by immediate cuttings or head cuttings in mid-spring or mid-summer. First treat the cutting, which must not be woody, with growth hormone, and then place it under double glass or plastic foil (see page 169 for cuttings) in a mixture of peat dust and sand. After six weeks roots will have grown and it can be placed in a 2½-in/6-cm pot. To get a good root ball, keep cuttings in the pot for the first year. For the next two years keep them outside in a greenhouse. Plant them in 4-5-in/10-12-cm final pots in mid-summer.
In mid-winter prune the plant back to two buds. In the following summer the first flower buds will appear on the shoots which have grown in the spring.

Natural environment

The plant's native climate is mild, rainy winters, a humid and warm spring, and hot dry summers with a rainy autumn. It is desirable to reproduce this climate for the plant as closely as possible. This means that the plant must be watered frequently in the spring, autumn and winter, but sparingly in the summer. However quickly the buds grow, spraying must be discontinued, or they may rot. Camellia does very well in a fibrous RHP frozen peat potting soil. Shield the plant against strong sunlight, but continue to grow it in as much light as possible.
Because of the long growing period of four to six years Camellia is not a cheap plant. But it is a splendid, strong plant which will do well in the house if you observe the rules and, in particular, do not let the temperature rise too high.

Treatment table

	cutting	growth	rest (autumn)
pot	3 in/7 cm	4-5 in/11-13 cm	—
soil	fibrous	RHP	—
watering	frequently	moist	moist
temperature	68° F/20° C	> 64° F/18° C	50° F/10° C
rel. humidity	85-95%	80-95%	80-95%
flowers	in winter		
growth hormone	Rhizopon BT 0.2% or AT 1%	none	none
special features	When flowering begins, water less frequently and raise the temperature to 60° F/15° C with a relative humidity of 60-70%. Avoid strong sunlight. Do not spray the buds. The temperature in the spring should be 72-77° F/22-25° C with a relative humidity of 60-70%.		

A delicate bell

Campanula means 'bell' in Latin. It is the name of a relatively small group of plants.

The bells are mostly blue or purple, though sometimes they are white like the Star of Bethlehem.

Campanula isophylla ('with identical leaves'), which we know as a houseplant, grows in the lime-rich regions of Liguria in northern Italy.

It is a perennial which flowers for about eight weeks, after which the stems can be pruned back to a length of 2 in/5 cm. The plant lasts for years. Large, old plants are usually seen grown as a hanging plant.

Pay attention to the bleeding

If, after pruning, the plant is provided with light from a TL 33 (10-15 Watt per yd²/m²), you will get more cuttings more quickly. Cut these back to a length of about 2 in/5 cm from late autumn to mid-spring. Plunge them immediately in luke-warm water to staunch the bleeding, and dip the wound tissue in rooting powder. Place the cuttings in a frame with peat-based potting compost at intervals of about 1¼ in/3 cm. In order to prevent damping off, give the compost a light covering of river sand (see page 169 for cuttings). Cover the cuttings with newspaper to prevent them from drying up. The roots will appear after four weeks. Two weeks later, place six to seven cuttings in a 4-in/10 cm final pot.

If you place fewer cuttings in the pot, you must top them after ten to fourteen days in order to get the cuttings to branch out. The growing period is six weeks longer with topping.

Long day

The plant normally flowers in the summer and is a long-day plant. Flowering may be advanced into the spring by long-day treatment combined with spraying with inhibitor. The plant thereby retains its compactness. Two weeks after potting, light the plant from 11 o'clock in the evening to 6 o'clock in the morning with a TL 33 (5-7 Watt per yd²/m²). Before the flower buds have formed, spray the plant with inhibitor, which takes effect after about seven weeks. The plant will flower about three months after the start of the lighting.

During the growing season, keep the soil moist at all times. After pruning, give it slightly less water at first. Do not feed the plants at this time, but during the growing season give them an extra feed every two weeks. Place the plant in the full light, but avoid strong sunlight. Campanula is by nature a creeper. Before flowering it can be tied back with wire. It may also be grown as a hanging plant.

Campanula isophylla 'Alba'　　　　　　　*Campanula isophylla 'Norsk'*

Campanula isophylla 'Alba'
Alba means 'white'. This Star of Bethlehem with white flowers is the most widely distributed.

Campanula isophylla 'Mayi'
A harder-to-grow variety which is somewhat less common, this Campanula has pinky-blue flowers and silver-grey leaves.

Campanula isophylla 'Norsk'
A profusely-flowering plant with blue flowers, this is somewhat smaller than the 'Alba' variety.

Treatment table

	cutting	growth	rest
pot	frame	4 in/9-10 cm	—
soil	peat-based compost river sand	humus-rich RHP based on frozen peat	—
feeding	—	1 tsp compound fertilizer per pt water/2 g per litre	none
watering	generously	generously	moderately
temperature	64-68° F/ 18-20° C soil 55° F/13° C air	55-60° F/ 13-16° C	—
rel. humidity	80%	60-70%	—
light	—	plenty	plenty of light
flowers	—	summer	—
inhibitor	—	½ fl oz B9 per pt water/15 ml per litre	—
growth hormone	Rhizopon AT 0.7% or BT 0.1% or Stimroot II		
special features	Shield against strong sunlight. The temperature in sun should not be more than 68° F/20° C. The temperature of young plants should be 60-65° F/ 15-17° C. The plant flowers in the spring if given light.		

Capsicum annuum

Capsicum annuum

The varieties grown as pot plants are generally dwarf varieties with small round, oval or oblong fruits in the colours red, orange and yellow. The little fruits are first of all purple-coloured and turn their true colour later.

Capsicum annuum, a variety with oblong fruits

Capsicum annuum 'Friesdorff'

This is a high-growing variety with red, yellow, orange and white fruits. The fruits are about 4 in/10 cm long and grow on branches about 30 in/80 cm long. These fruits are much used in floral arrangements at Christmas time. They are grown in the greenhouse to a limited extent.

Houseplant and food

Capsa is the Latin for 'oblong box', in which scrolls were kept and the fruit of Capsicum is oblong and box-shaped. Capsicum belongs to the nightshade family (Solanaceae), a family which is very important for man, because it contains plants which provide us with food, such as the potato, the tomato and the paprika. The last-named plant is a cultivated variety of the Spanish Pepper which we know both as a houseplant and as a food.
Peppers in earlier times saved the lives of many seafarers suffering from scurvy, who were given them to eat by the American Indians. The plant was introduced into Europe from America as early as 1514.

Sowing

Capsicum is an annual and therefore has to be propagated from seed.
Do this in early to mid-spring in a good sandy seed soil at a temperature of 68° F/20° C. Keep the soil constantly moist. One gram of seed contains 150 seeds which provide about 100 plants. Do not sow the plants too close together.
The seeds will germinate in two-and-a-half weeks.
Two weeks later, set out the plants at intervals of 1 in/2.5 cm. About five weeks after this, place the plants in a 3-4-in/8-10-cm pot in a sandy moisture-retaining mixture.
The pot should be repositioned regularly to prevent root penetration and stop the roots from growing through the pot into the ground. Growth then becomes wild and when the pot is repositioned, the roots break off and the plant loses its leaves.

Lots of light, little water

Capsicum is a simple, sturdy houseplant whose seed is easily obtainable each year by picking and drying the ripe fruits. The plant flowers from mid-summer onwards and the fruits start to turn colour in late summer, reaching full colour in early autumn. Keep the soil moderately moist, though not too wet, because excessive moisture will rot the roots and make the leaves drop.
Give the plant as light a position as possible in order to get consistent growth, profuse flowering and good fruit setting. If you keep the ripe fruits at a temperature between 59° F/15° C and 64° F/18° C, with a relative humidity of 60%, they will keep their shape and colour for up to ten weeks.

Treatment table

	seeds	growth
pot	frame	8-9 cm
soil	RHP and river sand 3:1	RHP and river sand 3:1
feeding	—	1 tsp compound fertilizer per pt water/2 g per litre
watering	moist	fairly moist
temperature	68° F/20° C	60-77° F/15-25° C (in sun)
rel. humidity	90%	70%
light	plenty	plenty
flowers	—	mid-summer
special features	Water sparingly in the autumn. A full-grown plant can tolerate a relative humidity of less than 70%. With excessive feeding the plant grows luxuriantly, but sets few fruits.	

A large family
Carex is the Latin word for 'sheer-grass', or 'sedge'. Originally it was a general name for prickly shrubs. The word 'garrigue' is still used in the south of France for scrubland and is said to be derived from it. More than 50 species of sedge occur in the wild in woods, locks and meadows and along roads. Sedge is a member of the rush grass family, Cyperaceae (Cyperus), as is the well-known bulrush. Mats are still made from bulrushes, and in earlier times the bulrush was also used as a chair covering and as a raw material for rush baskets.
The Carex which we know as a houseplant is a foliage plant with slender, variegated, grass-type leaves.
The plants came originally from eastern Asia and the green species is almost hardy.

Division
The variegated sedge can be propagated by division. Remove the plant from the pot in the spring and divide it with its roots and put the new plants into a number of other pots. Five to six weeks after division, the plant is again fully-grown. Division, which should be carried out each year in order to obtain beautiful fresh plants, is as important for Carex as annual repotting is for most perennials.

Marsh plant
Carex grows in marshy ground in the wild and if we want to give it its natural environment as far as possible, we must ensure that it gets a plentiful supply of water. The potting soil should be constantly wet and highly nutritious. During the growing season in the spring and in the summer, feed the plant each week. In the rest period, in autumn and winter, feed it every two to four weeks. You must ensure that the relative humidity is at least 80% or more, in order to prevent the leaf tips from turning brown or dying.
Carex likes slight shade. In high summer temperatures shield the plant to prevent the water evaporating and to maintain the correct air humidity.
The plant is prized for its leaves; the brown, grass-like inflorescences contribute little to its decorative value. For modern rooms with high temperatures and relatively dry air, Carex is a difficult plant. It does best in a cool position with a high air humidity.

Carex brunnea 'Variegata'

Treatment table

	young plant	growth	rest
pot	3-3½ in/8-9 cm	3-3½ in/8-9 cm	—
soil	RHP	RHP	—
feeding	1 tsp compound fertilizer per pt water/2 g per litre	1 tsp compound fertilizer per pt water/ 2 g per litre	seldom
watering	wet	wet	wet
temperature	50-60° F/10-15° C	50-60° F/10-15° C	46° F/8° C
rel. humidity	80-90%	80-90%	80-90%
light	slight shade	slight shade	light
flowers	—	of no importance	—

Carex brunnea 'Variegata'
Brunnea means 'brown', the colour of the inflorescence. *Variegata* refers to the variegated leaves, which are the only reason why this houseplant is grown. The genus Carex contains about 50 species.

Catharanthus roseus 'Coquette'

Catharanthus roseus 'Bright Eyes'

Catharanthus roseus 'Bright Eyes'
The flowers of this plant are white with a bright red eye.

Catharanthus roseus 'Coquette' (Pinky)
The flowers of this variety are light pink with a dark-red eye.

Catharanthus roseus 'Blanche'
This Catharanthus has pure white flowers.

Catharanthus roseus 'Ocellatus'
The white flowers of this Catharanthus have a reddish tinge.

Catharanthus roseus (Vinca rosea)
This plant is a native of Brazil and now grows wild everywhere in the tropics.
It is a semi-shrub which in the wild grows to a height of 30-35 in/80-90 cm.
As a houseplant it is mostly grown as an annual, but it can easily last for several years.

Symbol of purity
The name Catharanthus is derived from the Greek words, *katharos*, which means 'pure' or 'unspotted', and *anthos*, which means 'flower'.
The name refers to the pure pink colour of the flowers. The plant belongs to the family Apocynaceae.
The Catharanthus which we know as a houseplant is also known, incorrectly, as Vinca. The plant comes from Brazil, was cultivated in England in 1757, and now grows wild throughout the tropics.

Seeds rather than cuttings
Although it is possible to produce large, long-lasting plants, at least if you treat them well, it is simpler to propagate the plant from seed than cuttings.
One gram of seed contains about 800 seeds, more than enough for most purposes. In order to prevent damping off, the seed must first be disinfected with a fungicide.
Sow in a good sowing soil from late autumn for flowering in the spring and throughout the winter for flowering in late summer.
Prick the plants out after four weeks. Six to eight weeks later, place them in a 3-4-in/8-10-cm final pot.
Catharanthus branches out spontaneously and grows into a beautifully branched, profusely-flowering plant.

Genuine long-flowerer
Catharanthus flowers spontaneously without interruption from mid-winter to late autumn. In the garden centre you will usually see it in flower from mid-spring to late summer.
Flowering does not have to be advanced artificially.
Great care must be taken to see that the plant has a light position. For best results, allow it to rest in direct sunlight in the winter.
Keep the soil moist, but not too moist; otherwise the leaves will turn yellow. Give it slightly less water in the winter. During the growing season, feed the plant once every two weeks, in the winter once a month, depending on the size of the plant.
Rest the plant in the winter, and in the early spring, when the plant is again growing well, prune the branches back slightly.
Flowers will appear on the new shoots which are then formed.

Treatment table

	seeds	growth	rest
pot	frame	3-3½ in/8-9 cm	—
soil	RHP	RHP	—
feeding	—	1 tsp compound fertilizer per pt water/2 g per litre	—
watering	moist	moist	moderately
temperature	64-68° F/ 18-20° C	64° F/18° C	57-60° F/ 15-16° C
rel. humidity	80-85%	70-80%	50-60%
light	light	plenty of light	sunlight
flowers	—	late winter to mid-autumn	—

special features The soil should not be too moist.

Celosia/Cockscomb

Celosia argentea 'Cristata Jewel Box'

A flower for drying

There is some doubt about the origin of the name Celosia. The Greek word *kelis* means 'blemish' or 'shame' and this may refer to the blood-coloured patch which appears on the leaves of a particular species.

Kelon means 'arid' or 'dry'. When the beautiful, comb-shaped flowers of Celosia are dried, they still retain their colour.

Celosia, which belongs to the family Amaranthaceae, comes originally from Indonesia. Thanks to man, the plant has now spread over all tropical regions and is universally present in cultivated or wild form.

The houseplants are mainly dwarf varieties with combs or plume-shaped flowers in all sorts of colours. Higher-growing varieties are also cultivated, but mainly for cut flowers. These flowers are particularly suitable for drying, since they keep their fresh colours for a very ong time.

Annuals, therefore sow from seed

Celosia is an annual which is propagated from seed. One gram of seed contains about 1,500 seeds.

The commercial grower sows 500 seeds per tray. You can sow from mid-winter to early spring. The growing period up to flowering is four months. About five weeks after sowing, place the plantlets about 1½ in/4 cm apart. One month later place them close to one another in 3-4-in/8-10-cm pots. Then place the pots more apart once again and about two months after potting the flowers will appear.

You then have a few months in which to enjoy the brilliant flowers, after which the plant dies.

Avoid intense sunlight

Celosia is a simple, summer-flowering houseplant which needs plenty of light, but must not be allowed to stand in the full glare of the sun.

The plant grows well in a mixture of three parts RHP potting soil to one part river sand, so that the soil is highly porous. Keep the soil moderately moist, though never excessively wet.

About three weeks after potting, start feeding once a week.

Treatment table

	sowing	growth
pot	frame	3-3½ in/8-9 cm
soil	RHP and river sand 3:1	—
feeding	none	1½ tsp compound fertilizer per pt water/3 g per litre
watering	moderately	moderately
temperature	68°F/20°C	68-77°F/20-25°C (in direct sunlight)
rel. humidity	95%	70%
light	plenty	plenty
flowers	—	summer

special features Shield against excessively strong sunlight. The temperature may rise to 77°F/25°C in the sun.

Celosia argentea 'Plumosa'

Celosia argentea 'Cristata'

Argentea means 'silver-coloured' and *cristata* means 'combed'. This refers to the inflorescence.

This Celosia is obtainable in a large number of tints of purple, red, orange and yellow.

Celosia argentea 'Jewel Box'

A dwarf Japanese variety with big heavy combs in splendid colours and tints, a true 'Cristata' shape.

Celosia argentea 'Plumosa'

The 'Plumosa' varieties have a plume-shaped inflorescence in the colours purple, red, orange, golden yellow and yellow.

Chamaecereus silvestrii

Chamaecereus silvestrii

The Caterpillar cactus is a native of western Argentina, where it grows on lightly wooded slopes. *Silvestri* means 'wood-inhabiting' in Latin. Commercial varieties of Chamaecereus silvestrii are often crosses of Chamaecereus silvestrii and Lobivia famatimensis. These crosses have larger flowers and the plants are less fragile.

'Creeping stems'

Because Chamaecereus is one of the most profusely-flowering Cacti species, and is therefore popular as a houseplant, it is treated separately here (see Cactaceae). The name Chamaecereus comes from the Greek word *chamai*, meaning 'on the ground', and the Latin word for 'candle'. *cereus*, which in turn comes from the Greek word for 'beeswax', *kerion*. The stems of this dwarf Cactus, which creep along the ground, are somewhat like caterpillars. and the flower buds arise from the stems just like candles. The Cactus comes originally from western Argentina and was cultivated in 1904 in the United States.

Cuttings from stems

In order to propagate the plants, take the stems of profusely-flowering specimens. In late spring break off the finger-shaped stems at the base and place them in a 3-4-in/8-10-cm final pot filled with a mixture of four parts river sand and two parts clay. Replace this soil later with a mixture of two parts RHP potting soil, two parts river sand, and one part clay.

Spray before flowering

During the growing season in the summer, keep the potting soil moist. In the winter, water seldom, but take care that the plant does not dry up.

From mid-winter onwards, spray the plant lightly to stimulate the formation of flower buds. In mid-spring, when the buds are clearly visible, give the Cactus just enough water to moisten the potting soil. Maintain this during the growing season. The rest period starts in the autumn.

Feed during the growing season every two weeks, thereafter not at all.

Grow the Caterpillar cactus in as light a position as possible. Like nearly all Cacti, it can withstand the fiercest sunlight. The plants flower from mid-spring to early summer with a mass of fiery-red flowers 2 in/5 cm in diameter.

The Caterpillar cactus is an easy-to-grow houseplant which can be enjoyed for many years and from which many offspring can be obtained from cuttings, provided you give the plant as much light and sun as possible.

In order to get profuse flowering, allow the plant to winter in as cool a spot as possible and give it the maximum sunlight. Repot annually and if you want to have fine, strong stems, do not forget to feed it, particularly in the growing period.

Treatment table

	cutting	growth	rest
pot	3-3½ in/8-9 cm	3-3½ in/8-9 cm	—
soil	sand and clay 4:2	RHP and sand and clay 2:2:1	—
feeding	—	1 tsp compound fertilizer per pt water/2 g per litre	none
watering	moist	moist	dry
temperature	68° F/20° C	60-95° F/ 15-35° C	40-50° F/ 5-10° C
rel. humidity	60%	50-60%	50%
light	light	sunlight	light
flowers	—	spring and early summer	—

special features The temperature may rise again towards the end of winter. The night temperature must be as low as possible, even in the summer.

Chamaedorea/Mexican dwarf palm

Heat-lover

Chamaedorea is one of about 250 genera containing 3,500 species of tree-like plants which are given the family name of Palms.

Some characteristics of the palm family are that the stem is unbranched, growth is columnar and the stem ends in a rosette-shaped crown of feather- or fan-shaped leaves. Nearly all Palms originate from the tropics, some from the sub-tropics, and there is one species, Chamaérops humilis, which grows wild in Europe in the Mediterranean area. Chamaedorea owes its name to the Greek words, *chamai* and *dory*, meaning 'on the ground' and 'double spear' respectively. The plant remains very small — it is sometimes called Mexican dwarf palm — and the spear-shaped leaves sometimes end in a double point. The Palm comes originally from Mexico, where it grows at an average temperature of 77° F/25° C in a region with a low rainfall (24-36 in/600-900 mm). It is therefore a glutton for heat.

Irregular germination

The Palm is propagated from seed, but because the seed germinates very irregularly, commercial growers usually buy the seeds in germinated form or as young plants to obtain a uniform lot.

If you start from non-germinated seeds, soak them for 24 hours in water at 77-86° F/25-30° C before sowing them in peat dust sowing soil. Cover the seeds with a thin top layer of sowing soil. Because of the irregular germination, the first little palms will be suitable for pricking out or potting in a 3-in/8-cm pot after three months. The plant is fully grown after a year. Large plants can be grown by transplanting three plants from a 3-in/8-cm pot into a 5-in/13-cm pot.

Flowers as well as leaves

Chamaedorea is grown mainly as a foliage plant, but after three or four years of life the palms can also produce a beautiful bunch of yellow flowers.

Although called the Mexican dwarf palm, it forms with age a stem which may be up to 6½ ft/2m long, and the name 'on the ground' becomes scarcely appropriate. Grow the Palm in standard RHP potting soil kept moderately moist. Water it seldom in winter. During the growing season, feed the plant weekly and place it in a light position. It must be borne in mind that the plant does not tolerate strong sunlight, even though it comes from the tropics. Chamaedorea is a sturdy houseplant with a somewhat limited life. It should be repotted annually.

Chamaedorea elegans

Chamaedorea elegans

Elegans means 'decorative' in Latin, certainly an apt description of this slender-leaved Mexican dwarf palm.

Treatment table

	sowing	growth	rest
pot	frame	3-6 in/8-14 cm	—
soil	peat dust	RHP	—
feeding	—	1 tsp compound fertilizer per pt water/2 g per litre	none
watering	moist	moderately	keep dry
temperature	77° F/25° C	> 68° F/20° C	57-64° F/ 14-18° C
rel. humidity	85%	70-80%	60-70%
light	light	light	light
flowers	—	after 3 or 4 years	—

special features The minimum night temperature for the seed is 68° F/20° C. Avoid strong sunlight.

A tough plant

Chlorophytum is one of the toughest of all houseplants, and you will find it in almost every home. It does well both on window sill and further inside rooms. It does not require excessive sunlight, but if the light is insufficient, the variegated leaf colour may well fade.
Chlorophytum comes from the Greek words *Chloros* and *phyton*, meaning bright-green and plant respectively. A bright-green plant? Not always, because one often sees the variety "Variegatum" with a creamy-white leaf decoration or the variety *"Mediopictum"* with a cream-coloured central stripe.
The original *Chlorophytum* species are native to South Africa. These plants, such as *Chlorophytum capense* (Cape), are green-leaved. The first species was cultivated as early as 1731.
The plant belongs to the lily family, Liliaceae.
This is a very widespread family, many members of which grow in our country, i.e. the Van Dalen Lily, the hyacinth and the tulip.

Suckers from peduncles

Chlorophytum can flower the whole year. The small white, lily-shaped flowers have little decorative value, but the peduncles are important, because young plants grow from them and cuttings can therefore be taken.
Wait until the cuttings are almost fully grown before using them. Place them in a 3 in/8 cm pot and let them grow undisturbed there for 4-6 months. They will already be handsome plants by this time. Then repot them into a 4½-5 in/11-12 cm pot, where they will grow into splendid plants with long, beautifully decorated leaves and lots of young plants on the peduncles.

A plant for high spaces

Although *Chlorophytum* is not really a hanging plant, it is very often seen suspended or placed high up in a room to give it more space. It then enjoys good growth and the long peduncles with the young plants can develop to their full extent.
Grow the plant in a humus-rich nutritive RHP potting soil. The plant requires frequent watering during the growing season. If the temperature drops, give it less water. The plant reacts favourably to a rich feed.
Give the plant some nitrogen-rich fertilizer weekly during the growing season, and repot it annually.
The plant is also suitable as a water plant.

Chlorophytum comosum "Variegatum"

Comosum means crested. The peduncles, which first grow up vertically and later hang down, form at the top a sort of crest of piled-up bracts.
The peduncles are set very close together with rosettes of young plants. The leaves have a cream-coloured edge and are ¾-1½ in/3-4 cm wide. This species is native to South Africa and was first cultivated in Germany in 1828.

Chlorophytum bichetii

This is a smaller, less common species with a narrow yellow leaf-edge.

Chlorophytum capense "Variegatum"

A variegated-leaf variety with yellow leaf-edges.

Chlorophytum capense "Mediopictum"

This variety has a cream-coloured central stripe. It is a somewhat weaker-growing variety.

Streptocarpus hybrid "Wiesmoor"
This variety is grown to a limited extent. It produces numerous beautiful colours in white, pink, red and blue and is propagated from seed.

Treatment table

	cutting	growth	rest
pot	3 in/8 cm	4½-5 in/11-12 cm—	
soil	RHP potting soil	RHP potting soil	—
feeding	—	¾ tsp compound fertilizer per pt water/3 g per litre	none
watering	moist	frequently	moderately
temperature	61-64°F/ 16-18°C	61-64°F/ 16-18°C	—
rel. humidity	> 70%	70%	
light	plenty	plenty	plenty
flowers	—	year round	
special features	The plant's leaves turn green is there is insufficient light. Higher temperatures are acceptable, provided the relative humidity does not drop below 70%.		

Potchrysant

Symbol of courage and longevity

In Japan they celebrate an annual "Day of the Chrysanthemum", and the Japanese imperial coat of arms contains a chrysanthemum. The plant has an important symbolic significance there, symbolizing longevity and courage.

The plant has great importance as a cut flower. The chrysanthemum is the most important flower crop in many countries, including America, England, Japan and Scandinavia.

The Dutch imported the plant from Japan and China, where it had been cultivated from the earliest times. They named it Chrysanthemum indicum, because it came to Holland via the East Indies (now Indonesia). The word Chrysanthemum comes from the Greek words *chrys* and *anthemon*, and means 'golden flower'. Even today, 50% of the selected species still consist of yellow varieties; 18% consist of white and 11% of pink varieties. The plant was first cultivated in Europe in 1688.

The chrysanthemum belongs to the family Compositae. This is a very large family of plants, many members of which grow wild. The chrysanthemum itself is one of these, in the form of Chrysanthemum leucanthemum or Ox-eye daisy.

Cuttings from cuttings

When taking cuttings, select vigorous healthy plants. For a good production of cuttings, the stock plants must be kept cold and fairly dry for six to eight weeks beforehand (41°F/5°C). A month before taking cuttings, add water and raise the day temperature to 61°F/16°C and the night temperature to 50°F/10°C. Too high a temperature can cause budding of the cuttings.

You can also adopt a different approach and take cuttings from a cutting.

To do this, either take cuttings from a carefully selected plant or else buy some cuttings, for example of meristem culture, which are virus-free.

About three weeks after planting the cutting will be approximately 6 in/15 cm high. A small tip is then broken off. The plant will now form side-shoots which are ideal for using again as cuttings. When a cutting is about 3 in/7 cm long, break it off above an internode. Cutting with a knife can lead to virus-infection. Pick the cuttings in the morning, when there is no shortage of moisture.

After treatment with fertilizer, place the cuttings about 2 in/5 cm apart in a mixture of 3 parts peat litter and 2 parts perlite (see taking of cuttings page 169). The ideal pH is 5.8 (see acid level page 168).

Mist propagation is the ideal method, but you can also cover the cuttings with newspaper and spray them a few times. Under double glass or plastic foil there is a high rot risk. After 10-15 days the cuttings will have rooted. You can then place them in individual 3-3½ in/7-8 cm plastic pots or in groups of three to nine in a larger pot. In the latter case the cuttings should be grown spaced out at the edge of the pot. If a pot contains a single plant, top the plant in the summer 10-14 days after the potting off, and in the winter after two to three weeks. Here again, only a small tip should be removed. Two weeks after topping, spray the plants with growth inhibitor in order to get good compact growth.

With strongly growing varieties, repeat the spraying after 10-15 days.

The total cultivation period is 12-15 weeks on average, depending on the short-day requirement.

Chrysanthemum moriflorum hybrid

Chrysanthemum Morifolium Hybridum
Morifolium means "with the leaf of the mulberry.".

These hybrids are obtained by crossing Chrysanthemum indicum and Chrysanthemum morifolium as main species with a number of other species such as Chrysanthemum ornatum, Chrysanthemum japonense, Chrysanthemum zawadskii and other species.

'Neptune'
This is a widely grown species with white flowers.

Potchrysanten

Chrysanthemum 'Yellow Delaware'

'Yellow Delaware'

This is also a yellow chrysanthemum, as the name implies. The variety is widely cultivated as a pot plant.

'Blanche Poitevine'

This is an old variety with big white flowers. The variety flowers naturally on All Saints' Day and is widely used for decorating churches. Take cuttings from this plant in April. Place the plants in a 4-4½ in/11-12 cm final pot in May. Top the young plants and in the summer keep them outside in the garden. Take them indoors before the night frosts come, and allow them to flower in as light a position as possible at a temperature of about 60°F/15°C.

'Princess Ann'

This is a yellow variety that is widely cultivated; white, orange and pink varieties also exist.

Long day — short day

The chrysanthemum normally flowers in the autumn (fall), i.e. when the days are getting shorter. If you want flowers at that time, therefore, you have no problems with the light. For the growth of stems and leaves, so-called vegetative growth, the natural day length from late summer to late autumn (fall) is quite sufficient. And for good bud formation, or generative growth, the days from the end of early autumn (fall) to early spring are sufficiently short.

If you want plant growth at another time, you must advance the vegetative growth by extra lighting if the natural day is too short. If you want flowers at a time of year when the day is still too long, blacking out is required.

The long day for vegetative growth lasts 14-14½ hours. In late autumn (fall) you must give two hours extra lighting to get this, and, in the winter, four hours. Coarse-growing varieties receive a long-day treatment up to topping, other varieties until the shoots formed after the topping are about ½-1 in/1-2 cm long. For a long day, light with 150 watt bulbs. Give this lighting as a nightly interruption, e.g. from 11 p.m. onwards. The short day for bud formation lasts 10 hours. Black out preferably from five o'clock in the afternoon until seven o'clock in the morning.

Black plastic foil or black plastic sheeting can be used for this. Not more than 1% of light must penetrate the blacking out material. The length of the short-day treatment — the reaction time — varies according to variety. The gardening enthusiast can simply continue with the treatment until the flower buds are full in colour. This takes place after 9-14 weeks. During the blacking out the temperature and the relative humidity must not rise unduly.

By a judicious choice of long and short-day treatment, chrysanthemums can be made to flower the whole year round.

Treatment table

	cutting	growth	rest
pot	3-3½ in/7-8 cm	4½ in/12 cm	—
soil	peat litter and perlite 3:2	RHP mixture: 40% peat litter 60% frozen peat	
feed	¼ tsp compound fertilizer per pt water/ 2 g per litre	¼ tsp compound fertilizer per pt water/ 2 g per litre	
water	moist	moist	moderate
temperature	61-64°F/ 16/18°C	64°F/18°C	41°F/5°C
light	—	full	—
flowers	—	year round	—
growth hormone	Stimroot 11, 0.4%	—	—
rel. humidity	80-85%	70%	60-70%
special features	Root the cuttings at a soil temperature of 62/64°F/ 17-18°C and an air temperature of 68°F/20°C. In summer the maximum temperature is 75°F/23°C and in winter 70°F/21°C. Inhibit strongly growing varieties with Fosfon D.		

Ivy in the home

Kittos or *kissos* is the Greek name for ivy.
This strudy decorative foliage plant sometimes forms very long tendrils and it is therefore particularly suitable as a hanging or climbing plant for modern interiors. There is the additional advantage that the plant requires little light. It can therefore be used to brighten up the darker corners of a room, for example those formed by a cupboard, with its beautiful, luxuriant leaves.
The plant belongs to the Vitaceae family and is closely related to the vine.

Cuttings from the long branches

All *Cissus* species can be propagated by the taking of cuttings. Take an intermediate cutting with two leaves (see cuttings page 169) from long branches. Care must be taken that there are no tendrils growing in the leaf axils, because if there are the plant will not form any new tendrils. Cuttings can be taken throughout the year, except in the shortest days in mid-winter. For good rooting, treat the cuttings with growth hormone and place them in peat-based potting compost under double glass, plastic foil or mist.
They will have formed roots in a month's time. Place them then in a 2½-3 in/7-8 cm pot, and leave them to grow until the shoots are 12 in/30 cm long.
Support these shoots by tying them to a bamboo stick. In order to get a fine big plant, place 3-5 cuttings in one pot. Run the tendrils along bamboo canes or overhead along walls. In 6 months the plants will have grown sufficiently to be transferred to a bigger pot.

Don't forget to feed it

The plant needs frequent feeding particularly when it is growing. Give it a very high concentration of nitrogen-rich fertilizer once a week. In the darker winter months feed it once every two weeks with a potassium-rich mixture.
Cissus is not fussy as regards soil. It grows excellently in an RHP potting soil.
Keep the soil moderately moist in general, but in the growing season water it frequently. Only *Cissus discolor* needs constant and generous watering. This plant is more difficult to grow.
Cissus tolerates a position with reduced light. It even grows in shadow, for example in a very dark room. In a sunny position the leaves lose their colour and growth is stiff and sluggish.
Cissus cannot be persuaded to flower, but as a green-leaved foliage plant it is one of the sturdiest houseplants with great powers of adaptation. Only the juvenile form of this plant is cultivated, and propagated by taking cuttings. The only points requiring attention are that they get sufficient food during the growing season and that the pot is not too small; this ensures that the plant can absorb sufficient water for the tendrils.
Repot the plant in late winter and if you want to rejuvenate it, prune the tendrils right back.

Cissus rhombifolia "Ellen Danica"

Cissus rhombifolia (Rhoicissus rhomboidea)

This *Cissus* has a composite leaf consisting of three leaflets in the shape of a lozenge (rhombus). The variety "Ellen Danica" has weirdly-shaped indented leaves. This *Cissus* comes from the Cape area of South Africa.

Cissus striata

This *Cissus* comes from Chile and has a composite leaf with small leaflets. This plant is not so big as the other species.

Cissus incisa (Cissus juttae)

This *Cissus* is grown for its short thick stem and it is a cactus/succulent-type *Cissus* which is not often encountered. It grows in the wild in Namibia. (For treatment, see Succulents on page 156).

Cissus antarctica

The most well-known *Cissus*. The plant is a native of Australia (*antarctica* means South Pole) and was first cultivated in England in 1790.
The stems of this *Cissus* can grow very long indeed.

Cissus discolor

This *Cissus* is slightly harder to grow and has red-tinted leaves with light veins. A particularly beautiful foliage plant, it comes from Java and requires a temperature of at least 68°F/20°C with a relative humidity of 80%. A splendid climber, therefore, for the hothouse or greenhouse.

Treatment table

	cutting	growth	rest
pot	2½-3 in/7-8 cm (rooted)	4½-5 in/11-12 cm—	
soil	peat-based potting compost	RHP	
feeding	—	¾ tsp compound — fertilizer per pt water/3 g per litre	
watering	moist	moist	moderately
temperature	64-68°F/ 18-20°C	59-64°F/ 15-18°C	41-50°F/ 5-10°C
rel. humidity	85%	> 60%	> 60%
light	moderate	less strong	moderate
growth hormone	Rhizopon BT 0.1-0.2%	—	—
special features	The concentration of growth hormone depends on the hardness of the cutting. *Cissus discolor* cuttings prefer a temperature of 77-86°F/25-30°C with a relative humidity of 90-95%. The cultivation temperature is 70-77°F/22-25°C with a relative humidity of 80-85% and the minimum temperature is 64°F/18°C with a relative humidity of 70-80%. Other *Cissus* species are happy in direct sunlight up to a temperature of 86°F/30°C, provided that the relative humidity remains above 60%.		

Citrus sinensis

Citrus microcarpa

Citrus microcarpa (Citrus mitis)

Microcarpa means 'with small fruit'. This species comes from the Philippines. It has white sweet-smelling flowers and very flat fruits 1½ in/4 cm to 2½ in/6 cm in size.

Citrus sinensis

This is the original orange, *sinensis* meaning 'from China'.
The flowers of this Citrus are purplish in colour and the round fruits are lengthened at the top to form a navel. They are bigger than the fruits of Citrus microcarpa.

Sweet-smelling family

Citrus means 'lemon tree'. The lemon tree was already known in antiquity, not simply for its fruit, but also for its valuable wood. This originally African tree flowers and bears fruit the whole year round. The Citrus species which we know as houseplants are not lemons, but oranges. This species is called 'China apple' and most of the species come from China.

The numerous orange fruits provide the decorative value of these plants. When grown for eating, the fruits are naturally bigger, juicier and sweeter, but real oranges also grow on the houseplants. Citrus belongs to the family Rutaceae ('lozenge-shaped').

This is a family of strongly aromatic plants.

Cuttings and ringing

Take cuttings from the plants in mid-winter. When they have roots, place them in a 3-in/8-cm pot. Top them a few times in the summer to get a well-branched plant and in the following spring place them in a 4-in/10-cm pot. After two or three years, when they are fully grown and can flower and bear fruit, stand them in pots up to 5 in/12 cm, depending on their size. The plant can also be ringed, in which case the growing period is shorter. For this make a wound in the woody stem, and wrap around it some moss in plastic to retain the moisture (see page 170 for ringing). As soon as the plant has sufficient roots, cut it off and place it in a 3-in/8-cm pot.

If you want to experiment, you can also sow some pips of a normal orange or mandarin. Provided you have lots of patience — it may take a matter of several years — you will get a newly-grown houseplant, though it will never flower in a normal home.

Iron-containing soil mixture

Citrus is a beautiful houseplant which requires proper care. The most important item is the correct potting soil. This should contain 20% river clay and 80% Calceolaria soil. Water it frequently during the growing season, hardly at all in the winter. The plant can tolerate strong sunlight, but shield it from the light at temperatures above 86° F/30° C. Feed it once a week, except during the rest period. It is essential to repot the plant each year and then to keep the soil temperature at 75° F/24° C until the plant is growing strongly again.

In the summer it is best to set the plant outside in a sheltered spot.

Treatment table

	cutting	growth	rest
pot	3 in/8 cm	4-5 in/10-12 cm	—
soil	RHP Calceolaria with clay (4:1)	RHP Calceolaria with clay (4:1)	—
feeding	—	1½ tsp compound fertilizer per pt water/3 g per litre	
temperature	75° F/24° C	68-75° F/ 20-24° C	> 60° F/ 16° C
rel. humidity	90%	75-80%	60-70%
water	frequently	frequently	seldom
light	light	light	light
flowers	—	early spring and mid- to late summer	fruits
special features	The temperature may rise to 86° F/30° C in the sun, with a minimum relative humidity of 70%. The soil temperature after repotting should be 75° F/24° C. The night temperature in summer should be 64° F/18° C		

Inhibit before flowering

The name Clerodendrum comes from the Greek words *kleron* and *dendron*, which mean 'fate' and 'tree'. The plant is called the Chance tree because there are both poisonous and medicinal species of it. Only an expert can tell the difference. The plant is a member of the family Verbenaceae.

When growers did not yet have the use of inhibitors, this plant was chiefly regarded as a large, profusely-flowering climber in greenhouses and glasshouses. Now it is a beautiful houseplant which can flower the whole summer. Clerodendrum originates from tropical west Africa and was cultivated in England in 1861.

Cuttings with growth hormone

The plant can be propagated by taking an intermediate cutting with a leaf pair (see page 169 for cuttings). Take the cutting from long branches not treated with inhibitor. Place five such cuttings in a 4-in/10-cm pot filled with frozen peat potting compost. Under plastic foil they will have roots after four weeks, provided that they are treated with growth hormone. Remove the tops four weeks later. Each cutting will now grow two branches, which can be trained along a wire or a plastic fence. If you take cuttings in the summer or late summer, you will get a rich profusion of handsome flowering plants in the following spring and early summer.

Short-day treatment

In order to get a fine compact plant, the shoots must be inhibited after topping when they have grown to a length of 10 in/25 cm. Spray them twice at an interval of ten days with the inhibitor Reducymol in a concentration of 12 cu in/30 cm^3 per 2 pt/1 l of water. All other inhibitors have no effect on Clerodendrum. It is not essential to shorten the day before flower initiation, but if you want to get uniform flowering you must darken the plant so that it gets only eight hours of light a day. This is necessary from early spring until the autumn, the period with naturally long days. Keep the potting soil fairly moist and four weeks after potting add some fertilizer weekly. Give the plant as light a position as possible and simply shield it from very strong sunlight. Allow the plant to rest in the winter, with little water and no fertilizer.

If you want to have uniform flowering on a well-grown plant again the next year, cut the plant back and again inhibit and darken the new shoots.

Treatment table

	cuttings	growth	rest
pot	3½ in/9 cm	4-5 in/10-12 cm	—
soil	frozen peat	RHP	—
feeding	—	1 tsp compound fertilizer per pt water/2 g per litre	—
watering	moist	moderately	moist
temperature	72-77° F/22-25° C	68° F/20° C	40-50° F/ 10-15° C
rel. humidity	95%	70-80%	70%
light	light	light	light
flowers	—	summer	—
growth hormone	Rhizopon BT 0.2%	—	—
inhibitor	—	Reducymol ½ fl oz per pt water/30 ml per litre	—

special features At temperatures lower than 68° F/20° C a growing plant's leaves turn yellow. Shorten the days for uniform flowering.

Clerodendrum splendens

Clerodendrum thomsonae

Clerodendrum (Clerodendron) thomsonae

One of the many species which are encountered as a houseplant, this plant is named after W.C. Thomson, an English missionary who in 1861 sent a specimen of it from tropical west Africa to England.

Clerodendrum splendens

Splendens means 'brilliant' and refers to the flaming red flowers of this relatively rare Clerodendrum. The plant flowers after a long-day period. The genus Clerodendrum contains many other species, including small trees and numerous climbing plants.

Clivia miniata

Clivia miniata

Clivia miniata

Miniata means 'red-lead-coloured'. This refers to the magnificent, orange-red flowers of this stately plant, which has spread throughout the world, chiefly from Belgium.

An aristocratic plant

Lady Charlotte Florentine Clive was governess to Queen Victoria of England, and Clivia, which is named after her, flowered for the first time on her estate at Almwick. Now practically anyone can get this stately houseplant, with its bunches of magnificent orange-red flowers, to flower by keeping a check on the temperature and humidity at just the right time. The plant comes from Natal in South Africa and was described for the first time in England in 1849.

Clivia is a member of the Amaryllis family, Amaryllidaceae. This family includes individual well-known species such as the snowdrop and the narcissus.

Cuttings and sowing

Large plants form suckers which should be separated carefully from the mother plant and planted, together with the roots, in another pot. These shoots grow without undue problems into fully-grown plants which flower again if treated correctly. You can also try to get seeds from fine, large mother plants. The seed is ripe about nine months after pollination. The fruits are then red-coloured. As soon as they are ripe, sow the fruits. When the young plants are just two years old, place them in a 4-in/10-cm pot. They have a flowering life of three years. They grow in the summer months and flower from mid-winter to early spring, but the flowering can also spread spontaneously over the whole summer and autumn. The rest period for Clivia begins in mid-autumn.

Dry and cold regime

Grow Clivia in a mixture of equal parts of clay, river sand and frozen peat.

As soon as the seedlings have leaves, feed the plant every week until it is a year old. Thereafter feed every week, apart from the rest period from mid-autumn to mid-winter. In the rest period place Clivia in the full light; during the growing season, stand it in a slightly shaded position.

To get it to flower, you must keep it warm and moist in the growing season and cool and dry thereafter. Stand the plant in the light at a temperature of 50-54° F/10-12° C. As soon as the flower buds appear in mid-winter, raise the temperature to 68° F/20° C and water generously again.

Treatment table

	sowing	growth	rest
pot	frame	4½ in/11 cm	—
soil	sowing soil	clay-river sand-frozen peat 1:1:1	—
feeding	—	1 tsp compound fertilizer per pt water/2 g per litre	none
watering	moist	frequently	seldom
temperature	72° F/22° C	64-72° F/18-22° C	50-54° F/10-12° C
rel. humidity	90%	70-80%	60-70%
light	—	slight shade	light
flowers	—	late winter to mid-spring	—
special features	In sun the maximum temperature is 86° F/30° C. For good flowering a dry-cold regime from mid-autumn to late winter is necessary. As soon as the flower buds appear, increase the temperature to 68° F/20° C and water generously.		

Lover of warmth and humidity

Codiaeum is also called, though incorrectly, Croton. The true Crotons are not found as houseplants; they are bushes. two species of which are grown to obtain aromatic flavours used in the tobacco industry. The so-called croton oil is pressed from the seeds of Croton tiglium. This is an extremely powerful laxative.

Codiaeum belongs to the spurge family, Euphorbiaceae. This is a widely-distributed plant family with individual, well-known members such as Thorn of Christ and Christmas Star. There are also cactus-type Euphorbias.

Codiaeum is a native of tropical Asia, where it grows as a bush in a climate with an annual rainfall of 52 in/1300 mm, a maximum temperature of 88° F/31° C and a minimum temperature of 63° F/17° C.

The plant was cultivated in England in 1803.

Take care when moving

The most beautifully formed plants are obtained by propagation via a head cutting (see page 169 for cuttings). but only a limited number of head cuttings can be taken from a single plant.

Commerical growers therefore propagate on a large scale by means of intermediate cuttings with one or two leaves. The new plant grows from the topmost leaf axil and, in fact, starts with small leaves.

For good rooting treat the cuttings with growth hormone and then place them in a 2½-in/6.5-cm plastic pot filled with peat-based potting compost.

The cuttings will have rooted after four weeks, when they should be repotted into a 4-in/10-cm final pot for fine-leaved varieties or a 5-in/13-cm final pot for the other varieties. The plant is fully grown after six to seven months. For better growth, the professional grower increases the amount of carbon dioxide in the air to 0.12%.

If you want to move Codiaeum, for example from the greenhouse or hothouse to inside the house, you must do so only when the leaf rosette is fully grown. Otherwise growth will be stunted.

Codiaeum can also be grown from seed, by pollinating with a brush when the pollen is ripe. The plant is monoecious, which means that male and female flowers are found on the same plant. The seed is ripe after a month and should be sown immediately at 75° F/24° C. The seed germinates quickly and you will soon have pretty plants which will be fully in colour the following year. In most cases you will get predominantly green plants, but beautiful specimens in other colours are occasionally obtained.

Sunlight gives colour

The plant is at its most colourful in the late summer and autumn, when it should have a good sunny position. Keep the soil moist during the growing season, but water less frequently in autumn and winter.

Care must be taken to avoid oversalting of the soil. Add some potassium-rich fertilizer weekly until the autumn and add fertilizer again from late winter onwards, after you have repotted the plant.

You can enjoy this beautiful foliage plant for a very long time; if it grows too large, cut it back in early spring. A plant that has become bald and straggly should be cut down to about 3 in/8 cm above the soil. It will then become a magnificent specimen again.

Codiaeum variegatum 'Mrs. Iceton

Codiaeum variegatum

This plant, with variegated leaves. is one of the most beautifully coloured of all foliage plants.

It is a bushy pot plant of which hundreds of different varieties exist. There is a great variety of colours, leaf size and leaf shape. Few named varieties are grown, however.

Codiaeum variegatum 'Bravo'

Treatment table

	cutting	growth	rest
pot	2½ in/6.5 cm	4-6 in/10-14 cm	—
soil	peat-based potting compost	RHP	—
feeding	—	1½ tsp potassium-rich compound fertilizer per pt water/ 3 g per litre	—
watering	moist	moist	moderately
temperature	75° F/24° C (soil)	64-68° C/ 18-20° C (soil)	60-64° F/ 16-18° C
rel. humidity	95-100%	75-80%	60-70%
light	plenty	sunlight	sunlight
growth hormone	Rhizopon AK 0.7% or BT 0.1%	—	—

special features   Sow at 75° F/24° C.
Harden off full-grown plants at 60-64° F/16-18° C, with a relative humidity of 60-70%.
The temperature must be more than 86° F/30° C and the relative humidity not less than 70%.
Potassium-rich compound fertilizer or nitrate of potash give a beautiful leaf colour.

Coffea arabica in the wild in Colombia

Coffea arabica

Coffea arabica

Coffea arabica

This is the standard Coffee plant, which is cultivated mainly for coffee-growing, but also as a houseplant.

For coffee-growing there is also a variety 'Mokka' and the species Coffea canephora (Congo coffee) and Coffea siberica (Siberian coffee); these are not grown as houseplants.

A real Coffee plant in the home

Coffee is one of the most widely consumed drinks in the world. There is one other property, however, which makes the Coffee plant important for man: it makes a splendid houseplant. In the wild a Coffee plant can be anything up to 25 ft/7.5 m in height, and though on plantations it is usually cut back to 10 ft/3 m, as a houseplant it can also be left to grow apace.

It is cultivated mainly for the decorative value of its leaves, but older plants (three to four years) also bear fragrant white flowers, which if treated well produce splendid red berries. These berries contain two seeds, which are peeled and then roasted for coffee-production.

The plant belongs to the star-leaved family, Rubiaceae. This name comes from Rubia tinctorum, the madder, a plant which was widely grown at one time for the dyestuffs industry. The Coffee plant comes originally from Arabia and was cultivated in Europe as a houseplant as long ago as the 16th century.

The beans are the seeds

You can grow Coffee plants yourself from seeds imported from Africa and other countries and available commercially. Sow them in a frame containing an airy soil mixture, allowing moisture to pass through. The young plantlets grow quickly and after six to eight weeks should be placed in a 3-in/8-cm pot. They do not, at first, need to be pricked out individually. Four to five months after potting, repot the plants into a 4-5-in/10-12-cm pot and eight months later into a 6½-in/16-cm final pot. The plants must never be topped, because then the central main branch will be destroyed and the side branches will never develop properly.

When the plant is about two-and-a-half years old, the first bunches of four or five flowers appear in the leaf axils. The white flowers have a heavenly smell and the red berries ripen after about six months.

Light, but no sunlight

Although the plant should be placed in a light position, it will not tolerate direct sunlight. Slight shade is an ideal place, but growth will be inhibited if it is too dark. Keep the soil fairly moist, but, especially at lower temperatures, make sure that it does not get too wet. Feed young plants every week, full-grown plants once every two weeks.

The plant requires a spacious pot to make certain that it never roots through the pot. The roots are sensitive and apparently attractive to lettuce-root aphid. On plantations the bushes last 15 years. In the house they can also be enjoyed for a long time, provided that you give them the attention they require.

Treatment table

	sowing	growth	rest
pot	frame	3½-5 in/8-12 cm, later 6 in/16 cm	—
soil	porous	RHP and clay	—
feeding	—	1½ tsp compound fertilizer per pt water/3 g per litre	—
watering	frequently	moist	moderately
temperature	72° F/22° C	64-68° F/18-20° C	> 64° F/18° C
rel. humidity	95%	70%	70%
light	light	light	light
flowers	—	after 2½-4 years	—
special features	Grow young plants at 68-72° F/20-22° C, with a relative humidity of 70%. Temperatures should not fall below 64° F/18° C during the winter or at night. Avoid strong sunlight in the spring and summer.		

A spicy family

If you take a look at your herb-rack in the kitchen, you will come across many members of the Coleus family: Basil, Savory, Thyme, Lavender, Marjoram, Mint, Sage. All these are labiates or Labiateae. The name, Ornamental nettle, suggests a kinship with the stinging nettle and indeed the shape of the leaves reminds one strongly of this plant. Coleus comes originally from Africa and tropical Asia (Java among other countries) and was cultivated in Europe in 1800. In addition to being a houseplant, it is found as a garden plant. Because it grows quickly, but cannot tolerate night frost, it is grown outdoors as an annual.

The name Coleus is derived from the Greek word, *koleos*, which means 'scabbard'. The filaments come together at the base to form a scabbard shape.

Cuttings and seeds

The old varieties such as 'Goudrand' and 'Bienvenue' are propagated by the commercial grower by taking cuttings from mother plants grown specially for the purpose. He places three of these cuttings together in a 4½-in/11-cm pot in late summer. They are placed in a light position and the soil is kept dry. From mid-winter onwards they are given water and the temperature is increased. The plants now grow very quickly and after only four weeks shoot cuttings may be taken from them (see page 169 for cuttings).

When you take cuttings, place them in individual pots and after topping repot them into a 4-5-in/10-12-cm final pot. Place three cuttings together in each final pot. Under double glass or plastic foil they will have rooted after fourteen days in peat-based compost. A number of beautifully coloured varieties, sold as 'Rainbow varieties', sometimes by variety name and sometimes by colour, come from Japan.

One gram of seed of this plant contains 3,500 seeds and can easily provide 2,500 plants, more than enough for the normal home. Sow in mid- to late winter in sowing soil (see page 168 for sowing), taking care not to place the seeds too close together. The young plants can then be placed directly into a small pot without pricking them out.

The growing time is four to five months, depending on the sowing time. The earlier you sow, the longer is the growing time.

Think about the size of the pot

Coleus is an easy-to-grow plant which does not make any great demands. During the growing season, however, it requires a great deal of water and it must therefore be given a spacious pot with enough soil to take up all the water consumed by the rapidly evaporating leaves.

Feeding the plant regularly will produce rapid growth and beautiful leaves, but the soil must be kept fairly moist to prevent it from salting up.

For a fine leaf colour, place the plant in strong sunlight. After three to four months it will develop clusters of blue and white flowers, which do not have much decorative value and should be removed as buds to obtain a beautiful foliage plant.

If the plant becomes too straggly, it can be inhibited with inhibitor. Old plants can be saved, but since young ones are more beautiful in colour, it is better to take cuttings or re-sow every year.

Coleus blumei

Coleus blumei syn. Solenostemon scutellariodes

The varieties of this plant are large-leaved. They grow strongly and have a wide colur variation with different leaf shapes. The leaves of young plants are the most beautifully coloured. This plant is therefore usually grown from seed each year.

Coleus pumilus (Coleus rehneltianus)

This small-leaved Coleus, with procumbent stems, comes in a number of varieties with different leaf colours. It is a particularly decorative plant which grows laterally and does not become tall. It survives the winter well and is usually grown as a perennial.

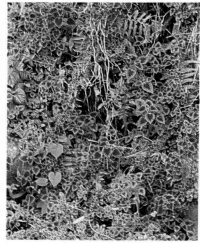

Coleus in the wild on Lombok

Treatment table

	cutting	growth	rest
pot	4-5 in/10-12 cm	4-5 in/10-12 cm or larger	—
soil	peat-based potting compost	RHP	—
feeding	—	1½ tsp compound fertilizer per pt water/3 g per litre	—
temperature	68°F/20° C	60-64° F/ 16-18° C	approximately 60° F/15° C
rel. humidity	90%	70%	70%
water	frequently	frequently	less frequently
light	—	sunlight	sunlight

Columnea 'Stavanger'
This hanging plant, a cross of the small-leaved Columnea microphylla and Columnea vedariensis, has magnificent flowers which can be enjoyed for many years.

Columnea microphylla
This plant, a native of Costa Rica, has been cultivated in Europe since 1881. *Microphylla* means 'small-leaved'. The plant flowers very profusely, though the leaves and flowers are somewhat smaller than those of 'Stavanger'.
Columnea microphylla 'Variegata' is a foliage plant which hardly ever flowers and requires the same treatment as 'Stavanger'.

Columnea gloriosa
A weaker Columnea which needs careful treatment to survive as a genuine hanging plant with decorative value.
The green-leaved species is a native of Costa Rica and was cultivated in Europe in 1904.
The rarely grown, brown-leaved variety, 'Purpurea' (superba), is a weak grower which is even more difficult to cultivate.

Columnea (x) banksii
This is a hybrid of Columnea oerstediana and Columnea schiedeana and was first cultivated in England in 1918.
The plant has glossy leaves and a somewhat upright habit. It is not grown as a hanging plant; the branches are tied to wire pins 16 in/40 cm long.

Columnea hirta
This species has hairy stems and leaves and flowers with a mass of light-orange flowers.

Columnea mortonii
This species has glossy, green leaves and orange-red flowers.

Columnea hirta

Columnea gloriosa 'Purpurea'

Many species and varieties
Columnea is named after a representative of an illustrious Roman family, Fabio Colonna, a scholar and author of botanical works who lived from 1567 to 1640. The plant belongs to the family Gesneriaceae. Columnea comes originally from Central America and South America.
The genus Columnea includes many species and varieties, some of which flower in the summer and some in the winter. Most Columneas produce orange-red flowers, but species with yellow flowers are also encountered. Although the plants are usually seen at commercial nurseries, shops or glasshouses in the spring, they are available practically the whole year round.

A hanging plant to take cuttings from
Most Columneas are cultivated as a hanging plant, which can be propagated by taking cuttings. Take cuttings from Columnea gloriosa in late autumn, the other Columneas in early spring. Take an intermediate cutting with one or two leaves (see page 169 for cuttings) from non-flowering tendrils.
Place five to seven cuttings of Columnea (x) banksii in a 3-in/8-cm pot, more in a larger pot.
If you treat the cuttings with growth hormone, they will have roots after five weeks under double glass or plastic foil. Two months later top the plants, and after another two months repot them into a 4½-in/11-cm pot.
Repot Columnea (x) banksii straight into a 5-in/12-cm final pot about two months after taking cuttings. Then top the plant two or three times. In order to get well-developed shoots which will form flowers, top for the last time in early summer.
With 'Stavanger', tie back the long branches in late autumn with six wire pins 16-in/40-cm long per pot. Leave the remainder of the branches hanging down.

Cold and dry treatment
Columneas are brilliant houseplants which with proper treatment can produce splendid hanging branches with masses of coloured flowers.
To begin with, you must see to it that the plant makes good growth each year and produces lots of new tendrils which will later flower. This is achieved by giving the right quantities of water and fertilizer at the right times. During the growing season, keep the soil moist at all times and feed weekly. Repot each year and where necessary cut off some of the old tendrils.
In the rest period (six weeks) keep the plants cold and dry. The maximum temperature is then 60° F/15° C, the minimum 46° F/8° C.
('Stavanger' must not be left in temperatures lower than 54° F/12° C.)
As soon as the flower buds appear, increase the temperature and start watering again. In the summer place in a slightly shaded position and in the darker months give them as much light as possible.
With all Gesneriaceae you must ensure that the water used is at room temperature in order to prevent leaf mottling.

Treatment table

	cutting	growth	rest
pot	3 in/7 cm	4-5 in/10-12 cm	—
soil	peat-based potting compost	RHP	—
feeding	—	1½ tsp compound fertilizer per pt water/3 g per litre	none
watering	moist	frequently	moist
temperature	68-72° F/ 20-22° C	64-68° F/ 18-20° C	46-60°F/ 8-15° C
rel. humidity	95%	> 80%	80%
growth hormone	Rhizopon BT 0.1 — 0.2%	—	—

special features   The minimum temperature of C. gloriosa during the growing season is 68° F/20° C, in the rest period 54° F/12° C.
The concentration of growth hormone with C. gloriosa is 0.1%.
Spray with 0.2% Benomyl (Benlate) to prevent foot rot (especially if under plastic cover).

Decorative and ornamental

Cordyline is a splendid foliage plant which, if it gets sufficient room, can grow into a substantial bush. In the wild it is actually a tree which originates from tropical Asia, although some species belong to Australia. It can flower beautifully as an older plant with big plumes of white or lilac flowers. It belongs to the lily family, Liliaceae.

Cordyline is often confused with Dracaena. Cordyline has white roots; it forms a rootstock and the fruit has six to fifteen seeds. Dracaena, with red-yellow roots, does not form a rootstock and the fruit has only one small seed.

Three methods of propagation

There are three ways of propagating Cordyline.

The simplest method of propagation is to separate the suckers, or 'tendrils', formed by the rootstock and grow them individually.

Ringing is also possible. Make a wound in the stem and wrap it in moisture-retaining material; new roots will then grow there (see page 170 for ringing). When you have cut off the newly formed plant, the old stem will grow into a handsome plant again.

Either head or stem cuttings can also be taken (see page 169 for cuttings). Treat the cuttings with growth hormone and place them in a 3-in/7-cm plastic pot filled with peat-based potting compost. They will have rooted after a month and should then be planted outside to stimulate further growth. When they are sufficiently large — this may well take more than a year — place them in a 5-6-in/12-14-cm pot, where they will probably grow less quickly.

Special soil

Cordyline requires a highly porous soil, one based on coarse peat or coarse pine needle litter, for example. Growers in Belgium — the cradle of Cordyline growing — use a mixture of 30% fresh oak leaves and 70% pine needle litter, a compost in which Azaleas are often first grown.

If you grow outside, the layer of earth must be 5-6 in/12-15 cm thick. The potting soil must be rinsed well at regular intervals, or excessive salt will produce dead spots on the leaves. Between these liberal rinsings with water (every two to three months) keep the soil moderately moist; also in the winter time. Feed weekly during the growing season. Cordyline needs plenty of light, but will not tolerate strong sunlight. Too dark a position causes the leaf colour to fade.

The plant may flower after two to three years, inside the house slightly later. The plumes of white or purple flowers shorten the growing length of the stem, but the plant continues to grow via side-shoots.

Cordyline fruticosa

Cordyline fruticosa (C. terminalis).

Fruticosa means 'bush-shaped'. A splendid foliage plant can indeed grow into a bush. There are numerous varieties with predominantly red and dark-red leaf colours. Green and red with white are also sometimes seen as leaf colours. A common variety is the red 'Firebrand'.

Cordyline (x) rubra

This plant is probably a cross between Cordyline fruticosa and Cordyline stricta. In breadth and leaf colour it is exactly intermediate. The variety 'Bruantii' has, when young, beautiful, copper-coloured leaves with a reddish underside.

Cordyline fruticosa 'Tricolor'

Treatment table

	cutting	growth	rest
pot	3 in/7 cm	outside thereafter 5-6 in/12-14 cm	5-6 in/ 12-14 cm
soil	peat-based potting compost	very highly porous	—
feeding	—	1 tsp compound fertilizer per pt water/2 g per litre	none
watering	moist	moderately	moderately
temperature	77-86° F/25-30° C	77-86° F/25-30° C	> 64° F/ 18° C
rel. humidity	95%	75%	70%
light	light	light	light
flowers	—	after 2 or 3 years	—
growth	Rhizopon BT	—	—
hormone	0.2%		

special features Shield against strong sunlight.

Crossandra infundibuliformis

Crossandra flava

This Crossandra with golden-yellow flowers is a popular flowering plant.

Crossandra infundibuliformis

Crossandra infundibuliformis 'Mona Walhed'

This is a deep orange-red variety which comes from Sweden.
Infundibuliformis means 'of an inverted funnel shape' and refers to the leaves.

A difficult houseplant

Crossandra is one of the flowering houseplants which frequently disappoint people. In the shop window or glasshouse it displays magnificent flowers and an even greater number of buds, all of which give promise of flowering. But once it is brought home, wrong treatment can soon cause the flowers to drop, while the buds do not materialize.

The plant requires plenty of light and a humid atmosphere, and this is a combination which is not so easy to achieve in a house as in a greenhouse. But with care it should still be possible to obtain a beautifully flowering Crossandra in the home.

Crossandra owes its name to the Greek words, *krossotos* and *andro*, which mean 'fringe' and 'male'. The male reproductive organs, the anthers, have long hairs.

The plant belongs to the family Acanthaceae.

The plant comes from southern Asia and was cultivated for the first time in England in 1880.

Cuttings for seven months

Cuttings can be taken of Crossandra from mid-winter to late summer.

Take head or intermediate cuttings with one leaf pair at that time (see page 169 for cuttings).

Place the cuttings in twos or threes in a 3½-in/8-cm pot filled with frozen peat potting soil. More cuttings should be placed in a larger pot.

To prevent rotting (damping off) make sure that the leaves do not overlap. Under mist or plastic foil the cuttings will have rooted after about a month.

Light and humidity

The Crossandra is a long-day plant and to get it flowering well, grow it in as light a position as possible. Simply shield it from strong sunlight. Six weeks after taking cuttings, feed the plant every week. The plant can flower from late spring to the autumn, but most plants begin to flower only in summer, when they have had sufficient light.

The plant can be overwintered, but it must then be cut back in late winter. The young shoots then formed will flower.

Treatment table

	cutting	growth	rest
pot	3½-5 in/8-12 cm	3½-5 in/8-12 cm	—
soil	frozen peat potting compost	RHP	—
feeding	—	1 tsp compound fertilizer per pt water/2 g per litre	—
watering	moist	moderately	seldom
temperature	72-77° F/ 22-25° C	64-68° F/ 18-20° C	—
rel. humidity	95-110%	70-80%	60-70%
light	light	strong	strong
flowers	—	late spring to mid- autumn	—
special features	In sunny weather the temperature may rise to 86° F/30° C, provided that the correct relative humidity is maintained.		

Cryptanthus

Concealed flowers

Kryptos means 'concealed' in Greek and *anthos* means 'flower'. Cryptanthus thus means the plant with the concealed flower. Cryptanthus is a Bromeliad (see Bromeliaceae) and Bromeliads are usually grown specially for their flowers. This is not so, however, with this Bromeliad. The plant forms flat low rosettes and the small, mostly white, flowers grow inside them; the gaudy bracts break off.

Most Bromeliads come originally from tropical America, where they commonly grow on tree trunks. Cryptanthus grows in the wild in the forests of eastern Brazil, both epiphytically (on tree trunks) and on the ground. The soil in this region is very dry and allowance must be made for this when growing this beautiful foliage plant.

The genus Cryptanthus contains about 20 species, all of them with beautifully coloured and decorative leaves. Their main use is for planting in baskets and pans, but the young plants in particular are also particularly suitable for floral arrangements, for example in bridal bouquets.

Young shoots

As with all Bromeliads, the plant dies when it has flowered. On a Cryptanthus many young shoots then appear, which, if placed in individual pots, will subsequently become full-grown plants.

If you want a lot of plants, you must grow the young shoots outside in the greenhouse, where high soil temperatures (up to 68-77° F/20-25° C) will produce sturdy growth.

After a year you will have mature plants, which both before and during flowering will produce many young shoots again.

Dryness and light

Although Cryptanthus is by nature a forest plant, it can withstand plenty of light, even a certain amount of sunlight. Indeed light makes the leaf colour even more beautiful. But because the region where it occurs in the wild is fairly dry, the potting soil must never be wet.

These plants grow best in a moderately moist to dry soil, which should be very humus-rich and highly porous.

Bromeliad soil is a mixture specially formulated for these plants and is universally obtainable.

Many varieties and hybrids of the 20 Cryptanthus species are cultivated, among them some marvellously coloured plants which are obtained by spraying the young plantlets with the toxic, aminotriazole (Weedazol), in the proportions $1/32$ fl oz Weedazol per pt of water/2 ml per litre.

Cryptanthus zonatus

Cryptanthus bromelioides 'Tricolor'

Cryptanthus bromelioides 'Tricolor'

Treatment table

	suckers	growth	rest
pot	3½-4 in/8-10 cm	—	—
soil	Bromeliad	Bromeliad	Bromeliad
feeding	—	1 tsp compound fertilizer per pt water/2 g per litre	—
watering	moist	seldom	dry
temperature	68-72° F/20-22° C	68-72° F/20-22° C	> 64° F/18° C
rel. humidity	70%	70%	70%
light	strong	strong	strong
special features	During the growing season, feed weekly with a mixture in the proportions 10:5:20. The ideal nitrogen-to-potassium ratio is 1:2.		

Cryptanthus zonatus 'Fuscus'

Zonatus means 'with a belt-shaped stripe' and *fuscus* is Latin for 'brown'. One of the many cultivated Cryptanthus species with a red-brown stripe, this is a coarse-leaved species.

Cryptanthus zonatus 'Viridis'

This zonatus is predominantly green-coloured (*viridis*).

Cryptanthus bivitattus

This plant has a smaller and narrower leaf than *Cryptanthus zonatus*.
Bivitattus means with two stripes.

Cryptanthus beuckeri

This is a plant with brownish-pink spotted leaves. Growth is on the erect side. The plant is named after Beucker.

Cryptanthus lacerdae

This *Cryptanthus* has a silver-white centre stripe.
The petals are divided into lobes.

Cryptanthus bromelioides 'Tricolor'

This Bromelia-like *Cryptanthus* has variegated leaves.

Cryptanthus acaulis

Acaulis means stemless.

Crypthanthus fosterianus

The plant is named after Foster.

Ctenanthe oppenheimiana 'Variegata'

Ctenanthe

Ctenanthe oppenheimiana 'Variegata'
This species is a native of north-east Brazil. The weaker-growing variety 'Variegata', is the most widely grown.

Ctenanthe lubbersii
This Ctenanthe comes from Brazil and was introduced into Belgium in 1883.

Ctenanthe kummeriana
This species, which also comes from Brazil, does not grow quite so high. The leaves are dark-green and have a silvery sheen along the veins.

A difficult name

The name, Ctenanthe, comes from the Greek *ktenion* for 'little comb', itself derived from the Greek for 'comb', *kteis*.
The numerous closely-packed bracts of the inflorescence of this plant (*anthos* is the Greek for 'flower') indeed resemble a comb.
Like its family name, Calathea, Ctenanthe is often incorrectly called Maranta.
The plant admittedly belongs to the Maranta family, Marantaceae, and this clearly has something to do with the similarities with the well-known Ten Commandment Plant, Maranta leuconeura. The shape of the magnificent leaves is often similar and the brilliant decoration may present similarities. Maranta, however, is much smaller, and its flower differs in certain respects. Most Ctenanthe species come originally from Brazil, a few from Peru.

Shoot cuttings

A Ctenanthe which is growing well forms young shoots which can be used to propagate the plant.
After taking cuttings and treating them with growth hormone, place them under double glass or plastic foil in peat-based potting compost (see page 169 for cuttings).
The young plants will have rooted after two to three weeks. Place them then in a 3½-in/8-cm pot and after two months repot them into a 4-5-in/10-12-cm final pot.
The growing time from cutting to full-grown plant is 10 to 12 months.
The plant can also be propagated by division.

Decidedly a foliage plant

Ctenanthe is grown mainly for its beautiful leaves. It is a herbaceous plant which grows quickly, but as a houseplant it suffers from the low relative humidity of the average house. It is an ideal plant for mixed planting in large boxes or pans. In a greenhouse these plants will shoot up in no time.
Ctenanthe requires an airy, fibrous, highly porous potting soil. The special Bromeliad soil is very suitable.
Water liberally during the growing season, but take care that the sub-soil does not get too wet. Add a compound fertilizer solution weekly and in the darker winter months once every three weeks. The plant grows best in a shady position.

Treatment table

	cutting	growth	rest
pot	3-3½ in/8-9 cm	4½-5 in/ 11-13 cm	—
soil	peat-based	Bromeliad soil	—
feeding	—	1 tsp compound fertilizer per pt water/2 g per litre	—
watering	moist	liberally	moderately
temperature	68° F/20° C	64-68° F/ 18-20° C	64° F/18° C
rel. humidity	95%	80%	80%
light	moderate	shade	light

special features In the sun, the maximum temperature is 77° F/25° C, with a minimum relative humidity of 80%.

Spontaneous improvement

Anyone walking in a wooded region around the Mediterranean, for example on the island of Corsica, suddenly confronted with a bank of flowering Cyclamen would never guess that they belonged to exactly the same species of which so many different varieties are grown as houseplants, namely Cyclamen persicum. But closer inspection would show that the flowers, although much smaller, have the same curling shape and that the coloured flower stalks and the heart-shaped leaves strongly resemble those of the houseplant varieties.

The name persicum is out of place; the plant is not found in Persia, but in the Mediterranean area, where it grows in the half-shade of woods, in a lime-rich, loamy soil, its round, disc-shaped tuber buried deep beneath the ground. Cyclamen takes its name from the tuber, *kuklos* meaning 'round disc' in Greek.

The plant has its rest period in the summer, when the soil is very dry and the temperature in the shade rises as high as 105°F/40°C.

The large-flowered varieties which we know are not the result of human tinkering. In about 1870 a grower in England suddenly got some large flowers on one of his Cyclamens. He called this spontaneous mutation 'Giganteum' and was pleased to find that this large-flowered character was hereditary. He was thus able to reproduce it.

In the same chance manner flowers with fringes (*fimbriata*) and frizzy flowers (*cristata*) were obtained on Cyclamen towards the end of the last century. Cyclamen was described for the first time in England in 1731.

Cyclamen belongs to the primrose family, Primulaceae.

Cross-pollination

To propagate Cyclamen you need to obtain the seed, choosing handsome, sturdy, healthy plants for this purpose. For the best results it is preferable to apply cross-pollination in the spring and autumn, making sure that the pollen from the one plant is brought into contact with the stigma of the pistil of the other.

This can be done by collecting the pollen with a teaspoon (by careful tapping against the peduncle) and bringing it into contact with a stigma. Do this at a temperature of 54-59°F/12-15°C and a relative humidity of 75-80%. If the fertilization is successful, the flower crown falls off and the stem droops. The plant must therefore be secured beforehand.

The seed is ripe when the fruit bursts (after four to six months). It remains viable for four to five years. One-year-old seed gives the best results. Fresh seed takes about six months to germinate.

Sowing

Seeds can be sown from mid-summer to mid-spring, depending on the desired size of the plant, the flowering time and the variety. Seeds for sowing must first be disinfected for two hours in an anti-mould agent. Let them dry out afterwards and then sow them in a frame at intervals of about 1 in/2.5 cm. Cover the seeds with a layer of sowing soil to the thickness of the seed grain. The seed should germinate in five weeks. Not all the seeds, of course, will germinate: 70-80% is a good proportion. About 13 weeks after sowing, set the best plantlets out approximately 2 in/5 cm apart.

They can be pricked out once more after this or potted off into a 3½-4 in/8-10 cm final pot after three months. Large, sturdy specimens can be grown in a 4-5 in/10-12 cm pot. Keep the soil dry before pricking out or repotting; the plants will then grow better when they are placed in the new soil.

Cyclamen hybrid

Treatment table

	sowing	growth	rest (tuber)
pot	frame	3½-5 in/9-12 cm	—
soil	RHP sowing soil	RHP	—
feeding	—	1 tsp compound fertilizer per pt water/2 g per litre	—
watering	liberally	frequently	dry
temperature	60-64°F/16-18°C	60-68°F/16-20°C	68-86F°/20-30°C
rel. humidity	90%	70%	dry
light	light (after germination.)	light	—
flowers	—	mid-autumn to mid-winter	—
seed disinfecting	Benlate 1 tsp per pt water/2 g per litre	—	—
heart-rot fungicide	—	Rovral	—
soil fungicide	—	Daconil, 2½ tsp per 10 pt soil/5 g per 10 litres or 1¼ tsp/2.5 g Polyram Combi M.	—
special features	Shield against strong sunlight in spring and summer. The soil mixture should have 13 lb Dolokal per yd³ RHP frozen peat potting soil/6 kg per m². The pH (=6) must not be less than 5.2.		

Cyclamen persicum hybrid

Cyclamen persicum 'Anneke'

Cyclamen persicum 'Rococo Rose'

'Beacon-light'
This is the most widely grown variety. It belongs to the large-flowered, entire varieties which are tetraploid and single-coloured.

'Anneke'
This white, small-flowered, entire Cyclamen belongs to a large group of varieties which were grown from crosses of large-flowered varieties with the botanical species. The varieties have girls' names, such as 'Sonia' (with white eye) and others. They flower with medium-sized, brightly-coloured flowers and are not very widely grown.

Rococo Cyclamen
These Cyclamens are also called papiliocyclamen. They have frizzy flowers and are difficult to cultivate. This type originated in 1886 and is hardly ever grown now.

'Franz Schubert'
This lilac-pink variety is also large-flowered and entire. It belongs to a group of diploid varieties, with soft colours and beautiful leaf decoration, which are given composers' names. These varieties keep particularly well, but are slow growers.

'With white eye'
This is a large-flowered, entire Cyclamen which is one of the so-called oculatum varieties. These are single-coloured, diploid varieties with a dark-coloured eye.
There are also striatum (striped) varieties, for example 'Harlequin', and sweet-smelling varieties, but they are seldom grown.

Cyclamen persicum 'With white eye'

'Swan Lake'
This white variety is one of a group of so-called F1 hybrid varieties. They excel in rapidity of growth, uniformity and profusion of flowering. There are many pink and white Cyclamens of this type. The seed is about ten times more expensive than that of a non-hybrid variety. Some of the varieties have the names of musical works, such as 'Swan Lake', and some of constellations, such as 'Orion' (with white eye).

'Sylphide'
This variety belongs to the most important Cyclamen group, the large-flowered, entire varieties which make up more than 95% of all Cyclamens. The lilac 'Sylphide' is a so-called diploid, single-coloured variety. White Cyclamens are of the same type.

Fimbriata Cyclamen
These Cyclamens have fringed flowers and are seldom grown. A distinctive variety is 'Victoria', with white flowers, a red eye and a narrow red border. Double-flowered Cyclamens also exist. There are many double-flowered F1 hybrids in Japan and they are also very widely grown in France.

Think about root rot and heart rot
CyClamen is very sensitive to moulds which cause root rot and heart rot. You can do various things to prevent this. To begin with, use soil which is properly disinfected. Commercial growers disinfect soil by steaming it and then mixing anti-mould agents into it. To prevent heart rot, spray the heart of the plant liberally with the agent Rovral. For each plant, use 1 fl oz/25 ml of a solution in which 1 tsp of agent with spreader is added to 1 pint of water/2 g per litre. This agent works only as a preventative, so that spraying the plant before it is attacked by mould is essential.
If these precautions have been taken, the plant can be watered liberally during its growing season in the summer. In warm weather the plant can be given a good spray, including the heart (when the plant is not in flower). Keep the potting soil moist by means of underground irrigation (see page 167 for water). In addition, because this leads to an increased salt concentration in the pot, plunge the plants once every 14 days in a bucket of water, allowing them to drain afterwards.
Place flowering plants in saucers of water. Because of the required air humidity, there must be a good distance between the plants, so that air can circulate between them.

Pay attention to temperature and humidity
Collect pollen at a temperature of 63-70°F/17-21°C and a relative humidity of 75-80%. The best temperature for fertilization and ripening is 54-59°F/12-15°C, with a relative humidity of 75-80%. Keep the seed at a temperature of 64-68°F/18-20°C. Higher temperatures have a harmful effect. The best temperature for germination is 70°F/17°C; the relative humidity should then be about 90°. Grow seedlings at a temperature of 64-68°F/18-20°C; in overcast weather this can be 59-64°F/15-18°C; the relative humidity is then about 70%. Pricked-out plants require (with some variation depending on the light) a temperature of 59-68°F/15-20°C and a relative humidity of about 70%. At the beginning, a temperature of 68°F/20°C and a relative humidity of 80% are favourable for smooth, continued growth after pricking-out or repotting. Reduce high temperatures by shielding the plant slightly, by spraying with water, and by ventilation. This is naturally simpler in a greenhouse than in the house. The turn yellow at high temperatures because the plant 'thinks' that the rest period is beginning.
Flowering rest plants need a temperature of 59°F/15°C and a relative humidity of 60%.

Overwintering
Cyclamen is a beautifully flowering plant with finely decorated leaves which can give you pleasure for many years if you control the temperature and humidity. If a fire is used for heating, the window sill is the coolest place in the room, but in houses with central heating Cyclamens have a hard time on the window sill. When the plant has flowered, set it in a warm position and keep the soil as dry as possible. After the leaves have died, keep the pot ball for four months at 68-86°F/20-30°C. Then grow it on as a young Cyclamen at 59°F/15°C. Old plants give a large number of smaller flowers which can nevertheless last for many years.

Cymbidium

An orchid

As with all orchids, the flowers of Cymbidium are of exotic beauty and keep for a very long time. This is just as well, because in other respects the plant does not have much value as a houseplant. During flowering, however, Cymbidium is a beautiful houseplant for just a few months. The name Cymbidium comes from the Greek and means 'little boat'. This refers to the shape of the stigma. Only hybrids are found as houseplants. They are crosses of botanical species which are natives of the high-lying, cool, mountainous regions of tropical Asia.

Sowing and division

If you wish to propagate Cymbidium, this can be done by sowing from seed. Large, old plants can also be propagated by division. Commercial growers propagate Cymbidium by means of a meristem culture (tissue growing).
Grow young plants in plastic pots. Older specimens are best placed two to four together in so-called 'styropur' cucumber frames. Plants grown from seed will have a flowering life of three to five years. Light the youngest plantlets (seedlings and meristem plantlets) for 16 hours a day at a light intensity of 9,000 mW per yd²/m² over a period of a few months.

Special potting soil

Cymbidiums grow best in a highly porous, terrestrial (earth-type) mixture. Commercial growers use a coarse-fibred peat litter substrate. To every 10 pt of this are added 30-40 tsp Dolokal/60-80 g per litre in order to increase the pH to 5.8. In order to provide sufficient micro-elements, 1¼ tsp/2.5 g Sporumix PG and ⅛ tsp/.25 g chelate sequestrene 138Fe are also added. As soon as the pH drops below 5.5 during the growing season, the lime content of this mixture must be increased again. Orchids cannot tolerate too acid a soil.
Give Cymbidium plenty of water regularly during the summer growing season, so that the soil remains moist. Give it slightly less water in the winter months. In the summer feed the plant every 10 days, in the winter every 15 to 20 days. Grow the plant in as light a position as possible, but shield it against strong sunlight in the summer.
Cymbidium can be grown completely indoors, provided that you follow the growing rules as closely as possible. In the summer months the plants can be placed in a sheltered position outside. When the plants flower they must be shielded against bees and bumblebees, because fertilized flowers wither within a few days.

Treatment table

	young plant	growth	rest
pot	frame	frame	—
soil	Cymbidium mixture		Cymbidium mixture
feeding	—	½ tsp compound fertilizer per pt water/1 g per litre	none
watering	moist	moist	moist
temperature	68°F/20°C	64-70°F/18-21°C in sun < 77°F/ 25°C	60-68°F/ 16-20°C
rel. humidity	80%	70-80%	70%
light	light	light	light
special features	Light young plants 16 hours a day with 9,000 mW per yd²/m². In summer the ideal night temperature is 57°F/14°C. During flowering the temperature should be 54-57°F/12-14°C. Shield somewhat against strong sunlight.		

Cymbidium hybrid

Cymbidium hybrid

The woody Cymbidium hybrids are crosses of botanic species such as Cymbidium lowianum, Cymbidium eburneum, Cymbidium giganteum and Cymbidium insignes. The large-flowered varieties are often tetraploid (they have twice the number of chromosomes). The woody varieties are of a high quality. The miniature Cymbidiums are crosses of the large-flowered hybrids with the small-flowered Cymbidium pumilum from Japan and Cymbidium devonianum. These miniatures are developed in California.

Cyperus alternifolius

This plant has a slightly different leaf from most other Cyperus species. It is about 1 cm wide and the involucral leaves are rough on top, the inflorescences having lanceolate scales. The stems are round to triangular.

The plant is a native of Madagascar.

Cyperus alternifolius

Cyperus argenteostriatus (Cyperus diffusus)

Argenteostriatus means 'with silver-coloured stripes' and refers to the three white, longitudinal nerves of the involucral leaves.

The plant has numerous root leaves with a rough edge. Each leaf is about ¾ in/2 cm long. It comes originally from Mauritius.

Cyperus gracilis

This 'slender' Cyperus is regarded as a variety of alternifolius. The plant comes from Australia and is about 20 in/50 cm high. A notable feature is that it forms more peduncles than root leaves.

Cyperus haspan (Cyperus profiler)

This delicate Cyperus is a species with fine grass-type leaves on supple stems. If you want to propagate the plant, the stems must be supported with a bamboo cane. The species is a native of Surinam and tropical Africa.

Cyperus papyrus

This Cyperus is a native of tropical Asia and can reach a height of 6½ ft/2 m to 13 ft/4 m. It grows wild in Sicily. The cut-off 'flower stems' have been introduced to the West and are used in floral arrangements.

A very old cultivated plant

Cyperus has been connected with man's activities from the earliest times.

The best-known rush grass is Cyperus papyrus. More than 4,000 years before our era, the Egyptians were already making paper from this plant, by sticking together strips of flattened pith from te stalks and then pressing them. Our word 'paper' comes from this, and from paper comes in turn the word 'papp,qrush grass was popular with the ancient Greeks as horse fodder. It was described as the plant with sweet-smelling roots called Kupeiron. The name Cyperus comes from this. Kupeiron was probably Cyperus esculentus, the chufa or earth almond. This plant is still grown in the Mediterranean area today. The tubers are eaten raw and cooked (esculentus R edible); oil is pressed out of it and in Spain a well-known refreshing drink is made from it: horchata de Chufas.

The particular Cyperus species which we know as houseplants are native to tropical Africa and Madagascar. The plants which are grown in the West as foliage pot plants are without exception marsh plants. Commercial growers also use the long stems with leaves of Cyperus papyrus in floral decoration.

It is not only man who likes Cyperus; cats are also mad about it. They love to eat the leaves, which act as an emetic if they have swallowed too many hairs. People who live in flats or houses where they cannot let their cats out frequently grow smaller species of rush grass specifically for this purpose.

Sowing and cuttings

It is quite easy to grow Cyperus from seed. This often happens spontaneously when the plant grows in marshy ground. But the seed can hardly ever be obtained commercially. You must get the seeds yourself from plants which have ffowered. If you sow them in fibrous potting soil which has been made thoroughly wet, you will succeed every time.

It is also very easy to take cuttings of Cyperus. Choose a big, fully-grown stem (which is not flowering nor has already flowered) and cut off the leaves to a length of about 1¼ in/3 cm. Place this top with about 2 in/5 cm of stem in water. Roots will now grow on the stem and the new stems will arise out of the rosette.

Seedlings are fully-grown after six months, cuttings after three to five months.

Plenty of light and little water

Cyperus is a free-growing and decorative foliage plant, which can be enjoyed for many years if you give it plenty of water. Cut off old stems and ones that have finished flowering and the plant will form new ones of its own accord. For good growth and a beautiful leaf colour, give the plant slight shade. It does not tolerate sunlight and will do extremely well in a shady position.

Repot the plant annually into a spacious, preferably plastic pot (the soil stays more moist in plastic than earthenware). Feed it once a week. It does best in a humus-rich, fibrous and highly moisture-retaining soil, one based on frozen peat, for example. You can approximate best to the plant's natural marshy environment by ensuring that it always stands in a small amount of water.

Treatment table

	cutting	sowing	growth
pot	3-3½ in/8-9 cm	5 in/12 cm	larger
soil	humus-rich, fibrous, moisture-retentive		
feeding	—	1 tsp compound fertilizer per pt water/2 g per litre	—
watering	plenty	plenty	plenty
temperature	68-72° F/ 20-22° C	68-72° F/ 20-22° C	64-72° F/ 18-22° C
rel. humidity	95-100%	95-100%	> 75%
light	slight shade	slight shade	slight shade

Cold lover from the tropics

Cyrtomium, with its splendid glossy, leathery leaves, is a Fern which does not require too much attention to keep as a houseplant. It can be enjoyed for many years so long as it does not get excessive light or heat.

The plant comes originally from eastern Asia and South Africa, where it grows in wooded, mountainous regions. Although it is, therefore, a tropical plant, it cannot tolerate high temperatures because high in the mountains it is always cool.

The name Cyrtomium comes from the Greek *kyrtos* for 'curved' or 'waved'. The leaves of this Fern are slightly curved in shape.

Cyrtomium probably owes its popular name, Iron fern, to the metallic lustre of its leaves, though some people say that it refers to the rust-coloured spores.

Spore plant

Like all Ferns. Cyrtomium has to be propagated by means of its spores (see page 168), which arise spontaneously. Sow them in clean soil which is not too acid; otherwise the spores will not germinate. The spores first form a green mossy layer, the so-called prothallium, and the actual fertilization takes place in this layer by the fusing of the male and female prothallia.

After about three months plant out individual pieces of prothallium, from which the young Ferns will then grow; and after another three months place them in a 3-in/7-cm pot. Six months later the Ferns will have grown into beautiful houseplants, which should be repotted annually into pots of increasing size.

Plenty of water

Cyrtomium requires plenty of water. Even in the rest period, during the darker winter months, keep the soil moderately moist.

Cyrtomium is a sturdy Fern for a not too warm room. Because of its leathery leaves, from which little water evaporates, it is also resistant to a low relative humidity. Grow it exclusively in RHP potting soil and place it in a well-shaded spot. It will grow well even in a very dark room. Feed it weekly during the growing season.

In shops Cyrtomium often stands in a small pot. It can therefore be repotted directly after purchase into a 4-5-in/10-12-cm pot.

Cyrtomium falcatum 'Rochfordii'

Cyrtomium falcatum 'Rochfordii'
The leaf of this Cyrtomium is a little more deeply indented.

Cyrtomium fortunei
These Ferns are grown to a very limited extent.
The leaf is regular in shape and consists of a row of narrow leaflets. The species is a native of southern Asia.

Cyrtomium fortunei

Cyrtomium falcatum
Falcatum means 'sickle-shaped' and refers to the leaf shape of this splendid, sturdy Fern.

Treatment table

	growth	rest
pot	4-5 in/10-12 cm	—
soil	RHP	—
feeding	1½ tsp compound fertilizer per pt water/3 g per litre	none
watering	generously	moderately
temperature	50-60° F/10-15° C	41-45° F/5-7° C
rel. humidity	70%	70%
light	shade	—
special features	The maximum temperature is 77° F/25° C, with a relative humidity of 70%.	

Cytisus racemosus 'Genista'

Cytisus (x) racemosus

This Indoor broom is probably a cross of Cytisus canariensis (from the Canary Islands) and Cytisus maderensis (from Madeira). *Racemosus* means 'bunched-shaped' and refers to the inflorescence.

Nitrogen fixers

Cytisus belongs to the family of papilionaceous flowers, in Latin, Leguminosae, from which is derived the French word for vegetables, *légumes*. Many of our commonest vegetables, in fact, belong to this family: peas, beans, field peas and all other pulses. Practically all papilionaceous flowers have the ability to fix nitrogen from the air and convert it into protein.

Many papilionaceous flowers, such as the Lupin, have nitrogen nodules by which they themselves release nitrogen into the soil. These plants are therefore often planted in nitrogen-poor areas which are being brought into cultivation. The name Cytisus is very old. The Greeks used it for Medicago, the Lucerne clover.

In some places Cytisus is called Indoor broom and although the bushes which we know as Broom belong to another genus of the family, this beautiful plant with its brightly-coloured yellow flowers is certainly very like it.

Side-cuttings and top cuttings

From early to mid-summer take the tops off the Cytisus plants which are to flower the following spring. Treat these tops with growth hormone and place them in a 3-in/7-cm pot filled with a mixture of equal parts of frozen peat and river sand. Cuttings can also be taken in late spring from the side-shoots, which are then cut with a 'heel' (a piece of the stem which is cut off with the cutting). Cover the cuttings with paper to protect them against strong sunlight. They will have rooted after six to eight weeks. The rooted cuttings must overwinter outside, the pot being placed in pits. Bring them inside in the spring and when the branches have started to grow well, cut their tops off. (These can be used as cuttings). Mid-summer is the latest time for this. In mid-spring place the plants in a 4-5-in/10-12-cm pot. At the beginning of summer move them into the garden. In the autumn, before the night frosts come, bring them inside again. Overwinter them at 46° F/8° C; the first flowers will appear from late winter onwards.

Outdoor plants

Although they flower indoors, grow the plants outside in the sun. When they are indoors in the autumn and winter, give them as much light as possible. Water them sparingly then; in the summer they need plenty of water. The plant grows in a mixture of three parts RHP potting soil and one part river sand. Feed them once every two weeks during the growing season. You can enjoy your indoor Broom for many years if you grow it outside and then allow it to overwinter cool but frost-free. If the temperature is kept to 61-64° F/16-18° C during flowering, the plants will flower for six or seven weeks.

Treatment table

	cutting	growth	rest
pot	3 in/7 cm	4-5 in/10-12 cm	—
soil	peat-based potting compost	RHP and river sand 3:1	—
feeding	—	1½ tsp compound fertilizer per pt water/3 g per litre	
temperature	60° F/15° C	60-64° F/ 16-18° C	41-46° F/ 5-8° C
rel. humidity	75%	60%	70%
light	light	light	light
flowers	—	late winter to mid-spring	—
growth hormone	Rhizopon 0.1 or 0.2%	—	—

special features Shield from strong sunlight indoors. Treat herbaceous cuttings with a lower concentration of growth hormone.

Didymochlaena

Double coat

Like Cyrtomium, Didymochlaena is a Fern which comes from hot regions. This beautiful foliage plant is indigenous to all tropical regions throughout the world. Although a forest plant, Didymochlaena does not grow in the cool forests of high mountain areas and can tolerate somewhat higher temperatures.

These Ferns have splendid glossy, leathery leaves, somewhat browner in colour than those of Cyrtomium. Both plants belong to the same family, Aspidiaceae.

Didymochlaena was cultivated as a houseplant in 1838. The name comes from the Greek words, *didymos* and *chlaina*, which mean 'two-fold' and 'coat'. The name therefore means 'plant with a double coat' and refers to the two-fold membrane covering the spores.

Spores and division

Didymochlaena can be propagated by collecting the spores and sowing them in a clean, not too acid, soil (see page 168 for propagation by spores). The prothallium, a mossy layer, appears first. If pieces of this are pricked out after three months, the young Ferns will grow out of them; these should be potted on into a 3-in/7-cm pot after about three to four months. Repot them into a 4-5-in/10-12-cm pot after six to seven months.

Not strong

Compared to its relation Cyrtomium, this Fern is not a strong plant, but it is a particularly beautiful and decorative houseplant which can be enjoyed for many years if properly treated.

The most important requirement is the correct relative humidity, relatively simple to achieve in a greenhouse or hothouse, more difficult in a house. During the growing season water the plant liberally and in the rest period keep the soil moderately moist. Feed it once every three weeks then, every week during the growing season.

The plant should be placed in a slightly shaded position and it will also be content with somewhat more shade. It requires a great deal of heat, but will not tolerate sunlight. In shops it will usually be seen as a very large plant in a 4-5-in/10-12-cm pot.

Treatment table

	growth	rest
pot	4-5 in/10-12 cm	—
soil	humus-rich RHP	—
feeding	1½ tsp compound fertilizer per pt water/3 g per litre	1½ tsp compound fertilizer per pt water/3 g per litre
temperature	68-72° F/20-22° C	> 64° F/18° C
rel. humidity	70-80%	70-80%
light	slight shade	light
special features	The maximum temperature in the sun is 86° F/30° C, provided that the correct relative humidity is maintained.	

Didymochlaena truncatula

Didymochlaena truncatula

Didymochlaena truncatula

Truncatula means 'slightly truncated' in Latin and refers to the somewhat compact leaf shape of this magnificent Fern. D. truncatula is the only species which is grown as a houseplant.

Dieffenbachia bowmanii 'Exotica'

Dieffenbachia amoena 'Tropic White'

This Dieffenbachia, with large, white-blotched leaves, comes from Costa Rica. Another variety of this species is 'High Colour', whose leaves have a smaller number of blotches.

Dieffenbachia bowanii 'Exotica'

This Dieffenbachia comes from Colombia and has light-green stems and irregular, white-blotched leaves. 'Exotica Perfecta' has even more white blotches. This species contains many varieties.

Dieffenbachia seguine

This species comes from Central America. The top side of the petiole is sheath-shaped with white blotches. Many varieties of this species are grown.

Dieffenbachia maculata (Dieffenbachia picta) 'Rudolph Roehrs'

This is the most common variety. The leaves are dark-green with irregular yellow-to-white decoration. In addition to 'Rudolph Roehrs', 'Superba' is also a well-known variety.

Dieffenbachia x bausei

This is one of the Dieffenbachia species which has been created by selective breeding and cross-breeding. The leaves are a striking yellow-green with white specks. This species is a very weak grower.

Dieffenbachia maculata

Dieffenbachia x bausei

Beautiful, but poisonous

This splendid foliage plant, which may flower on occasions, has a somewhat dubious reputation as a houseplant. It is a beautiful, decorative and sturdy plant, but it is extremely poisonous. The tissue contains prussic acid compounds and calcium oxalate crystals. The sap is therefore strongly irritant to the skin. Some people react if their skin merely comes in contact with the plant. So take care!

Dieffenbachia is an arum-type plant and belongs to the family Araceae. It is named after Joseph Dieffenbach, the 19th-century keeper of the Botanical Gardens at Schoenbrunn in Austria. It is indigenous to South America.

Take care

If you take cuttings of the plant in order to propagate it, make sure that you do not come into contact with the sap. The wearing of rubber gloves is advisable. And you must also ensure that the mother plant is not infected with bacteria. The cutting knife must therefore be carefully disinfected on each occasion. Imported stems may be used for the taking of cuttings and you can also take head, stem or shoot cuttings yourself (see page 169 for cuttings). Make sure to take them from rapidly growing, virus-free plants.

Under plastic foil the cuttings will root in peat-based potting compost after three weeks. A shoot cutting can be placed either in a pot for cuttings or straight into a 5-in/12-13-cm final pot; a stem cutting forms after rooting a young plant, which can be potted on after two to three months. In eight or nine months you will have a fine specimen.

Think about diseases

Dieffenbachia is very sensitive to bacterial diseases. It must therefore be repotted annually and grown in conditions that are neither too warm nor too humid. It grows exceptionally well in a humus-rich RHP soil, which should be somewhat fibrous to provide good porosity.

Keep the potting soil moderately moist, and never allow it to dry out. Dieffenbachia is very salt-sensitive. It is therefore a good idea occasionally to plunge it in a bucket of water, allowing it to drain afterwards. Feed it weekly in the summer and once every two weeks in the winter. Given slight shading in the summer and as much light as possible in the winter, it will last for many years and can grow into a large plant. It is therefore in great demand for planting inside buildings. In America, where most varieties currently come from, Dieffenbachia is one of the most widely grown foliage plants.

Treatment table

	cutting	growth	rest
pot	3 in/7 cm	5 in/12-13 cm	—
soil	peat-based potting compost	fibrous RHP	—
feeding	1½ tsp compound fertilizer per pt water/3 g per litre	1 tsp compound fertilizer per pt water/2 g per litre	—
temperature	77° F/25° C	68-77° F/ 20-25° C	64-68° F/ 18-20° C
rel. humidity	85%	70-80%	70-75%
light	—	slight shade	light
water	moist	moderately	moderately
special features	The temperature must fall at night with no increase in relative humidity. The plants grow exceptionally well under sufficiently strong lamp light.		

Dipladenia

Exotic beauty

The prefix *dipl* in Greek means 'double' and *adinos* means 'close together'. The flower buds of Dipladenia mostly come out in twos, so that the flowers lie close to each other and seem to crowd one another out.

Dipladenia is a member of the periwinkle family, Apocynaceae.

Dipladenias, which are natives of tropical America, are climbing plants with delicate exotic flowers and beautiful glossy leaves. They are usually supplied by commercial growers on wire bows or plastic frames.

Staunch the bleeding

Dipladenia can be propagated by means of a stem cutting with one leaf pair. Immediately after taking the cutting, plunge it in luke-warm water to staunch the bleeding and prevent the sap or wound tissue from congealing. The tissue must remain fluid in order to absorb the growth hormone with which the cutting has to be treated. Place the cuttings in a highly porous frozen peat potting soil under plastic foil or mist (see page 169 for cuttings). As soon as the cuttings have rooted, place a number of them individually, no more than nine, in a 5-in/12-cm pot. Do not top the plants, but provide them with ventilation to ensure that they do not grow wild.

Depending on the size of the plant, Dipladenias flower nine to eighteen months after the taking of cuttings.

Not easy to grow

Dipladenias are not easy to grow as houseplants: they require a high temperature, a high relative humidity and lots of sunlight if they are to flower well.

Shield them from excessively strong sunlight in the summer and spring, but do not leave them in the shade or growth will be wild and flowering diminished.

In the growing season, keep the potting soil moderately moist and feed weekly. In the darker winter months water sparingly and add no fertilizer. Wet potting soil in the winter is fatal to Dipladenias.

The plants can flower from mid-spring to mid-autumn, though most specimens flower hardly at all after the summer. In the house they are awkward customers, but in a hothouse or greenhouse they make ideal climbing plants with profusely-flowering stems up to 3 ft/1m long.

Treatment table

	cutting	growth	rest
pot	—	4-5 in/10-12 cm	—
soil	high-porosity frozen peat potting soil RHP		
feeding	—	1 tsp compound fertilizer per pt water/2 g per litre	none
watering	moist	moderately	dry
temperature	77-81° F/ 25-27° C	64° F/ 18° C	60-64° F/ 15-18° C
rel. humidity	95%	65-70%	60-65%
light	light	light	light
flowers	—	mid-spring to mid-autumn	—
growth hormone	Rhizopon AK 0.7%	—	—
special features	Grow young plants at 72-77° F/22-25° C, with a relative humidity of less than 80%. Avoid strong sunlight in spring and summer.		

Dipladenia sanderi 'Rosea'

Right: *Dipladenia sanderi*. Left: *Dipladenia boliviensis*

Dipladenia (X) amoena 'Rubiniana'

This is a strongly-growing Dipladenia with large, dark-pink (*rubiana*) flowers. *Amoena* means 'lovely'.

Dipladenia sanderi

This Dipladenia flowers with bunches of light-pink flowers with a diameter of 2-3 in/5-8 cm. It can flower profusely as a small plant.

Dipladenia boliviensis

This is a strongly-growing Dipladenia with large, white flowers which have a yellow throat. The flower tube is long, and the flowers break off easily in transit. For this reason they are grown to only a limited extent.

Dizygotheca elegantissima

Dizygotheca elegantissima

This Dizygotheca comes from the Pacific Islands and was cultivated for the first time in England in 1873. The variety 'Castor' has a little brother, called 'Pollux', which has a different leaf shape. These varieties are spontaneous mutations.

Dizygotheca veitchii

This plant is a native of New Caledonia. The original species has wider leaves than Dizygotheca elegantissima. The plant was first cultivated in England in 1870. The variety 'Gracillima' is decorative and fine-leaved.

Dizygotheca elegantissima 'Castor'

Non-climbing ivy

Dizygotheca is a member of the family, Araliaceae, and is often wrongly called 'Aralia'. The name Dizygotheca means 'with a double set of anthers'.
The Dizygotheca species which are known as houseplants all come originally from islands in the Pacific Ocean.
They are decorative foliage plants which do not require much attention and can last for years.

Cuttings, sowing and grafting

The varieties 'Castor' and 'Pollux' can be propagated by placing an intermediate cutting in a mixture of two parts peat-based potting compost and one part river sand. Under plastic foil they will root in three weeks. Place the 'Castor' cutting in a 3-in/8-cm pot and the 'Pollux' cutting in a 4-5-in/10-12-cm pot. The growing period is 11 to 12 months. Imported Dizygotheca elegantissima seed is available in the shops. Sow it in a mixture of equal parts of peat dust and river sand. After two to three months, set the plantlets out individually and four months after this place them in a 3-in/8-cm pot. Finish them off four to six months later in a 4-5-in/10-12-cm final pot. The whole growing period from seed to mature plant is 18 to 20 months.
Dizygotheca can also be grafted on to the rootstock of Oreopanax reticulata (Aralia reticulata). As well as 'sticking' the two obliquely cut stems, the graft can also be 'set aside'. To do this, place the top firmly on the rootstock and cut open a piece of bark down to the cambium. This is the cell layer between the wood and the bark. The obliquely-cut graft is then bound with the wound tissue on to the cambium of the rootstock. Place the graft under double glass or plastic foil. It will set in two weeks.
Propagation by grafting or cuttings is possible with Dizygotheca veitchii. 'Gracillima' must be grafted.

Not too much water

If Dizygotheca is repotted annually and root rot is prevented by not giving the plant too much water, this splendid, decorative foliage plant can be enjoyed for many years. It grows best in a mixture of three parts RHP potting soil and one part river sand. During the growing season, keep the soil moderately moist and feed it weekly. Water sparingly in the winter. Growth is almost nil then and the plant requires no fertilizer.
It is a plant which needs slight shade and does well even in very dark rooms. It will not tolerate strong sun.

Treatment table

	cutting	growth	rest
pot		4-5 in/10-12 cm	—
soil	peat-based potting compost and river sand 2:1	RHP and river sand 3:1	—
feeding	—	1 tsp compound fetilizer per pt water/2 g per litre	none
watering	moist	moderately	sparingly
temperature	77° F/25° C	68-86° F/ 20-30° C	> 64° F/ 18° C
rel. humidity	85%	70-80%	70-80%
light	—	shade	—
special features	Sow from seed and graft at the same temperature and relative humidity as for cuttings. The sowing soil should be a mixture of equal parts peat dust and river sand.		

Dracaena/Dragon's blood tree

Female dragon

The name Dracaena comes from the Greek word, *drakaina*, the female form of *drakoon*, which means 'dragon' or 'serpent'. The stem of some Dracaena species contains a red resin and in tropical Africa, where many Dracaenas originally came from, this resin is called 'dragon's blood'.
Many Dracaena species are imported as stems.

Stems and cuttings

Dracaena is a beautiful foliage plant which has come to the fore in recent years. Many cuttings and stems are grown in South America and exported. You can, however, take your own head or stem cuttings (see page 169 for cuttings). If a bare stem is laid horizontally in a nursery bed, shoots will appear on it which can be used as cuttings. Take cuttings from fully-grown stems in the autumn and spring.
When the roots have appeared, after three to four weeks, pot them in a 3-in/8-cm pot. A month later place them in a 5-in/12-cm final pot. They will root at a temperature of 75° F/24° C and a relative humidity of 95%. Three or four weeks after the shoots have started to grow, the plants can be grown on as fully-grown plants.
Dracaenas can also be ringed (see page 170 for ringing) The procedure is to make a wound in the stem, bind the latter up with porous material, and then cover it with plastic. If this material is kept moist, roots will grow in it, while the plant continues to grow normally. Once the tip has grown enough of its own roots, cut if off and you have a new plant.

Think of the salt content

Dracaenas are excellent houseplants which last for a long time, provided that you ensure a good relative humidity and prevent the salt concentration in the potting soil from becoming too high. This can be avoided by repotting the plant annually and plunging the pot weekly in a bucket of water and then allowing it to drain. Dracaena grows in a fibrous, airy and highly porous soil. Keep this soil moderately moist throughout the year. The plant cannot tolerate a wet potting soil. During the growing season, feed it weekly; restrict feeding in the rest period. Shade the plant slightly from direct sunlight. The variegated Dracaenas do not tolerate a dark position. When the shoots are three or four years old, Dracaena will flower with a wide plume of white flowers.
The plant can be rejuvenated by cutting back to the bare stem. It then forms new shoots of its own accord.

Treatment table

	cutting	growth	rest
pot	3½ in/8 cm	5-6 in/12-16 cm	—
soil	extra-high porosity		—
feeding	—	1 tsp compound fertilizer per pt water/2 g per litre	less
watering	moist	moderately	moderately
temperature	82-86° F/ 28-30° C	68° F/20° C	> 64° F/ 18° C
rel. humidity	95%	80%	70-80%
light	—	slight shade	light
flowers	—	after 3 or 4 years	—

special features These data apply to Dracaena fragrans and Dracaena godseffiana. Grow the other species at 60-64° F/16-18° C.

Dracaena marginata 'Tricolor'

Dracaena fragrans 'Massangeana'

This is the most common variety of Dracaena, the leaves of which are sweet-smelling (*fragrans*). The species grows as a tree in tropical West Africa and was cultivated in the Netherlands in 1697. Other varieties are 'Lindenii', with broad, yellow leaf-edges, and 'Victoria', the yellow of which is more cream-coloured, while the leaf-edges are wider and more wave-shaped.
Dracaena fragrans 'Massangeana' is the most widely grown. Many stems of the originally green-leaved species come from the Ivory Coast and South America.

Dracaena deremensis 'Warneckii'

This species comes from Usambara in tropical Africa. The leaves are narrower than those of Dracaena fragrans. The variety 'Warneckii' has white, longitudinal stripes of differing widths on the green leaf and the variety 'Bausei' has one yellow-white, central stripe.

Dracaena sanderiana

This Dracaena comes from tropical West Africa and has narrow, green leaves with broad, white, longitudinal stripes.
The base of the leaf narrows like a stem in a striking manner.

Dracaena reflexa 'Song of India'

This Dracaena species is a native of Mauritius. The leaves are curved in a decorative fashion and have two light-yellow edges. The plant has a fine, compact habit and the leaves sit close together.
'Song of India' can also branch out. It is a plant for a controlled, greenhouse atmosphere.

Dracaena godseffiana 'Florida Beauty'

The white patches on the leaves of this

Flowering 'Dragon tree' in the wild

Dracaena fragrans 'Massangeana'

Dracaena are larger than those of other species. The plants branch out strongly. The leaf is oval and not so long as on other species. The species, which comes from tropical West Africa, is not so strong as other Dracaenas.

Dracaena marginata 'Tricolor'

This beautiful three-coloured variety of a narrow-leaved Dracaena is indigenous to Madagascar.

Epiphyllum hybrid

Epiphyllum hybrid
The Epiphyllum hybrids are crosses of
the Epiphyllum genera with the
Nopalxochia, Heliocereus, Selenicereus
and other Cactus species.
Florists sell mainly red-flowered varieties,
but there are also many varieties in white,
yellow, orange, pink, violet and purple
tints.

Flowers on the leaf

Epiphyllum is a Cactus which in its natural habitat grows in a
completely different environment from that of other Cactus
species. Most Cacti grow in hot, sandy areas where rain only
falls a few times a year. Epiphyllum is indigenous to Mexico,
where it grows in humid forests either on a humus-rich, acid
soil or epiphytically, that is to say on the bark of a tree or a tree
trunk. It requires a different sort of treatment from other Cacti
and is therefore dealt with separately here. Epiphyllum comes
from the Greek prefix, *epi*, and the word, *phyllon*, and means
'together on the leaf'. This name refers to the splendid flowers
which grow on what appears to be a leaf, but is, in fact, a
broadened stem. The leaves of a Cactus are actually the
spines.

Allow cuttings to dry out

The leaf Cactus can be propagated by cutting up the top
leaves of young specimens after flowering into pieces about
4 in/10 cm long. Allow the wounds to dry out properly for a few
days and then place them in a mixture of equal parts of river
sand and peat dust, covered with a layer of river sand. When
they have grown sufficient roots, after about six or seven
weeks, plant them in 3-in/7-cm pots. In the following spring
repot them into 4-5-in/10-12-cm final pots. In order to get a
well-branched Cactus, remove the top immediately. This top
can be used again as a cutting. The first flowers will appear in
late spring the following year. The plant will flower for almost
two months.

Cold and dry treatment

Epiphyllum is an excellent houseplant which will flower
profusely each year in late spring if kept in a cold, dry place in
the autumn and winter months. Grow the Cactus in a very
humus-rich RHP soil.
In the summer growing season keep the soil constantly moist
and feed it weekly. Add no fertilizer in the rest period and
keep the soil fairly dry, at the same time taking care that the
soil does not dry out completely. The leaves must not get
wrinkled.
As soon as the first flower buds appear, begin to water and
feed again. The plant can be repositioned again, but at the
risk of the buds dropping. Repot the plant immediately after
flowering.
The natural habitat of this cactus is forest, and it should
therefore be shaded slightly from direct sunlight in the spring
and summer. Otherwise, grow the plant in as light a position
as possible. Epiphyllum can last a long time and reach a good
size.
Support the long stems by tying them fast to bamboo sticks or
wire pins.

Treatment table

	cutting	growth	rest
pot	3 in/7 cm	4-5 in/10-12 cm	—
soil	river sand and peat dust 1:1	humus-rich RHP	—
feeding	—	1 tsp compound fertilizer per pt water/2 g per litre	—
temperature	68° F/20° C	64-77° F/ 18-25° C	50° F/10° C
rel. humidity	85%	70-80%	60-70%
light	light	slight shade	light
flowers	—	early to mid-summer	—
special features	After taking cuttings, allow them to dry out for a few days.		

Not really a houseplant

Erica is the ancient Greek word for 'heather'. Erica gracilis, which we know as a houseplant, is one of more than 600 species and grows in South Africa. Although actually an outdoor plant, which continues growing even with night frosts, it has been popular as a houseplant for the last 100 years.

Difficult to take cuttings from

Erica can be propagated by taking cuttings. Take a head cutting or intermediate cutting (see page 169 for cuttings) which is neither herbaceous nor woody. The judging of this requires some experience. The cutting length is about 1¼ in/3 cm. Place the cuttings in three parts peat dust and one part dunesand. The topmost layer is sand in order to prevent mould (mold) formation. Cuttings can be taken in winter to early spring or in high summer. In general, place them under plastic foil or double glass, though in summer mist propagation is also successful.

Cover the cuttings as a protection against direct sunlight and place them immediately in a 3½-in/8-cm pot. Pot spring cuttings at the very end of summer or later and autumn cuttings in the following spring. In order to get a good compact plant, the spring cuttings must be topped regularly until mid-autumn. Overwinter the plants in a cool but light position and bring the plants into growth again from the beginning of spring.

Repot them into a 4-5-in/10-12-cm pot and at the beginning of summer plant them in the garden in highly porous sub-soil. New shoots will be formed and blooms will follow in the autumn.

The growing period is two years. After a hot summer, the plants will start early and produce many flowers. Plants which flower late, or whose flowers are still in the bud or have failed to open, will not tolerate night frosts.

Difficult to feed

The feeding of Erica is a very difficult task. The plant is particularly salt-sensitive, and it is therefore essential to give it exactly the right amounts of fertilizer at the various stages. The ideal proportions of nitrogen, phosphorus and potassium are 4:1:2, though during the main growing season even more nitrogen is required (6:1:2). Add no feed in the winter. If the plant is due to set flowers in summer, stop feeding. Grow the plant in as light a position as possible in a highly porous soil kept moist at all times. Avoid excessive watering as this stunts the plant. The water used must be lime-free and the soil must be clean. A mixture of peat litter and frozen peat with one-fifth part river sand is widely used.

Treatment table

	cutting	growth	rest
pot	3½ in/8 cm	4-5 in/10-12 cm	—
soil	see text		
feeding	see text		
temperature	64-68° F/ 18-20° C	60-68° F/ 15-20° C	41° F/5° C
rel. humidity	80-90%	80%	60-70%
light	light	light	light
flowers	—	autumn to early winter	—
special features	Flower-setting takes place during the long day, with a high light intensity and a temperature of 68-75° F/20-24° C. In the autumn keep the flowering plants at 50-60° F/10-15° C. Use for feed high-concentration, compound fertilizers to which spore elements are added.		

Erica wilmorel hybrid

Erica gracilis 'Glasers Rote'

This decorative (*gracilis*) plant is the most common variety. In Germany, where most of the plants come from, it is often used to adorn graves on All Souls' Day. Ericas are not really houseplants, because a shortage of light often causes the flower colour to fade. It is, however, an ideal plant for outdoor window boxes, since it tolerates slight night frost, even during late flowering.

Erica gracilis 'Hasler' ('Geiger')

This variety has glossy, dark-red flowers.

Erica gracilis 'Globularis'

This variety has salmon-coloured to copper-red flowers.

Erica gracilis 'Auerbachs Weisze'

This is a somewhat compact-growing variety with a mass of white flowers which frequently turn a light-pink colour.

Erica Wilmorei hybrids

These plants, which flower in the spring, are grown only to a limited extent. They have large flowers in many different colours.

Euonymus japonicus

Euonymus japonicus 'Silver Queen'

Euonymus japonicus 'Yellow Queen'
The leaves of this variety often have a somewhat indeterminate yellow edge.

Euonymus japonicus 'Albomarginatus'
This large-leaved variety, with its narrow, brilliant-white edge (*albomarginatus*), is widely grown.

Euonymus japonicus 'Aureomarginatus'
This variety has dark-green leaves with a sharply-defined golden-yellow edge.

Euonymus japonicus 'Silver Queen'
This Euonymus has silver-white edges to its leaves.

Euonymus japonicus 'Aurea' ('Mediopicta')
This is the most widely grown variety. The leaves have a golden-yellow central stripe.

Euonymus japonicus 'microphyllus Variegatus'
This is a small-leaved (*microphyllus*) variety with bright silver leaves which is becoming more popular.

Euonymus japonicus 'Duc d'Anjou'
The large, glossy leaves of this variety are dark-green and flaming yellow. This old variety is still seen today as a large plant in country house collections.

Poisonous seeds

The Euonymus which we know as a houseplant comes from China and Japan. It was cultivated in England in 1804. The meaning of the name is somewhat ambiguous. Euonymus comes from the Greek words, *eu* and *onoma*, which mean 'good' and 'name'. The 'good name' of this plant must be qualified, however, because its seeds are poisonous. The Romans were aware of this, since they used the seeds as a remedy against head lice. Its related Asiatic species, also used as a houseplant, does not flower and thus produces no seeds.

Cuttings from fully-grown shoots

The plant can be propagated by taking cuttings. Take a shoot cutting (see page 169 for cuttings) when the shoot has developed and is resting. This can be in late summer or the spring. Intermediate cuttings may be taken throughout the year, because they are always sufficiently 'woody'. Place the cuttings in peat-based potting compost with river sand, after first treating them with growth hormone.
Protect them against drying out by covering them with paper or placing them under mist. After about a month the roots will have grown sufficiently for the cuttings to be placed in a 3-4-in/8-10-cm pot. In order to get a well-branched plant, remove the tops with four to five leaves regularly. If you want large plants, repot them in the spring before growth begins. Prune the plant to the required shape in the autumn.

No flowers

Because the plant is topped and pruned regularly, it will neither flower nor produce its beautiful fruits. Nowadays, the plant is kept small and grown solely for its leaves. In the last century, however, when the plant was popular in country houses, it was kept in tubs, grew large and naturally flowered well. The plant requires a nutritious RHP potting soil, which for older specimens is mixed with equal parts of clay. Keep the soil moist during the growing season, but water it sparingly in the winter. Feed it weekly from spring until autumn. The plants require a light position and in the greenhouse should simply be shielded from strong sunlight. Outside they like to be shielded from the wind and kept out of the sun.
Euonymus is a splendid, sturdy plant with a long life. It is a shrub which needs proper winter resting. Repot the plant in late winter or early spring.

Treatment table

	cutting	growth	rest
pot	3 in/7 cm	3½ in/8-9 cm	—
soil	peat-based RHP potting compost and sand 2:1	—	
feeding	—	1½ tsp compound fertilizer per pt water/3 g per litre	—
watering	moist	moist	moderately
temperature	64-68° F/ 18-20° C	64° F/18° C	40-50° F/ 5-10° C
rel. humidity	90%	60-70%	50-60%
light	plenty	plenty	plenty
growth hormone	1-naphthalena-cetic acid 0.2%	—	—
special features	Shield against strong sunlight. Set older plants outside in the winter and overwinter frost-free.		

A strange family

A close look at Christ's Thorn, Christmas Star or the cactus-type Euphorbia grandicornis scarcely gives the impression that they are related to each other. But these plants do not simply all belong to the spurge family; they also all belong to the same genus Euphorbia.

A noticeable similarity between all Euphorbias is that a white or pale-coloured 'milk' is exuded when a twig is broken off. The differences, however, are so great that two groups are described separately here.

The name Euphorbia is probably derived from Euphorbos, the personal physician to King Jaba II of Numidia, who lived in the first century BC. This doctor is said to have discovered the medicinal properties of the vegetable milk. The well-known Euphorbia milii, or Christ's Thorn, originates from Madagascar and was cultivated for the first time, in France, in 1826.

Short-day plant

Euphorbia milii is a flowering houseplant which is one of the succulents. It sets flowers in winter and flowers from late winter to mid-spring. It is thus a short-day plant.

It can be propagated by taking cuttings in high summer. Use the thin side-shoots for this and treat the cuttings with growth hormone before placing them in a 2-in/5-cm pot filled with three parts sand and two parts peat dust. Cover the cuttings with paper to prevent drying out. Roots will form in three to four weeks. About two months after taking the cuttings, repot them into a 3-4-in/8-10-cm final pot.

Long-day treatment

Before the plant sets flowers, growth can be promoted by a long-day treatment. Light the plant with 1,100 mW per 3 ft²/1 m² and prolong the day to 14 to 15 hours.

Water the plant sparingly during this growth period. Give it slightly more water from mid-autumn until flowering, though too much will make the leaves drop. When the plant flowers, give it more water again, but ensure that the soil never gets really moist. The plant grows well in a mixture of three parts RHP potting soil to one part river sand. Feed weekly up to October.

Christ's Thorn is a sturdy houseplant which can become quite large after a few years. It begins to set flowers when the day-length becomes less than 12½ hours. It also sets flowers if the temperature is maintained constant at 60° F/15° C.

Grow Euphorbia in full sunlight. It needs a short day to set flowers, however, and even street or house lighting have a harmful effect.

Prevent leaf-drop by watering sparingly and avoiding fluctuations in temperature.

Euphorbia milii

Euphorbia milii (Euphorbia splendens)
This Christ's Thorn is mostly seen with orange flowers.
There are, however, also varieties with yellow-white and yellow flowers.

Euphorbia milii 'Bojeri'
This Christ's Thorn has thin, round stems with more slender prickles than those on the usual Christ's Thorn.

Treatment table
Euphorbia milii (Christ's Thorn)

	cutting	growth	rest
pot	2 in/5 cm	3½ in/8-9 cm	—
soil	sand and peat dust 3:2	RHP and river sand 3.1	—
feed	—	1 tsp compound fertilizer per pt water/2 g per litre	none
water	moist	moderately	moderately
temperature	77° F/25° C	84-86° F/ 29-30° C	> 60° F/ 16° C
rel. humidity	75%	60-70%	60%
light	plenty	plenty	plenty
flowers	—	spring-summer	late winter to end of spring
growth hormone	3-indoleacetic acid 0.1%	—	

special features	The minimum growing temperature is 60° F/16° C. The plant has no real rest period. During the flower-setting period in the winter, keep the plants at a minimum temperature of 60° F/16° C and a relative humidity of 60%. Temperature fluctuations cause leaf drop.

The most well-known Christmas Star in its natural habitat in Colombia.

The most beautiful Euphorbia?

There is, of course, no disputing as to taste, but the species name of the Euphorbia which we know as Poinsettia or Christmas Star is pulcherrima, which in Latin means 'very beautiful' or 'fairest of all'. Indeed, the often highly-coloured bracts or top leaves — not the flowers because they are small and sometimes drop immediately — retain their decorative value for months at a time when any touch of colour in the house is welcome.

The Christmas Star is a native of tropical America, especially Mexico, and was cultivated for the first time in the United States in 1828. It can be brought to flower throughout the year by means of long- and short-day treatment. For the growth of stems and leaves (vegetative growth) a day length of 14 hours is required. From early autumn to the end of winter, the day must be lengthened by lighting the plant with 300 mW per yd²/m². The plant will then grow about 2/5 in/1 cm a day. This period lasts for two weeks with an untopped plant, for up to five weeks with a branched plant. After this, give it a short-day treatment for nine weeks (by darkening it) and you will get a magnificent flowering plant.

Grow cuttings with long-day treatment

When the plant is growing well during the long-day treatment, cut the shoots off when they are about 4-5 in/10-12 cm long. Plunge them immediately into lukewarm water to staunch the 'bleeding' and treat them with growth hormone, using charcoal or talc as a carrier (see page 170 for growth hormones).

Place the cuttings in small pots filled with equal parts of peat dust and river sand.

The cuttings grow best under mist (see page 169 for cuttings). Alternatively, they can be sprayed frequently and covered with paper. Under plastic foil inadequate ventilation turns the leaves yellow.

The cuttings will have roots after about four weeks, when they should be placed in the desired pot and given the long-day treatment immediately. If you want them to flower at Christmas, you must start with the short-day treatment not later than three months before. The unbranched plant must then be at least 4 in/10 cm high.

It is also possible to grow a branched Christmas Star by removing the top as soon as the cutting has started to grow. The plant will then form four or five side-shoots. Pot the plant up in a 4-5-in/10-12-cm plastic pot and remove a small growth point three days later so that four or five leaves are left. The side-shoots will now grow.

Instead of removing the top, you can also give the plant a short-day treatment for one to five days. Ensure during this period that it does not receive more than 9 to 10 hours light a day. The top will then stop growing and the side-shoots will develop. Now give the plant a long-day treatment for five weeks, starting from the potting. When the side-shoots have become 1¼ in/3 cm long, the short-day treatment for flower formation can be started.

High or low plants

The Christmas Star keeps for several months. When it has finished flowering it can be made to flower again by cutting the plant back to 4 in/10 cm and giving it a long-day treatment for five weeks, followed by a short-day treatment for about nine weeks. If you want a compact plant, you must spray with inhibitor before the start of the s or-day treatment.

Spray topped plants seven to ten days after the topping, repeating the spraying every ten to twelve days until the short-day treatment begins.

Euphorbia

Spray untopped plants once, or at the most twice, four to seven days after potting. If you use the expensive, but effective, agent, Chlormequat, spray the topped plants wh the side-shoots are about ⅓ in/1 cm long. Spray untopped plants five to six days after potting.

Salt-sensitive
Grow Christmas Star in a highly porous mixture of four parts RHP frozen peat potting compost to one part river sand. The pH must not be low (about 6); any lower and it will cause yellow leaves or scorched leaf-edges (see page 168 for acid level).
Keep the soil moderately moist. If it is too wet, the risk of root rot and yellow leaves arises. The salt concentration in the soil must not be too high. The soil must therefore be washed regularly by placing the pot in a bucket of water and then letting it drain. Replace the potting soil every six months by repotting the plants.
Feed the plants twice a week during the growing season. One week after potting, add ½ tsp compound fertilizer per pt water/1 g per litre for two weeks and thereafter double the amount.
When the umbel begins to change colour, add a solution of 1 tsp nitrate of potash per pint water/2 g per litre. Give Christmas Star as light a position as possible, but shield the plant from strong sunlight.

Treatment table

	cutting	growth
pot	frame	3¼-4½ in/9-11 cm
soil	peat dust and sand 1:1	RHP frozen peat potting soil and sand 4:1
watering	moderately	moderately
feeding	—	see text
temperature	72° F/22° C	62-77° F/17-25° C in sun
rel. humidity	85%	70-80%
light	light	light
inhibitor	—	Cycocel or CCC ¹/₁₀-⅛ fl oz per pt water and spreader or Chlormequat 3-4 ml per litre
growth hormone	3-indoleacetic acid 0.5-1% on talc or charcoal	
special features	Never place cuttings under plastic sheeting. The temperature during the last weeks of the short-day treatment should be 60-62° F/16-17° C with a relative humidity of 60-70% (for a deeper colour).	

Euphorbia pulcherrima

Euphorbia pulcherrima
This red Christmas Star is the ancestor of the most common 'Hegg' varieties which have been developed in Norway. Others are 'Dark Annette Hegg' (deep red), 'Heggs Diva' (bright-red with a big umbel), 'Heggs Topstar' (red and early-flowering), Heggs 'Hvit' (white), 'Annette Hegg Rose' and 'Annette Hegg Marble' (two-tone pink and white).

Euphorbia trigona

Problem-free
Exacum is a lovely plant which flowers in the summer and presents no problems as a houseplant. It is indigenous to Socotra, an island off the Arabian peninsula, now barren. The plant was cultivated in Europe in 1882.

The name Exacum probably comes from the old Gallic word, *exacon*, which was connected by Pliny with the word, *exigese*, which means 'expel'. By this was meant another plant, probably another Gentian, which was used in medicine.

Various Gentian species which were used in medicine were given names such as Bitter Plant, Bitter Herb and Bitter Leaf.

A single annual
In the wild Exacum is a biennial, but as a flowering houseplant it should be grown as an annual. Propagate the plant from seed; one gram contains 3,200 seeds and yields about 2,400 seedlings. Sow the seedlings from early winter to mid-spring in peat dust sowing medium with a pH of 5.5 (see page 168 for acid level). Cover the sowing frame with glass.

Lots of humidity and lots of light
Place Exacum in as light a position as possible, while shielding it from strong sunlight. Ensure that the potting soil is always moist. If you fulfil these two requirements, and also avoid excessive heat, you should have no problems and will get a splendid plant which sets beautiful mauve flowers from mid-spring to mid-autumn. The plant makes no great demands as to potting soil and may be grown in a normal RHP soil. Three weeks after potting, give it some fertilizer weekly. If the seeds are sown very thinly, they can be potted directly from the sowing frame. If the frame contains many seedlings, prick them out first about ¾ in/2 cm apart after six to seven weeks. Then place one or two seedlings in a 3½-in/9-cm pot or four to five in a low 4½-in/11-cm pot (the so-called Azalea system).

For compact growth, space the plants well apart and ventilate them often to prevent the temperature from rising too high. The growing period from seed to flowering plant is five to six months.

Exacum affine

Exacum affine
This is the only Exacum grown as a houseplant. There are a few named varieties, all of which have mauve flowers.

Treatment table

	sowing	growth
pot	frame	3½-4 in/9-11 cm
soil	peat dust	RHP
feeding	—	1 tsp compound fertilizer per pt water/2 g per litre
watering	moist	moist
temperature	68° F/20° C	> 60° F/16° C (up to 68° F/20° C in the sun)
rel. humidity	95%	70%
light	light	light
flowers	—	late spring to mid-autumn

special features Grow young plants at a temperature of 64° F/18° C and a relative humidity of 80% until they are potted up and growing.

X Fatshedera

A successful experiment

A successful experiment with plants was carried out in 1914 by the French grower, Lizé, in Nantes. He succeeded in crossing a Finger Plant (Fatsia japonica) with an Ivy (Hedera helix) and obtained a plant which combined all the best features of these two plants. It was given the name X Fatshedera.

This generic hybrid — ie, a cross between two genera — has proved to be a decorative plant which makes few demands and lasts a long time. It is one of our sturdiest houseplants and has good powers of adaptation. Although it must be grown in cool, light conditions, it does well in a rear corner of a normally heated room.

It is also used as a strong rootstock for grafting variegated varieties of Hedera helix, which has weak tendrils for a climbing plant.

Easy to take cuttings from

X Fatshedera can be propagated by means of intermediate cuttings from its long stems and, to a limited extent, by head cuttings (see page 169 for cuttings).

The best time for taking cuttings is early autumn. Place the cuttings in the usual potting soil under double glass or plastic foil and they will have roots in about three weeks. They can then be placed in a 3½-in/9-cm final pot.

A so-called clump can also be grown. This is a pot which contains individual plants on their own. For this, place four or five cuttings in a larger pot, eg a 6-in/15-cm pot. A compact plant with four or five branches will then be obtained.

The growing time for a small plant is six months, for larger specimens eight to nine months.

Easy-to-grow plant

X Fatshedera is an easy-to-grow plant which makes no special demands. Grow it in normal RHP potting soil and water generously during the growing season. The plant has its rest period in the autumn and winter, when the soil should be kept moderately moist. Do not feed the plant at this time, but add fertilizer weekly during the growing season. The plant grows best in a light position, but it also holds its own well somewhere more shady. It must be repotted annually.

Plants which have become too bare or straggly should be cut back to a stem length of 4 in/10 cm in the spring. The stem will then grow again and form fine young shoots. The top can also be cut off and used as a head cutting. Instant cuttings can be taken from the remaining stem.

Left: X Fatshedera x lizei 'Variegata'. Right: the original species

X Fatshedera (x) lizei 'Variegata'
This is an X Fatshedera with irregularly decorated, white leaf-edges.

X Fatshedera (x) lizei 'Annemieke'
This variety has variegated golden leaves. A small-leaved variety is less commonly grown.

Treatment table

	cutting	growth	rest
pot		3½-5½ in/ 9-14 cm	—
soil	RHP	RHP	—
feed	—	1½ tsp compound fertilizer per pt water/3 g per litre	none
water	generously	generously	moderately
temperature	64-68° F/ 18-20° C	64° F/18° C	41-54° F/ 5-12° C
rel. humidity	90%	70%	50-70%
light	light	light	light

special features Shield against strong sunlight. The plant is sensitive to attack by red spider and ivy mite.

X Fatshedera lizei

X Fatshedera (x) lizei
This splendid sturdy plant is named after the French grower, Lizé, who obtained it in 1914 from a crossing of Fatsia and Hedera.

Fatsia japonica 'Variegata'

Fatsia japonica

Fatsia japonica
As the name of this splendid foliage plant implies, it comes from Japan. This green-leaved variety is the most common.

Fatsia japonica 'Moseri'
This variety provides somewhat more compact plants.

Fatsia japonica 'Variegata'
This Fatsia has irregular, white-blotched leaves and is propagated from cuttings. The variegated form which is grown at 64° F/18° C is unsuitable for planting in gardens.

Leaf with eight fingers
In some countries Fatsia is called a Finger plant. The leaf of this magnificent foliage plant is indeed like a hand, but the hand usually has eight fingers (sometimes seven or nine, but never five). The plant was probably cultivated for the first time in Japan.

Fatsia is usually sold commercially about eight or nine months old. In recent years some beautiful specimens have also been seen as garden plants, which grow into a bush and flower profusely in the autumn with large white plumes. If there is a severe winter, the plants will die.

Fatsia is indigenous to a rainy area of eastern Asia with an average annual temperature of 61-63° F/16-17° C. It was cultivated in Europe for the first time in 1852 in the Netherlands. It is a member of the Araliaceae family.

Sowing and cuttings
The original species can be grown from seed. Seed imported from Japan is available in the spring and must be sown directly on arrival; otherwise the germinating power deteriorates. The seeds germinate quickly and the seedlings should be potted immediately from the sowing bed into a 3-4-in/7-10-cm pot, where they can remain. If you want large plants, pot them off after three to four months into a 5-in/12-13-cm pot. You will then have a sturdy plant by the beginning of winter.

The variegated variety grows more slowly and is always cultivated as a large plant.

Variegated varieties can be propagated by head cuttings and intermediate cuttings (see page 169 for cuttings) and should be grown in warmer conditions. Treat them with growth hormone and place them in a 3-in/7-cm pot filled with peat-based potting compost. They will root in three weeks. Four to five months later, repot the cuttings into a 5-in/12-13-cm final pot.

Plenty of light essential
The plant grows in a rainy area in the wild. During the growing season, therefore, the potting soil must be kept permanently moist. Feed the plant weekly, and place it in as light a position as possible, though not in direct sunlight.

In the darker winter months, the plant has its rest period. Growth is nil at that time and it therefore requires no fertilizer and little water.

Fatsia makes no great demands as regards potting soil. It does excellently in a normal RHP potting soil.

It is a strong, quick-growing plant with great powers of adaptation. It can also hold its own in a spot with little light, provided there is no excessive rise in temperature. Repot the plant annually, ensuring that the pot is always large enough to allow for good growth and expansion of the root system.

Treatment table

	cutting	growth	rest
pot	3 in/7 cm	5 in/12-13 cm	—
soil	peat-based potting compost	RHP	—
feed	—	1½ tsp compound fertilizer per pt water/3 g per litre	—
water	moist	very moist	moderately
temperature	68° F/20° C	60° F/15° C	46-50° F/ 8-10° C
rel. humidity	95%	70-80%	60-70%
light	light	light	light
growth hormone	3-indoleacetic acid	—	—

Ficus

Many different species

Ficus is a genus of which more than 1,000 species are known Most of them come from Asia and Africa, but some grow wild in Central and South America and even in Australia. The appearance of the various Ficus species, even those which we know as houseplants, varies enormously. In their natural habitat, they grow as trees and shrubs, horizontally or as climbers; and there are even species which grow as lianas in the primaeval forest or on trees and tree-trunks as epiphytes. With houseplants the leaf size and leaf shape show the most striking differences. Strange to say, the treatment of all Ficus species is virtually the same. They can be divided into two groups only as regards temperature requirements: the species with a tropical origin and the species from a more moderate climate.

Ficus is the old name for the Fig tree, grown in warm climates for its sweet fruits. The fig tree must always be grown in a very shaded spot, even in cooler locations. Ficus belongs to the mulberry family, Moraceae. The mulberry originated in China and Japan and was previously grown chiefly to provide food for the silk-worm.

Think about the roots

All Ficus species can be propagated by taking cuttings. Take shoot cuttings, intermediate cuttings or eye cuttings (see page 169 for cuttings). Treat them with growth hormone and then place them in peat-based potting compost under double glass or plastic sheeting.

After one to four weeks they will have roots and should be placed very carefully in the final pot, which should be 3½-5 in/8-13 cm in diameter depending on the species. Care must be taken not to damage the roots. Those of a large-leaved Ficus, in particular, break easily. Commercial growers, therefore, always place these plants in small pots.

The variegated silver variety 'Doescheri', of Ficus elastica, is also sometimes grafted by commercial growers on t a thick root of Ficus elastica.

Ficus also lends itself very well to ringing (see page 170 for ringing). Make a wound in the stem and wrap it in a highly porous material. Fix this in position with plastic sheeting and keep it moist. Roots will then grow there and can be cut off, together with the stem, when they are of sufficient size.

Prune the old stem to approximately 10 in/25 cm above the soil. It will then grow again with a number of good, strong shoots.

Ficus elastica

Ficus lyrata (Ficus pandurata)

Lyrata means 'lyre-shaped' and *pandurata* means 'fiddle-shaped'. These names refer to the shape of the large leaves. This Ficus comes from tropical western Asia and was first cultivated, in Belgium, in 1904. Grow this species in large-sized pots. It is not easy to grow and is always propagated by head cuttings.

Ficus rubiginosa (F. australis) 'Variegata'

Rubiginosa means 'with rust-brown hair'. This green-leaved species is seen as well as the variety 'Variegata'.

This Ficus was cultivated in England in 1789. It comes from Australia. Grow it in a 4-5-in/10-12-cm pot.

Ficus pumila (Ficus repens, Ficus stipulata or Ficus scandens)

Pumila means 'small'. This is a Ficus with small leaves.

Repens and *scandens* mean 'creeping' and 'climbing', and *stipulata* means 'close together'. This is a small-leaved climber with many leaves and aerial roots. It is usually grown in a 3½-in/8-9-cm pot. As a houseplant only the juvenile form, with sterile branches which do not flower, is grown.

The fully-grown form, which bears fruit, has branches with longer, stemmed leaves.

The white-variegated, marbled variety, 'Variegata', is grown only to a limited extent and requires more warmth. It comes from eastern Asia and was cultivated for the first time in Holland in 1720. The plant sticks to the wall and is difficult to remove.

Ficus elastica

Elastica means 'springy'. The sap of this Ficus was previously used for making rubber, but has now been replaced by Hevea brasiliensis.

The following varieties of the green-leaved Ficus elastica are the most common: 'Decora', with broad, glossy, dark-green leaves and a red leaf-sheath; 'Robusta', somewhat broader than 'Decora'; 'Abidjan', broad-leaved with very dark, bronze-green leaves and a deep-red leaf-sheath; 'Schrijveriana'; 'Tricolor', and a new variety, 'Belgaplant'. Ficus elastica comes from tropical Asia and was first cultivated, in England, in 1814. Grow it in a big pot at least 5 in/12-13 cm in size.

Ficus lyrata

Ficus pumila

Ficus benjamina ('Waringin')

This Ficus comes from India, where it grows as a tree.

It is one of the strongest houseplants and can grow to an enormous size even indoors.

There are a number of varieties which are also classed as species, eg, Ficus nitida. Grow it in a 5-in/12-13-cm pot or larger, depending on the size of the plant.

Ficus radicans 'Variegata'

This is the variegated variety of this climbing Ficus, which is very widely grown. The leaf is larger and more pointed than that of Ficus pumila.

The plant has roots over the whole length of the stems (*radicans* means 'with roots'). It comes from India and was cultivated in France in 1829.

Ficus deltoidea

Ficus deltoidea (Ficus diversifolia)

This is one of the few Ficus species which bear fruit, a mass of little figs. It has deltoid leaves and needs a large pot. It comes originally from tropical Asia and was cultivated in 1850 in England. For good fruit-setting a temperature of 68-72° F/20-22° C is required. Keep the potting soil dry at this time.

Ficus triangularis

This Ficus is indigenous to tropical Africa. The leaf is triangular in shape, a distinctive feature which has increased demand for the plant. Grow it in a 4-5-in/10-12-cm pot or larger.

Ficus benjamina

Ficus rubiginosa 'Variegata

Ficus buxifolia

This is a small-leaved, decorative bush that has leaves similar to those of the Palm tree, Buxus. More and more specimens of it are seen.
It comes from the Congo and should be grown in a 4-5-in/10-12-cm pot or larger. The plant is very sensitive to the insecticide, dichlorous, which is present in many aerosol sprays.

Ficus cyathistipula

This name comes from the Greek word, *kyathos*, for 'wine-ladle', and the Latin *stipulata,* for 'close together'.
The name comes from the ladle-shaped stipules which drop off other Ficus species, but remain in place under the leaves of this one. It is a large-leaved species which comes from tropical east Africa. It needs the larger pot sizes.

Ficus benghalensis

A Ficus from tropical Asia which has been cultivated ever since 1690, this species has very large leaves with fine hairs on both sides. It, too, needs larger-sized pots.

Ficus neckbuda

This Ficus comes from tropical Asia and was first cultivated in Belgium in 1903. The leaf is a distinctive, bright green and its clearly visible veins are almost white. Put this vigorously-growing Ficus in a 5-in/12-cm pot.

Ficus racemosa

This is the only Ficus which has clear, rather than white, milky sap. It comes from south-east Asia. It has a very narrow leaf and can grow into a well-branched bush. *Racemosa* means 'in bunches'.

Ficus carica

This Ficus, which comes from Karia, in south-western Asia Minor, is the genuine fig-tree, which bears green or blue-green fruits. In sheltered spots it is sometimes grown as an espaliered plant, when it also bears fruits. These do not ripen, however, until the second year.
It is not often encountered as a houseplant. When it is, it remains small in size.

Differences in temperature requirement

The only Ficus species which requires little heat is Ficus pumila.
Take cuttings from it at 68° F/20° C and a relative humidity of 90%.
Grow it at 61° F/16° C and a relative humidity of 70%.
The minimum winter temperature is 50° F/10° C; the relative humidity may then drop to 60%.
The other Ficus species can be divided into two groups. One group includes the following species of tropical origin:
Ficus cyathistipula,
Ficus elastica (the variegated leaf varieties),
Ficus triangularis,
Ficus benghalensis,
Ficus lyrata,
Ficus neckbuda,
Ficus rubiginosa 'Variegata'.
Take cuttings from these species at a temperature of 86° F/30° C and a relative humidity of 90%.
Grow them at 72-77° F/22-25° C and a relative humidity of 75%.
The minimum winter temperature is 64° F/18° C.
The species from a temperate climate are:
Ficus elastica (green-leaved),
Ficus benjamina,
Ficus deltoidea,
Ficus rubiginosa (green-leaved).
Take cuttings from these species at a temperature of 77° F/25° C and a relative humidity of 90%. Depending on the amount of light, grow them at a temperature of 64-68° F/18-20° C. For good growth a relative humidity of 70% or more is necessary. In winter the minimum temperature is 54° F/12° C, while the relative humidity must not be less than 60%.

Sturdy plants

Ficus is a sturdy houseplant which makes few demands apart from the differences in temperature requirement.
One or other species of Ficus will therefore be found in almost every plant-lover's home. Only Ficus elastica tolerates direct sunlight. The other species also require plenty of light, but they must be covered against strong sunlight.
Grow a Ficus in a normal RHP potting soil. During growth, give it plenty of water and feed it weekly. The bushy varieties can reach a good size in the house and can easily be cut back if they take up too much room. They make very popular houseplants and are widely available.

Treatment table

	cutting	growth	rest
pot	3 in/7 cm	3½-5 in/8-13 cm	—
soil	peat-based potting compost	RHP	—
feeding	—	1½ tsp compound fertilizer per pt water/3 g per litre	—
temperature	see text		
rel. humidity	90%	70%	60%
light	light	light	light
water	generously	generously	moderately
growth	3-indoleacetic acid	—	—

special features Except for Ficus elasticata, shield all plants against strong sunlight in the summer.

87

Fittonia

Splendid leaves

Fittonias are foliage plants with beautifully decorated and coloured leaves. They are poor houseplants because they require a high relative humidity. In the greenhouse they grow very quickly and form splendid ground cover beneath the propagating table.

The leaf, unfortunately, does not keep when cut off, even when placed in water.

The name Fittonia comes from the sisters Elisabeth and Sarah Fitton, friends of the Scottish plant collector and scholar Robert Brown. They wrote some popular botanical works in the mid-19th century.

The plant originates from the tropical rain forests of Peru and was first cultivated in Belgium in 1862.

Fittonia is a member of the family Acanthaceae.

A rapid grower

Propagate Fittonia by means of intermediate cuttings with two leaves (see page 169 for cuttings). These cuttings will grow roots more easily than the tip of a shoot. Treat them with growth hormone and place them in peat-based potting compost under plastic foil, at a relative humidity of more than 95%.

They will have roots within ten to twelve days, when they should be placed in a 3-in/7-cm pot. They will grow very quickly in the spring and summer and you will have a beautiful plant after two or three months. Four cuttings can also be placed in a 4-in/10-cm pot and a slightly sturdier plant will then be obtained.

A plant which is shy of light

Fittonia grows poorly in too much light, chiefly because the relative humidity then is also too low. It must, in any case, be well shielded from the sun. It makes no particular demands as regards potting soil and grows excellently in an RHP soil. Keep this soil moist in the summer and water it frequently. Fittonia is, after all, a plant which in the wild grows in a tropical rain forest. It therefore needs a high relative humidity. In the winter water it slightly less, depending on the temperature. Feed weekly during the growing season.

Fittonia is not an easy houseplant, but if you are able to grow it in warm, moist and slightly shady conditions you will have a brilliant foliage plant which grows quickly. Under propagating tables in the greenhouse they grow exceptionally well, although the leaves may be quickly attacked by woodlice and slugs.

The small-leaved variety 'Minima' is sometimes seen as an aquarium plant.

Fittonia verschaffeltii 'Argyroneura' Fittonia verschaffeltii 'Pearcei' (with red nerve)

Fittonia verschaffeltii 'Argyroneura'
Fittonia verschaffeltii is almost never grown now as a botanical species. The variety 'Argyroneura' has silver-white veins. The species is named after a famous Ghent flower grower, A.C.A. Verschaffelt, who lived from 1825 to 1886 and imported many new plants into Holland. The small-leaved variety 'Minima', which is grown as a water plant, also has silver-white veins, whereas the variety 'Pearcei' has bright-red veins. The red of these varieties is more distinctive than it is in botanical species.

Treatment table

	cutting	growth	winter
pot	3 in/7cm	3-4 in/7-10 cm	—
soil	peat-based potting compost	RHP	—
feeding	—	½ tsp compound fertilizer per pt water/1 g per litre, nitrogen-free	none
watering	moist	moist	moderately
temperature	68-72° F/ 20-22° C	64-86° F/ 18-30° C	64-86° F/ 18-30° C
rel. humidity	> 95%	> 95%	—
light	light	shade	light
flowers	3-indoleacetic acid 0.1%	—	—
special features	The plant holds it own, but does not grow at, lower temperatures. Shield, however, against the sun.		

Fuchsia hybrid 'Beacon'

Fuchsia hybrid 'Beacon'

Fuchsia hybrid 'Beacon'
This is a well-known, compactly-growing variety with a red calyx and a violet corolla.

Fuchsia hybrid 'Dollar Princess'

Fuchsia hybrid 'Dollar Princess'
This well-known Fuchsia variety has a pink calyx and a white corolla.

Fuchsia hybrid 'Gartenmeister Bonstedt'
This Fuchsia is a hybrid of Fuchsia triphylla, with dark leaves and orange, tubular flowers.
There are hundreds of Fuchsia varieties of which not more than 20 are cultivated by commercial growers. Many new varieties come from England.

A classical houseplant

Fuchsia is named after the Dutch professor, Leonhard Fuchs, who lived from 1501 to 1566 and wrote some botanical works. Fuchsia has been known as a houseplant for a very long time. The genus was named as far back as 1703 and obtained recognition as an ornamental plant in 1840. There are about 100 species, which are for the most part indigenous to South America, where they grow in mountain forests in a cool, rainy climate.
The varieties which we give as Fuchsia hybrids are mainly crosses of Fuchsia gracilis, Fuchsia corymbyflora and Fuchsia triphylla.
Fuchsia is a member of the evening primrose family, Onagraceae. It is a rewarding houseplant which should flower throughout the summer.

A flowering semi-shrub

In order to propagate Fuchsia, take a shoot cutting, for spring flowering in late autumn, for summer flowering from mid-winter to early spring. Treat the cuttings with growth hormone and place them in a mixture of three parts peat-based potting compost to one part river sand. Cover the cuttings with paper or place them under a mist (see page 169 for cuttings).
The cuttings will root after a few weeks, when they should be planted in a 3-in/7-cm pot and repotted into a 4-5 in/10-12 cm pot after two to three months. In order to get a sturdy plant, prune the tops a few times. Give the plant an open position for good, profuse flowering.
Many enthusiasts like Fuchsia as a standard. To get this effect, choose a quick-growing variety. Grow the plant only for its stem and remove all side-shoots as soon as they appear, while leaving sufficient leaves on the main stem for good growth. When the stem has reached the desired height, grow a crown on it by allowing the topmost side-shoots to grow and topping them a few times.
If you want to grow a slow-growing Fuchsia variety or a variety of pendulous habit as a standard, graft this variety in late winter or early spring on to the rootstock of a quick-growing variety by whip-and-tongue grafting (see page 170 for grafting).

Long-day plant

Fuchsia will flower only when the day length reaches 12 to 14 hours, since the light intensity has to be sufficient for the growth of the buds. If they get too little light, the flower buds drop off. Care must be taken that they do not stand in direct sunlight. Fuchsia grows well in an RHP potting soil, which must not be given excessive fertilizer. Nor must it be allowed to dry out completely, because the plant is sensitive to excessive soil salinity. Keep the soil structure moist, even in the winter months.
During the growing season, feed the plants weekly. Flowering can be advanced by lighting with lamps (15 Watt installed power per yd²/m²) as a four-hour nightly interruption from mid-winter to early spring.
Old plants can be overwintered in a cool, but frost-free, place and should be repotted in early spring before renewed growth has begun.
When buying a plant, take good care that the roots (if they have grown outside the pot) are not cut off or broken. If they are, growth problems will occur and the flower buds drop off.

Treatment table

	cutting	growth	rest
pot	3 in/7 cm	4-5 in/10-12 cm	—
soil	peat-based potting compost and sand 3:1	RHP	—
feeding	—	1 tsp compound fertilizer per pt water/2g per litre	—
watering	moist	moist	moderately moist
temperature	64-68° F/ 18-20° C	60-77° F/ 15-25° C	45-60° F/ 12-15° C
rel. humidity	75-80%	> 70%	> 70%
light	light	light	light
flowers	—	summer	—
growth hormone	3-indoleacetic acid	—	—

Guzmania

A natural spring flowerer

Guzmania is a Bromeliad which is greatly valued as a houseplant because its flowering can be so easily influenced. It can, for example, be made to flower in late autumn, so that the magnificent red or orange bracts of the flowers can be enjoyed until mid-winter, though this applies only to specimens which are at least two years old.

This Bromeliad grows in the wild in the forests of Central America, usually epiphytically, ie on trees or tree trunks, but also on the ground. This must be taken fully into account when growing it, particularly as regards potting soil and watering. Guzmania owes its name to an 18th-century Spanish pharmacist and nature-lover, A. Guzman.

Fluffy seed

As with all Bromeliads, the terminal bud of Guzmania dies when it has finished flowering. Young shoots are then formed which can be removed when they are almost full-grown. Commercial growers propagate Guzmania chiefly from seed, which is ripe six months after pollination. Sow it in a special humus-rich mixture. Because it is so fluffy, it is not easy to distribute evenly over the sowing ground. Very dense sowing is the best solution. After six months take pickings of the new plants and prick these out separately. Plantlets will now emerge which can be clearly distinguished from each other. Distribute the pickings after three months and again after another three months, so that each plantlet stands on its own. About a year later they will be large enough to be planted in a 4-in/10-cm final pot. Provided the plants are not set too close together, they will flower two years after the sowing.

Influencing the flowering

When the plants have developed sufficiently — after approximately two years — they can be made to flower throughout the year by influencing the flowering. Prepare 1pt./5l of solution for this purpose by diluting 1½ cu in/25 ml 2-hydrazinoethanol with water.

Empty the leaf sheath and pour about ⅓ fl oz/10 ml of the solution into the leaf sheath. After seven days remove the solution and fill the leaf sheath with water again. In summer the plants will flower two to three weeks after this treatment. In winter it sometimes takes four to six weeks.

Guzmania grows excellently in the special Bromeliad soil. Keep this soil moderately moist, at the same time ensuring that water is always present in the leaf sheath.

Place the plant in a lightly shaded position in summer; in winter it can tolerate direct sunlight. The light requirement is 6,000 mW per yd^2/m^2. Shield the plant if the light intensity reaches 17,000 lux.

In the summer give an extra feed by adding ¼ tsp of compound fertilizer (17-6-18 or 20-5-20) per pt water/½ g per litre one week, and the next week adding a solution of the same amount of potassium nitrate (13.5-0-45). In the winter reduce the concentration of these fertilizers by one-half. The solution can either be applied to the potting soil or poured over the leaves, which must then be washed down.

Guzmania minor 'Orange'

Guzmania minor

This is the most widely grown Guzmania, in the varieties 'Red' and 'Orange'. *Minor* means 'smaller'. The growing of Guzmania minor hybrids with a larger inflorescence is making some headway. Propagation is from seed.

Guzmania monostachya

Monostachya means 'with one ear'. This Guzmania has a pointed red inflorescence. It is propagated from seed and flowers only after three years.

Guzmania zahnii

This is a species grown from seed with a yellow inflorescence.

Guzmania lingulata

This Guzmania has a beautiful, large inflorescence. The bright-red variety 'Cardinalis' is propagated by means of suckers. The plant is often used to provide cut flowers. It is grown to only a limited extent.

Guzmania musaica

This Guzmania has a beautiful leaf decoration in the form of a mosaic. The inflorescence is red and yellow. Propagation is from seed.

Guzmania hybrids

Many new hybrids with beautifully coloured inflorescences have been grown in recent years. Their propagation is not simple, but propagation by tissue-growing in vitroculture is making some headway.

Treatment table

	sowing	growth	winter
pot	frame	3½ in/9 cm	—
soil	humus-rich	Bromeliad soil	—
feeding	—	see text	see text
watering	moderately	moderately	moderately
temperature	72-75° F/ 22-24° C	77-86° F/ 25-30° C	68-72° F/ 20-22° C
rel. humidity	95%	90%	80%
light	light	shade	light

Gynura procumbens

Gynura aurantiaca

Gynura procumbens 'Velvet Plant'
This splendid plant, with violet-coloured hairy leaves, has horizontal stems (*procumbens* meaning 'close to the ground').

Gynura aurantiaca
This Gynura species has thick stems and large leaves, which are less brightly coloured than those of procumbens. The species comes from Java.

Member of a very large family
Gynura is a splendid foliage plant with violet-coloured, hairy leaves. The gold-coloured, ox-eye-type flowers seldom drop and they have an unpleasant smell. Most people who have a Gynura in their house therefore make sure that it never flowers. This can be achieved by topping the flower regularly. The flower alone clearly shows that this plant belongs to the large family of composite flowers, Compositae. Almost 100 different genera of this family grow wild in Europe. The most well-known species are the dandelion, the daisy and the ox-eye daisy.
The name Gynura refers to the flower; *gynè* means 'woman' in Greek and *oura* means 'tail'. The pistil (the female reproductive organ) has something of a tail shape.
The plant comes from tropical Asia and was introduced into England in 1891.

Intermediate cutting under double glass
Propagate Gynura by taking an intermediate cutting with one leaf pair (see page 169 for cuttings). Place this cutting under double glass in a 3½-in/9-cm pot filled with peat-based potting compost. The cuttings can also be placed in a frame with peat-based potting compost (bed for cuttings) and after three weeks, when the plants have roots, repotted into the final pot. The plants are mostly seen grown in a 3½-in/9-cm pot, in which three cuttings are placed.

Think about wild growth
Gynura is a rapid-growing, easy-to-grow foliage plant which if watered too much will produce extravagant growth. Rapid growth sometimes makes the plant become very untidy.
The best plants are produced by the regular taking of cuttings. If you want to grow large plants, regular topping is necessary; this is also the way to prevent flowering.
The plant makes no great demands as regards potting soil. It grows excellently in the normal RHP potting soil.
During the spring and summer months, feed it weekly. In the winter months, add feed in a lower concentration once every two weeks.
Gynura requires plenty of light for steady growth, and also for producing its beautiful leaf colours. Shield it from direct sunlight.
The gold-coloured flowers appear on the fully-grown branches. If these are cut back regularly, the plant will be constantly rejuvenated and will never flower.

Treatment table

	cutting	growth	rest
pot	3-3½ in/ 8-9 cm	3½ in/ 9 cm	—
soil	peat-based potting compost	RHP	—
feeding	—	1 tsp compound fertilizer per pt water/2 g per litre	—
watering	moist	moderately	moderately
temperature	68° F/20° C	60-64° F/ 16-18° C	60-64° F/ 16-18° C
rel. humidity	90%	60-70%	60-70%
light	light	light	light

special features   Shield from direct sunlight in the summer.

Hebe

Not really a houseplant
In Greek mythology Hebe was the beautiful daughter of Zeus and Hera, goddess of youth and cup-bearer to the gods. When Hercules acquired immortality and became one of the gods, he took her as his wife.

The Hebe which we know as a houseplant is a cross between Hebe speciosa and Hebe salicifolia. Both species come from New Zealand. The cross was made in England and the plant was cultivated in 1848. Hebe is an evergreen shrub which flowers in the autumn with bunches of magnificent purple or mauve flowers. Hebe is also known as Veronica, but this is incorrect. The Veronica species, which are also called Speedwell, are all herbaceous. Hebe belongs to the family Scrophulariaceae. Strictly speaking it is not a houseplant. It grows best outside, but must be overwintered in a frost-free environment. Indoors, the flower colours look very gaudy.

Autumn and spring cuttings
Autumn cuttings should be taken from non-flowering shoots. If placed in peat-based potting compost they will have sufficient roots after six to eight weeks. Pot them to take for cuttings and overwinter them in a frost-free environment. The tops of the plants can be taken as cuttings in the spring. Cover them afterwards with paper in order to prevent drying out. When they root, place the plants in a 3-in/8-cm pot. A small plant will then be obtained which will make further growth the following year. Top the plants in late winter or early spring to get a well-branched plant. About two weeks after topping, the plant can be repotted into a 4-5-in/10-12-cm final pot. Place the plants outside in mid-spring and grow them in beds.

Although the first flowers will appear in late summer, most plants will not flower until the autumn.

Cool position
Because Hebe is not really a houseplant, it is important to find a cool position for it inside. It needs plenty of light, but should be shielded from strong sunlight.

The plant makes no great demands as regards potting soil and grows excellently in a normal RHP soil.

Keep the soil moist during the growing season in the spring and summer months. Overwintering young plants need a moderately moist potting soil; older specimens should be watered seldom in the rest period. Feed them weekly from mid-spring to early autumn. Hebe is a beautiful, decorative plant which lasts many years and eventually grows into a fairly large bush.

Hebe Andersonii 'Variegata'

Hebe andersonii

Hebe Andersonii hybrid 'Variegata'
This variegated Hebe is a cross between Hebe speciosa and Hebe salicifolia. It is named after Thomas Anderson, a medical officer in the British Army who lived from 1828 to 1870. He was a plant collector and superintendent of the Botanical Gardens in Calcutta. Many varieties have purple, violet and mauve tints.

Treatment table

	cutting	growth	rest
pot	3 in/7 cm	4-5 in/10-12 cm	—
soil	peat-based potting compost	RHP	—
feeding	—	1½ tsp compound fertilizer per pt water/ 3 g per litre	—
watering	moist	moist	moderately/ dry
temperature	46-50° F/ 8-10° C	50-54° F/ 10-12° C	36-41° F/ 2-5° C
rel. humidity	80-90%	80%	70%
light	plenty	plenty	plenty
flowers	—	autumn	—
special features	Overwinter in a frost-free environment. The plant can be placed outside in the full sun in the summer; shield against direct sunlight indoors.		

Hedera helix 'Pittsburgh'

Hedera canariensis

This plant has a larger leaf than Hedera helix. The species comes from North Africa and the Canary Islands. It was cultivated in England in 1833.
The most widely-grown variety is the variegated 'Variegata' ('Gloire de Marengo'), which requires more warmth than the variegated Hedera helix varieties. The variety 'Montgommery' is grown to only a limited extent. It has glossy green leaves.

Hedera helix 'Pittsburgh'

This is the most widely grown variety of Hedera helix. Helix is the old name for ivy. More than 100 varieties are known, all of them in immature form. The mature form does not climb and flowers with green-yellow flowers; it bears numerous black berries afterwards.

Hedera helix 'Herald'

Hedera helix 'Herald'

'Herald' is one of the silver-variegated Hedera varieties.
These varieties are often grafted on to the rootstock of a Fatshedera.
The silver-variegated tendrils then hang like the branches of a weeping tree along the stem.

Hedera helix 'Glacier'

This is a silver-marbled variety of Hedera helix.

Hedera helix 'Goldheart'

This Hedera is golden-yellow in the middle of the leaf.

A plant with an iron constitution

Hedera helix is one of the easiest houseplants to grow and causes hardly any problems inside.
It does not like excessive light or standing in the sun, however, because it may be attacked by tick or red spider mite, especially if the relative humidity is too low. Hedera helix is also, like the previous plant, Hebe, not really a houseplant. It is the common European Ivy, which grows in the wild in the woods with its evergreen leaves and black berries and is often grown in gardens.
Hedera helix is excellent at adapting to an indoor climate. The name, Hedera, comes from the Greek word *hedra*, which means 'fastened'. The plant has been cultivated since the earliest times.
Fatshedera is used as a rootstock on which to graft some variegated Hedera helix varieties. Twigs 4-in/10-cm long are grafted on to the stem by cleft-grafting (see page 170 for grafting). Fix the graft in position with twine and place the rootstock in the propagation bed under double glass or plastic sheeting. Coalescence will take place in three weeks and a splendid little weeping tree with variegated tendrils will be obtained.

Taking of cuttings is simple and quick

Take intermediate cuttings from Hedera with two or three leaves (see page 169 for cuttings). They will root quickly because roots are already attached to the stem. The stems can also be laid on the ground in the normal way. As soon as the roots appear, cut the stems into pieces and you will have rooted cuttings.
Place two cuttings in a 3-in/8-cm pot. To get large plants, repot them after three to five months in a larger pot. Support the young plants by tying the stem to a stick or wire. Train large plants along three bamboo canes tied together at the top.

Large enough pot

Care must be taken that Hedera always occupies a pot large enough to enable it to grow well. It can be given a larger one at the annual repotting.
The plant makes no special demands as regards potting soil. RHP soil is quite adequate. During the growing season, give it plenty of water. Water it slightly less frequently in the winter when the plant is resting. Feed weekly in the growing season and discontinue in the winter. The variegated varieties require a light position for good growth, but not excessive light, which they cannot tolerate. Set the green varieties in a shaded spot. If you want to rejuvenate the plant, cut back the long tendrils.

Treatment table

	cutting	growth	rest
pot	frame	5-6 in/10-14 cm	—
soil	peat-based potting compost	RHP	—
feeding	—	1½ tsp compound fertilizer per pt water/ 3 g per litre	—
watering	moist	generously	moderately
temperature	64-68° F/ 18-20° C	64-68° F/ 18-20° C	54° F/12° C
rel. humidity	90%	70-85%	60-70%
light	light	shadow	light

special features The variegated varieties require a higher winter temperature (64° F/18° C) and more light than the green ones.
The green varieties are hardy outdoors.

Summer flowerer

Hibiscus is a splendid summer-flowering pot plant which can flower from mid-spring to early winter, though most plants flower in summer.

Hibiscus is an old Greek name for the marsh mallow, which is now called Althaea officinalis.

Officinalis means 'medicinal' and the plant has been known as such for many centuries.

Like the marsh mallow, Hibiscus is a member of the family Malvaceae.

Hibiscus comes from eastern Asia and had already been cultivated there for a long time before it was described and cultivated for the first time, in the Netherlands, in 1687.

Half-leaves

Propagate Hibiscus by an intermediate cutting or a head cutting. In most cases the top is too weak to take cuttings from. Take cuttings from mid-autumn to early winter. Treat them with growth hormone and place them in pairs in a small pot. The leaves must be cut in half, or the axillary buds will get insufficient light for good growth.

Place Hibiscus under mist or plastic sheeting. The cuttings will root after four to six weeks.

About seven weeks after taking cuttings, pot the plants up in a 4-5-in/10-12-cm pot.

When the shoots are 2½ in/6 cm long, remove the tops in order to get a well-branched plant. When the largest shoots have grown to 4 in/10 cm and the smallest to 2½ in/6 cm, treat the plant a few times with growth inhibitor.

The growing time from topping to flowering is 10 to 12 weeks. If three cuttings are placed in a pot, do not top. The plant is supplied by commercial growers when the flower buds are fully grown but have not yet opened. With early flowering the buds sometimes dry out, because the plant gets too little light. The grower who wants to supply flowering plants for Mother's Day tops them in late winter. But if the following months are somewhat dark, with little sunlight, the buds will drop off.

Plenty of light

Hibiscus is a splendid flowering plant which requires a great deal of light; it will even tolerate direct sunlight, provided that the correct relative humidity is maintained. It makes no great demands as regards potting soil and grows exceptionally well in a normal RHP soil. The soil must be kept moist during the growing season, when the plants should be given a weekly feed. In winter, keep the soil moderately moist and stop feeding.

Cut back old plants in early spring, so that they can form new shoots on which the plant can flower.

The limiting factors for bud formation in the house is the light. The plants must be repotted annually.

Hibiscus schizopetalus photographed in Colombia

Hibiscus rosa sinensis

Hibiscus rosa sinensis

Hibiscus rosa sinensis

Hibiscus rosa-sinensis

This species has single-flowered and double-flowered varieties, most of which are grown by name. The flowers are red, pink, yellow and orange-yellow. Large-flowered varieties include the following: 'Lagos' (orange), 'Miami' (yellow) and 'Canberra' (pink). They are grown to only a limited extent because they root less easily and grow more slowly than the standard varieties, which are often of Danish or American origin.

Hibiscus rosa-sinensis 'Cooperi'

This is a rare variety with beautiful white, pink and green leaf decoration. The plant is grown mainly for its leaves and flowering is minimal.

Hibiscus rosa-sinensis 'Albovariegata'

This is a variegated variety with white patches which is grown to only a limited extent and then just for its leaves.

Treatment table

	cutting	growth	rest
pot	wire basket or Jiffy	4-5 in/10-12 cm	—
soil	peat-based potting compost	RHP	—
feeding	—	1½ tsp compound fertilizer per pt water/ 3 g per litre	—
watering	moist	moist	moderately
temperature	64° F/ 18° C	64-77° F/ 18-25° C	50-60° F/ 10-15° C
rel. humidity	95%	> 80%	80%
light	light	sunlight	light
flowers	—	mid-spring to mid-autumn	—
growth hormone	1-naphtha-lenacetic 0.1%	—	—
growth inhibitor	—	1/30 fl oz Cycocel or CCC per 30 pt water/1 ml per 15 litres	—

special features If growth is strong, inhibit with 1/30 fl oz per 20 pt water/1 ml per 10 litres. Repeat the spraying two or three times at 10-day intervals. The soil temperature with cuttings is 68° F/20° C.

Dutch speciality

Hippeastrum, which is better known as Amaryllis, is a very popular houseplant.

The plant comes originally from South America, from where the first plants were imported into the Netherlands in 1698. The most important parent species are Hippeastrum reginae, Hippeastrum vittatum, Hippeastrum leopoldii, Hippeastrum equestre, Hippeastrum aulicum and Hippeastrum rutilum. This last plant is the ancestor of the modern, small-flowered varieties. Dutch growers have carried out most of the improvement work and still provide some of the leading Hippeastrum experts in the world.

The name Hippeastrum comes from the Greek words, *hippeus* for 'knight' and *astron* for 'star'. The name 'Knight's Star' refers to the beautiful, somewhat star-shaped, flowers. The plant belongs to the family Amaryllidaceae, some members of which also grow wild, such as the 'Zomerklokje' ('summer bell'), the Snowdrop and the Narcissus.

Problem-free treatment

If you buy a 'flowering bulb', the flowers are already present in embryo. Keep these bulbs at a temperature of 55-63° F/13-17° C. As soon as the tip of the flower bud is visible, plant it with its nose just showing in a nutritious, highly porous RHP soil. It will flower eight weeks later. During the growing season, water it regularly and give it a weekly feed. Place the plant in as light a position as possible, but shield it slightly from strong sunlight.

If you want flowers again in the following year, let the plant come on normally at a temperature of at least 68° F/20° C and feed it weekly. The growing period must last at least seven to eight months.

Dig up the bulb in mid-autumn and keep it at a temperature of 55-63° F/13-17° C until planting out. It needs a 5-in/12-13 cm pot as a houseplant.

In order to combat various diseases and also to stimulate growth, commercial growers often give the bulbs a hot-water treatment. About two weeks after digging up, therefore, plunge them as a growth-stimulant in a hot-water bath for two hours at 104-108° F/40-42° C, and for disease control for two hours at a temperature of 110-115° F/43.5-46° C.

Ensure that the roots remain intact as far as possible when preserving the bulbs.

Seed and offset bulbs

If you want to propagate the plant yourself, try to collect the seed. Select for this purpose the first two flowers which open. The pistil is ripe when it is sticky, split in three, and curved in shape. Then apply to it a ripe anther of the same flower; this process is called self-pollination. After about seven weeks you will have a ripe fruit containing about 80 blackish-brown, flat, round seeds. Sow them out in a mixture of four parts peat dust to one part river sand, at a distance of about 3 in/7 cm apart. Cover the seeds with a layer of soil ½-in/1-cm thick. After four months, prick the young plantlets out individually and treat them thereafter as normal plants. In eighteen months time the bulbs will be 7 in/18 cm in diameter. Dig them up in mid-autumn of each year and plant them out again in the spring. In two-and-a-half years, the bulb will form flower buds which will flower eight weeks after planting.

The plant can also be propagated via the offset bulbs which the plant forms. The white varieties, in particular, provide the most offset bulbs. The small-flowered hybrid 'Gracilis' is always propagated from offset bulbs. This manner of propagation is very slow. After digging up and drying the parent bulbs, break off the offset bulbs. Keep them at a temperature of 55-63° F/13-17° C and plant them out again in mid-winter. Thereafter, treat them as normal bulbs.

Commercial growers also propagate the bulbs by 'scooping' and 'cutting' the bulbs. This is specialist work, which requires

Hippeastrum hybrid

Hippeastrum hybrid

There are a particularly large number of varieties in all tints of pink, salmon and red. There are also white and two-tone varieties. They are mostly sold not by name, but by colour. Small-flowered red varieties are also grown.

Hippeastrum hybrid

Hippeastrum hybrid

Hippeastrum hybrid

a great deal of patience and expertise, but could be done by a competent amateur. For scooping and cutting use carefully selected, three-year-old bulbs which have not been subjected to a hot-water treatment. Select for abundance of flowers among other things. The best time is the rest period from mid-autumn to mid-winter. Start by cutting off a slice of basal plate. A piece of soil will still be attached to the bulb scales. Remove the top of the bulb and cut the bulb perpendicularly and parallel with the leaves into two equal parts. Divide these two halves into 18 parts of equal size and cut these parts between the scales into two or three pieces. Individual pieces of bulb scale with basal plate will then be attached to each part. Place the pieces on a layer of river sand 2 in/5 cm thick, superimposed on 4 in/10 cm of potting soil. The pieces must be completely covered by the river sand. The soil temperature should be kept at 77-86°F/25-30° C. In about three months these pieces will form offset bulbs on the base between the bulb scales. The offset bulbs are capable of flowering in two years.

Early and late flowering

If you want a flowering plant at Christmas, the earliest time for digging up the bulb is the end of summer. Keep it for a month at a temperature of 63°F/17°C and then for four more weeks at 73°F/23°C before planting out. The bulb will flower six to seven months after planting out.

Hippeastrum normally flowers in the spring, but if the bulb is kept at 54°F/12°C after being dug up in mid-autumn and at a temperature of 41°F/5°C as soon as the flower bud is visible, flowering can be delayed by a few months. The plant will then flower three to four weeks after planting out.

Bulbs capable of flowering are usually three years old with a diameter of at least 8 in/20 cm. These bulbs can give two pedicles.

Treatment table

	sowing	growth	bulb
pot	frame	5 in/12-13 cm	none
soil	peat dust and sand 4:1	RHP	none
feeding	—	1½ tsp compound fertilizer per pt water/3 g per litre	—
watering	moist	moist	dry
temperature	75° F/ 24° C	> 68-82° F/ 20-28° C	46-62° F/ 12-17° C (ventilate well)
rel. humidity	90%	70-80%	—
light	light	light	—
flowers	—	all year, but chiefly in the spring	—
inhibiting	—	—	at 41° F/ 5° C

special features The air temperature for sowing is 68° F/20° C. In the sun the growing temperature may rise to 82° F/28°C.

Think about dead leaf patches

Howeia is one of the approximately 50 genera (with 3,500 species) of the Palm family. Palms are typically tropical or sub-tropical plants which have a hard time in our homes and are therefore somewhat unsuitable as houseplants. Howeia is grown for the decorative value of its leaves, but it is rare for it not to be damaged. Older specimens are usually seen with dead patches on the leaves, the result of excessively low relative humidity. Howeia comes from, and takes its name from, a group of islands in the Pacific at about 32° east of Australia, the Lord Howe Islands.

The plant was cultivated in England in 1858. Previously palm growing was a typically Belgian activity.

At the present time many Palms, as well as germinated or non-germinated seeds, are imported directly from their land of origin, from Australia or from the Mediterranean region.

Sowing

The seeds of Howeia germinate very irregularly and patience is therefore required. Sow in a sandy, substantial mixture which must be humus-rich. As soon as a germinated seedling has a seed leaf 3-4 in/8-10 cm in size, pot it in a 3-in/8-cm pot. A year later repot it into a 5-in/12-cm pot. It may well be three to four years after that before you obtain a reasonably large palm.

Plenty of light but no sunlight

In the sunny regions where the Palms come from, young specimens are for the most part shaded. The Palms which we keep as houseplants must therefore receive plenty of light, though they must never stand in direct sunlight. The plants grow best in a mixture of two parts RHP frozen peat potting soil to one part clay and one part sand. During the growing season, water generously and feed twice a week. In the darker winter months the plant has a rest period; water it sparingly then and discontinue feeding. Howeia is a large houseplant which can last a long time. A constant check must be kept on the relative humidity. It is content with slight shading, in which position, however, it will grow more slowly. Repot the plant once every two years. It is essential to feed it regularly when it is growing.

Howeia forsteriana

Howeia forsteriana (Kentia forsteriana)

This is the quickest-growing Howeia. The drooping leaves are very broad, they are finely-scaled on the underside, and are extended in almost uniform fashion on a long leaf stalk.

Howeia belmoreana (Kentia belmoreana)

This Howeia grows slightly more slowly than forsteriana and requires more heat. The leaves are more pendulous; they have woolly hairs at the edge, are not scaled, and they stand at right angles to each other on a short, somewhat reddish, petiole.

Treatment table

	sowing	growth	rest
pot	frame	5 in/12 cm	—
soil	sandy	frozen peat, clay and sand 2:1:1	
feeding	—	1 tsp compound fertilizer per pt water/ 2g per litre	—
watering	moist	generously	moderately
temperature	77° F/ 25° C	68-72° F/ 20-22° C	50° F/ 10° C
rel. humidity	95%	70%	60%
light	light	light	light

special features Shield against direct sunlight.

Hoya bella

Hoya carnosa

This flowering climber with flesh-coloured (*carnosa*) flowers comes from the region of the world stretching from southern China to Australia. The plant was introduced into England in 1802.

Hoya carnosa

Hoya carnosa 'Variegata'

This is a variegated Hoya variety. The leaves have a creamy-white edge which is reddish on the young leaf.

Hoya carnosa 'Exotica'

On this variegated variety the middle of the leaf is creamy-white to light-pink. The remainder of the leaf is slightly tinted with green.

Hoya bella

The beautiful Hoya bella comes originally from Burma. *Bella* is the Latin for 'beautiful'.
It is a hanging plant which is often supported with a frame or with wire clips. The plant was introduced into Europe in 1847.

Hoya micrantha

This is a small-flowered Hoya which is grown in the same way as Hoya carnosa.

Hoya australis

This is a strongly-growing, but rare, species with creamy-white flowers. Its treatment is the same as that for Hoya carnosa.

Exotic hanging plant

Hoya is a well-known houseplant with remarkable flowers which form splendid bunches and look as if they are made of wax. The droplets of nectar which often hang on them then look like molten wax. The name Hoya comes from Thomas Hoy, a famous English grower who lived in the late 18th and early 19th centuries. He cultivated the plant for the first time. Hoya belongs to the family Asclepiadaceae.

Cuttings in spring and summer

Take intermediate cuttings with one leaf pair from Hoya carnosa in mid-summer (see page 169 for cuttings). Place the cuttings in 3-in/7-cm pots filled with peat-based potting compost. They will root in four to five weeks, when they should be transferred to a 4-in/11-cm pot.
Train the quick-growing tendrils over a wire hoop or plastic frame. The plant will flower from the following spring into the summer.
Take head or intermediate cuttings with one leaf pair from non-flowering shoots of flowering Hoya bella plants from late summer to mid-autumn. In peat-based potting compost, under plastic sheeting, the cuttings will root after five to six weeks. Place them in a 4-in/10-cm pot about four months after taking cuttings. The plant will then flower in late spring or early summer the following year.

Great differences in treatment

Hoya carnosa is an easy-growing houseplant which will cause you fewer problems than Hoya bella. Treatment of the two species varies greatly.
Hoya carnosa grows in normal RHP potting soil; feed it weekly and water generously until the rest period. It can flower splendidly in the house provided it gets sufficient light. Do not cut off the old flower stalks; they will flower again. Repot the flower annually after flowering in the autumn.
Hoya bella grows more epiphytically, ie on trees or tree trunks, in the wild. It is more of a hanging plant than a climber and requires a fibrous, highly porous soil.
Give it a lower concentration of fertilizer and after the flower initiation feed it again once every two weeks. The plant is very sensitive to a high salt concentration and therefore requires more warmth than Hoya carnosa. It is a weaker plant and sets flowers with difficulty, unless it gets sufficient light and is kept dry. It should, however, be watered generously and fed weekly in the summer months.

Treatment table Hoya carnosa

	cutting	growth	rest
pot	3 in/7 cm	4½ in/11 cm	—
soil	peat-based potting compost	RHP	—
feeding	—	1 tsp compound fertilizer per pt water/2g per litre	—
watering	moist	generously	moderately
temperature	68° F/20° C	68° F/20° C	50° F/10° C
rel. humidity	90-95%	80%	60-70%
light	light	fairly light	light
flowers	—	spring and summer	—
special features	After the flower initiation in the spring the temperature should be 60-64° F/15-18° C with a relative humidity of 70-80%. A low winter temperature is necessary for good flowering. Shield against strong sunlight in the summer.		

Hydrangea Hortensia

A garden plant in the house

Hydrangea is an almost hardy semi-shrub which is just as suitable for the garden as for the house. It is sold in pots, however, because people find the bulb-shaped inflorescence with the white, pink, pink-red or blue sepals so attractive.

The name Hydrangea comes from the Greek words, *hydoor* and *aggeion*, and means 'water-jar'. This refers to the shape of the fruit when it bursts.

Hydrangea belongs to the family Saxifragaceae, some members of which occur in the wild or are cultivated, such as saxifrage, which is used as a culinary herb, and various species of berry, such as white, red and black currant and gooseberry. Hydrangea comes from Japan. It was cultivated in England in 1788. The plant is not known in the wild.

Two different times for taking cuttings

Shoot cuttings can be taken from the plant towards mid-summer. Plants which are kept outside are topped at this time and the tops can also be used as cuttings. Treat them with growth hormone and place them in peat-based potting compost under plastic sheeting or paper. When they have grown good roots, after three to four weeks, place them in 3-in/7-cm pots. Grow the plants in a cool, frost-free spot. In late winter or early spring cut them back to a height of 3 in/ 7 cm. In late spring remove them from the pot and plant or repot them outside in the garden. Towards mid-summer remove the tops once again (which can be used as cuttings). The plant now forms the branches which will flower the following spring. In late summer place the plants in a 5-in/12-cm pot. Keep them cool and frost-free, inside or outside, until they flower. Only at this stage do they become houseplants. To protect them against frost they can also be placed in pits, branches and all.

Cuttings can also be taken in the spring, in the form of the tips cut from leaf shoots of flowering plants. This can be done towards mid-summer. These late cuttings are usually grown simply for the stem.

If you want a branched plant, you must top it in mid-summer.

Special soil

Hydrangeas require a humus-rich soil with a weak acid pH of 5.5 (see page 168 for acid level). Unless you want blue flowers, the soil must also be free from iron and aluminium. Feeding with ammonia or potash alum will produce blue flowers. Add a good two spoonfuls of it to the potting soil in August. Due to the high salt concentration blue Hydrangeas are somewhat weaker and have fewer roots. Water the plants generously during the whole of the growing season, in some cases as often as once a day. Stand them outside in well-fertilized soil or add fertilizer weekly. When Hydrangeas are about to set flowers, give them slight shading, but grow them on in as light a position as possible. The early varieties will flower in late winter, the flowers lasting about two weeks. Commercial growers keep growth compact through a special treatment, eg with inhibitors. The flowers tolerate this fairly well.

Hydrangea is a somewhat old-fashioned houseplant which requires plenty of space. After flowering, cut the plant back and in late spring place it outside. The tops may also be removed at the time of the summer solstice. If too many new branches grow, remove the smallest ones. Pot the plants up in late summer (if you leave them in the pot feed them weekly) and bring them inside in mid-autumn to spend the winter cool and frost-free.

If the buds are visible, the plant can be placed in the warmth in a light position This may be from early winter to early spring, depending on the variety. The plant can also be left to grow normally in the garden. Although it will flower later there, it will grow into a magnificent large shrub, the leaves of which are very beautiful.

Hydrangea macrophylla 'Lemmenhof'

'Mme Emile Mouillière'

Hydrangea macrophylla 'Mme Emile Mouillière'

This is a well-known white variety of French origin.

Hydrangeas are grown by name in a large number of varieties. These varieties were mainly developed in Germany, Belgium, Switzerland and France.

Hydrangea macrophylla 'Sainte Soeur Thérése de l'Enfant Jésus'

This Hydrangea with the female name is a variety with particularly large, white flowers.

Hydrangea macrophylla 'Lemmenhof' and 'Holstein'

These varieties will have blue flowers if treated with ammonia or potash alum. The aluminium salts get into the sepals and form delphinide, a blue anthocyanine pigment.

Hydrangea macrophylla 'Alpengluehen'

This is a Hydrangea with pink-red flowers; it is a late-flowering variety.

Hydrangea macrophylla 'Alpengluehen'

Treatment table

	cutting	growth	rest
pot	3 in/7 cm	5 in/12-13 cm	—
soil	peat-based potting compost	humus-rich	—
feeding	—	1½ tsp compound fertilizer per pt water/ 3g per litre	—
watering	generously	generously	fairly generously
temperature	68° F/20° C	64-72° F/ 18-22° C	frost-free
rel. humidity	95%	80-90%	80-90%
light	light	light	light
flowers	—	spring	—
growth hormone	indoleacetic acid	—	—

Impatiens walleriana hybrid 'Deep Orange'

Impatiens walleriana hybrid 'White'

Impatiens walleriana hybrid 'Harlekijn'

Unapproachable but busy

Busy Lizzie is one of the few houseplants whose generic name is derived from Latin, not Greek. *Impatiens* means 'unapproachable' or 'not to be touched' in Latin. This refers to the ripe fruit's habit of bursting open and scattering its seeds when touched. This is, incidentally, a family trait; all Balsaminaceae, of which Busy Lizzie is one, behave in this way. A well-known relative is the large Spring Balsam, which comes from Indonesia and scatters its seed for several yards in gardens and in the wild. Impatiens owes its popular name, Busy Lizzie, to its capacity for extremely rapid growth.
The Impatiens which we know as a houseplant comes from tropical Asia. Although cultivated as an annual, it can last for many years as a sturdy, simple houseplant.

Sowing and cuttings

Although many people regard Busy Lizzie mainly as a plant propagated by cuttings, commercial growers propagate it from seed. The seed is small; there are about 2,000 seeds to a gram. Sow from mid-winter to early spring. One month after sowing, the seedlings will be large enough to be pricked out individually. About five to six weeks later, place them in a 4-in/10-cm pot.
The plants will flower for the first time in three to four months. They are naturally still fairly small at that time, but they grow at a great pace and in late summer will have reached about 16 in/40 cm. The whole plant is then covered with flowers.

Lots of light, water and food

A plant obtains the carbon it needs to grow from the air under the influence of light. Air is important in feeding a plant, and a plant which grows as quickly as Busy Lizzie needs a great deal to eat and drink. Make sure, therefore, that the potting soil is moist at all times and feed weekly. For profuse flowering it is necessary to give the plant a light position; but avoid direct sunlight in the spring and summer.
Impatiens makes no great demands as regards potting soil. The plant grows exceptionally well in a normal RHP potting soil. It is a sturdy houseplant which will flower splendidly in your house throughout the summer. If the plant becomes too large, cut it back in late winter or early spring.

Impatiens Walleriana hybrid

Busy Lizzie is named after H. Waller, an English plant collector.
There are varieties with large flowers and varieties with small flowers. They are seen in numerous shades of white, pink, carmine, red, chocolate, orange and lilac. There are also a number of two-tone varieties. Beautiful hybrids of Impatiens hawkeri come from the United States. They have bright, variegated leaves and distinctive flower colours.

Impatiens balsemina 'Plena'

This is an Impatiens species which flowers in the summer with mainly pink and salmon-tinted flowers. It is propagated from seed.

Treatment table

	seed or cutting	growth	rest
pot	3 in/7 cm	3½ in/9 cm	—
soil	peat-based potting compost or sowing soil	RHP	—
feeding	—	1½ tsp compound fertilizer per pt water/3 g per litre	—
temperature	68-72°F/20-22°C	64-77°F/16-25°C	50-60°F/10-15°C
rel. humidity	95%	80%	> 70%
water	moist	generously	moist
light	plenty	plenty	plenty
flowers	—	spring and summer	—
special features	Sow also at 68-72°F/20-22°C and a relative humidity of 95%. Shield against direct sunlight.		

Ixora

Not so suitable for the home

Ixora is a semi-shrub whose flowers form splendid red, orange and yellow large umbels. It is really a plant for the warm greenhouse and can be kept in the house to only a very limited extent.

The name Ixora is a corruption of a Sanskrit word for Master; it is the name of a Hindu deity in India and Sri Lanka. Ixora belongs to the family Rubiaceae.

The Ixoras which we know as houseplants are crosses of Ixora chinensis ('from China') and Ixora coccinea ('carmine red'). These species come from an area stretching from China to India and were introduced into France in 1782.

Cuttings under mist

Propagate Ixora by a head cutting or an intermediate cutting (see page 169 for cuttings) from mid-winter to mid-spring. Place the cuttings in 2-in/5-cm pots filled with a mixture of four parts peat-based potting compost to one part river sand. Depending on the hardness of the cutting, treat it first with 3-indoleacetic acid in a concentration of 0.1% or 0.2%.

The cuttings are best placed under mist. If they are placed under plastic sheeting the plastic must be removed twice a day in order to ventilate the cuttings. The cuttings will root in four weeks. Up to three cuttings should then be placed in a 4-5-in/10-12-cm pot, depending on the desired plant size. When two leaf pairs have appeared, the top can be removed. The flowering season will be delayed by later topping: the later you top, the later the plant will flower. The flowers will appear on the fully-grown shoots.

The flower buds will form only during the long day and only if the plant gets enough light. Ixora can flower from mid-summer to mid-autumn. The growing time is six to twenty-four months, depending on the plant size. Bring the flower indoors only when the flowers are open; unopened buds will stop growing and drop off.

Salt-sensitive

Ixora is highly salt-sensitive and can easily suffer from chlorosis, a condition in which the leaves turn yellow from a shortage of chlorophyll.

Grow the plant in RHP calceolaria potting soil. In direct sunlight give it a slightly shaded position; otherwise grow it in as light a position as possible. Keep the potting soil moist at all times during the growing season. Feed weekly also at this time. Discontinue feeding in the winter months, when the plant flowers, and also during the rest period. Keep the potting soil moderately moist then but never dry.

Ixora is a splendid greenhouse plant which requires a very high temperature and a high relative humidity. It is a poor houseplant, its durability being comparable to that of a fairly durable cut flower. It usually gets too little light in the house and the atmosphere is too dry.

Ixora hybrid 'Fraseri'

Ixora hybrid 'Biers Glorie'

This is a dark orange variety of Ixora. Although there are a very large number of Ixora species, only a few varieties are seen.

Ixora hybrid 'Fraseri'

This Ixora variety is an orange-salmon colour.

Treatment table

	cutting	growth	rest
pot	2 in/5 cm	4-5 in/10-12 cm	—
soil	peat-based potting compost and sand 4:1	Calceolaria	—
feeding	—	1 tsp compound fertilizer per pt water/2 g per litre	none
watering	moist	moist	moderately
temperature	74-86°F/23-30°C	68-86°F/20-30°C	60°F/16°C
rel. humidity	95-100%	90%	70%
light	light	light	light
flowers	—	mid-summer to mid-autumn	—
growth hormone	1-naphtha-lenacetic acid 0.1-0.2%	—	—

special features Depending on the hardness of the cutting, the growth hormone concentration should be 0.1% *or 0.2%. Shield from direct sunlight.*

Kalanchoë hybrid 'Annet'

Kalanchoë blossfeldiana 'Vulcan'

This is a common dwarf breeding variety of Kalanchoë.
The name blossfeldiana comes from the German, H. Blossfeld, a succulents specialist who brought back Kalanchoë from Madagascar.

Kalanchoë blossfeldiana 'Orange Triumph'

The flowers of this variety tend to be bright red. A variety with a pale yellow inflorescence is more rare.

Kalanchoë hybrids

Many named varieties of this are seen in various shades of red, pink, lilac, yellow and bright orange.
Well-known varieties are the red 'Paula' and the somewhat small-flowered, red 'Annet'. Many varieties of these hybrids, which were developed originally in Switzerland, now come from the United States.
For compact growth they are sprayed during vegetative growth with the growth inhibitor Alar (1½ tsp per pt/3 g per litre). The auxillary shoots are then about ¾ in/2 cm long.
If the peduncles become extended, they are sprayed again with Alar (1 tsp per pt/2 g per litre). These hybrids have a longer short-day period (approximately six weeks) at a temperature of 68°F/20°C

Kalanchoë blossfeldiana 'Vulcan'

Kalanchoë blossfeldiana 'Tom Thumb'

Kalanchoë blossfeldiana 'Tom Thumb'

This is one of the many varieties with bright-red flowers and a somewhat short body.

are sprayed again with Alar (1 tsp per pt/2 g per litre). These hybrids have a longer short-day period (approximately six weeks) at a temperature of 68°F/20°C.

Flowers the year round

Kalanchoë is the Latinized form of the Chinese popular name for Kalanchoë lacianata: Kalan chau.
The Kalanchoë which we know as a houseplant is a native of Madagascar and was introduced into Germany in 1828.
Kalanchoë belongs to the family Crassulaceae.
It is a flowering pot-plant which you will see in flower the whole year round at the florist's shop. Commercial growers are able to regulate the flowering by a short-day treatment.

Cuttings and seed

Like most succulents, Kalanchoë is very easy to take cuttings from. The large-flowered Kalanchoë is propagated by means of a head cutting in sand and peat dust.
Commercial growers always propagate the small-flowered Kalanchoë from seed. This is very small: 50,000 to 80,000 seeds weigh one gram. When sowing, therefore, it is best to mix them with some sand. Sow in a cold, glass-covered frame to prevent drying out. The seeds do not need to be covered with soil. Thin the seedlings for the first time after seven weeks. A month later this can be repeated and the plants placed straightaway into 3-in/8-cm final pots. If only one plant is placed in a pot, the top must be removed after four weeks in order to get a good sturdy plant. It is quicker to put two plants in a pot. Kalanchoë is sensitive to pesticides, which can damage the leaves and even cause them to fall off.
The stem and the leaves grow during a long day, and in order to stimulate this vegetative growth, the plant can be given extra light. Commercial growers use high-pressure mercury lamps for this, or sometimes TL 33 bulbs with a radiation energy of 10,000 to 20,000 mH per yd²/m².
In order to suppress flowering, they light during the short-day period with lamps or TL with an intensity of 1,000-2,000 mW per yd²/m². This is not necessary with seedlings. Flowering can be anticipated once each shoot has formed three fully-grown leaves by giving the plants a short-day treatment of nine to ten hours. If you have to darken for this purpose, use black plastic sheeting, taking care that the relative humidity under the plastic is not too high. This causes tissue growth on the leaves. This period lasts three to six weeks; about three months later the plant will flower at a temperature of 63-68°F/17-20°C.

Light and dry

Like most succulents, Kalanchoë requires a great deal of light and not much water. The potting soil must never be wet. Add fertilizer during the growing season and discontinue when the plant flowers.
It is not always easy to find an indoor position light enough for it. It usually does well on the window-sill. After flowering, it will grow vegetatively over a long day. The tops which are removed at that time can be easily used as cuttings.

Treatment table

	sowing	growth
pot	frame	3-3½ in/8-9 cm
soil	frozen peat potting soil and river sand 4:1	
feeding	—	1 tsp compound fertilizer per pt water/1 g per litre
watering	moderately	moderately
temperature	64-68°F/18-20°C	60-86°F/16-30°C
rel. humidity	85%	dry
light	light	light
flowers	—	all year

special features Shield against direct sunlight.

Laurus/Laurel

Not a real houseplant

Laurus is an evergreen tree native to the Mediterranean region. It is cultivated as a foliage plant, but is not a real houseplant. The plants are at their best planted in tubs in gardens and on terraces, where they are able to rest in the winter in a cool position in dry soil.

Laurus means 'laurel'. It is a plant which has been cultivated by man from time immemorial. To the Greeks, the plant was the symbol of fame and honour. They made laurel wreaths from its leaves and used them to crown victors.

Another well-known use of the Laurel leaf is in cooking, as an aromatic herb in many dishes.

The Laurel is grown in many different forms. One sees bulb-shaped, pyramid-shaped and even square-shaped specimens, and also little trees with a small crown on a long stem. The yellow-green flowers have little decorative value. The bigger plants are five to twelve years old.

No propagation

The Laurel can be propagated by taking cuttings in the late summer. Its growing is a typical Belgian activity. Laurels are much grown in and around Bruges in unheated greenhouses. A restricted group of commercial growers regulates the number of plants to be grown, the sales and the prices. If you want a Laurel tree to retain its shape, you must trim it. Do this in the late summer, never in the spring, summer or winter, when the branches will make insufficient growth or die. The Laurel grows in the spring.

As soon as there is no longer any risk of night frosts, place the plants outside for the whole summer.

In late autumn bring them inside to overwinter in the cool and dry. The best place for this is a cold greenhouse. The Laurel tolerates a certain amount of frost pretty well in autumn and winter, but it is better to keep it frost-free. If it is kept too warm in the winter, the buds will grow too early.

A genuine out-of-doors plant

The Laurel is usually in its element when it is placed outside in full sun in the spring and summer. It also grows best at this time, though it can also, of course, be kept in the greenhouse or inside the house during the summer. If so, it must get as much light as possible. Only in the rest period will a small amount of light suffice.

Laurel grows exceptionally well in RHP potting soil. Water it liberally from mid-spring onwards, and when the young shoots start to come, add fertilizer weekly.

After pruning in late summer, stop adding fertilizer and keep the soil dry in the winter to prevent premature growth.

The Laurel is a real tub plant which should be repotted annually before the renewed growth in the spring.

Because of its slow growth the Laurel is very expensive, but it can give pleasure for many years.

Laurus nobilis

Laurus nobilis

This is Laurus nobilis, the 'noble laurel'.

Treatment table

	growth	rest
pot	tub	—
soil	RHP	—
feeding	1½ tsp compound fertilizer per pt water/3 g per litre	—
watering	generously	seldom
temperature	68-77° F/ 20-25° C	32-50° F/ 0-10° C
rel. humidity		
light	light	

special features The temperature must under no circumstances exceed 50° F/10° C in the winter.

Maranta leuconeura 'Fascinator'

Maranta leuconeura 'Kerchoviana'

Maranta leuconeura 'Kerchoviana'
This Maranta is widely grown as a foliage plant in a small pot. *Leuconara* is the Greek for 'with white nerves'.

Maranta leuconeura 'Massangeana'
This is a beautifully coloured, though slightly weak, variety. The leaf colour is very dark with red and bronze-green tints.

Maranta leuconeura 'Fascinator' ('Tricolor')
This Maranta is often seen in a large pot trained above ground on a moss stick.

Popular but difficult

The Ten commandment plant has, through its beautifully decorated leaves, won very many admirers. It is not one of the easiest houseplants to grow since it has specific requirements as far as soil, temperature and relative humidity are concerned. For instance, if the relative humidity is too low, dead leaf margins and patches can easily appear. If the rules are strictly observed, it is a rewarding plant which can give pleasure for many years.
Maranta is named after the 18th-century Venetian doctor, Bartolomeo Maranta, who wrote about plants with medicinal properties, among them Maranta. The plant is still confused sometimes with Calathea. Both belong to the family Marantaceae, but Maranta has an unicellular ovary and Calathea a tricellular one.
The Maranta which we know as a houseplant is a native of eastern Brazil.

Sometimes round a moss stick

Maranta is propagated by means of shoot cuttings (see page169 for cuttings). After treating them with growth hormone, place them in peat-based potting compost. Under double glass they will have sufficient roots after two to three weeks, when cuttings of the variety 'Kerchoviana' should be put into a 3½-in/8-9-cm final pot. Place 'Fascinator' cuttings into a much larger pot (6 in/15 cm) in which a so-called 'moss stick' or a plastic pipe has been bound or has been planted. Train the shoots of 'Fascinator' along this stick overhead.

Moist but not wet

Maranta requires an airy, highly porous potting soil. The so-called Bromeliad soil is suitable. Keep this soil moist at all times, but not so wet that water can be squeezed out of it. Feed the plant weekly and place it in a shady position, where it grows best. Plants which are grown specifically for taking cuttings, so-called mother plants, are often seen under the staging in greenhouses, where they grow abundantly.
A Maranta often does well in a box under the shade of larger foliage plants; it does not get too much light there and its decorative leaves come into their own.
Although Maranta grows slightly less well in the darker months, it has no real rest period.

Treatment table

	cutting	growth
pot	frame	3-3½ in/ 8-9 cm
soil	peat-based potting compost	Bromeliad soil
feeding	—	1tsp compound fertilizer per pt water/ 2g per litre
watering	moist	moist
temperature	72° F/22° C	68° F/20° C
rel. humidity	95%	85%
light	light	shade
growth hormone	1-naphthalenacetic acid 0.1-0.2%	—
special features	The temperature may rise somewhat in the sun, but it must never exceed 77° F/25° C. The relative humidity must never drop below 80%.	

Medinilla

Exotic beauty

Medinilla is a plant which is becoming increasingly in demand because of its bunches of magnificent, exotic pink flowers. However, it is a very difficult plant to grow, particularly in a normal indoor environment. The plant is named after J. de Medinilla Piñeda, who in the early 19th century was governor of the Marianas, an island group in the Pacific to the east of the Philippines. Medinilla is indigenous there. It was introduced into England in about 1830. Medinilla belongs to the family Melastomaceae, a family of tropical plants which includes many beautiful foliage plants.

Lengthy growing period

Medinilla can be propagated from imported seed. The growing period from seed is three yers and the plants are not so uniform and do not flower so profusely. It is, therefore, better to propagate the plant by means of head or intermediate cuttings. The plant then flowers after one-and-a-half to two years (see page169 for cuttings). In mid- to late winter take a somewhat woody piece of stem about 1 ½ in/4 cm long with one leaf and a bud in the leaf axil, split the stem across and place it in a 3-in/7-cm pot filled with frozen peat soil with 20% clay.
If the cutting has first been treated with growth hormone, it will root after three months. About two to three months after taking the cutting, place the plant in a final pot. Give the plant a bigger pot regularly as it increases in size.

Flower initiation during a short-day period

Grow Medinilla in four parts RHP potting soil and one part clay. During the growing season, keep the soil moist and feed it weekly. In the rest period, discontinue feeding, but water sufficiently until the flower buds are visible.
During the rest period in the winter keep the temperature at 54° F/12° C. See that the soil remains moist. The flower buds will be visible in two to three months. The temperature should be raised to 68° F/20° C. In this short-day period the plant forms flowers, which appear in two to three months.
Medinilla is a true greenhouse plant which makes high demands as to climate. The required high relative humidity of 90% or more is extremely difficult to achieve indoors. The required low winter temperature and the shortage of light also cause problems. In the summer, the plant grows best in slight shade, but during the short-day it requires a great deal of light. In the greenhouse it is a fantastically beautiful plant, which can grow very large and last a very long time. Older plants produce more and larger flowers than young ones.

Treatment table

	cutting	growth	rest
pot	3 in/7 cm		—
soil	frozen peat and clay 4:1	RHP and clay 4:1	—
feeding	—	½ tsp compound fertilizer per pt water/1g per litre	none
watering	moist	moist	moist
temperature	77° F/25° C	68-86° F/ 20-30° C	54° F/12° C
rel. humidity	>95%	85-90%	70%
light	light	slight shade	strong light
flowers	—	spring and summer	—
growth hormone	1-napthalenacetic 0.1%	—	

Medinilla magnifica

Medinilla magnifica
Magnifica means 'large, splendid, very beautiful'.
This is a very apt name for this brilliant plant with its large, dark-green leaves and its luxuriant bunches of pink flower buds, which burst open by turns and flower a very long time.

Microcoelum weddelianum

Microcoelum weddelianum (Cocos or Syagrus)

This splendid, indoor Palm, with its distinctive ornamental growth, comes from tropical eastern Brazil. It is named after the 19th-century botanist H.A. Wedel, who travelled in Peru, Bolivia and Brazil, among other countries.

Expensive indoor Palm

The Palm family has about 250 genera with some 3,500 species. The distinctive features of these plants are the unbranched stem, columnar growth and, at the top, a crown or rosette of feather or fan shaped leaves. Most Palms are typical tropical or sub-tropical plants. In Europe there is a single species which grows in the Mediterranean region. Microcoelum is an ideal Palm for keeping indoors because it remains very small and tolerates very high heat levels in the winter. The danger of dead leaf patches caused by excessively moist potting soil and excessively low relative humidity must be guarded against, but provided the plant is treated properly it can develop into a splendid ornamental plant with a somewhat limited life. Microcoelum comes from the Greek words, *mikros* for 'small' and *koilos* for 'arched'. In the wild the Palm remains small and the leaves overhang like an arch. The Palm is a native of tropical eastern Brazil and was cultivated in Belgium in 1858. Belgium has ever since remained a cradle of Palm growing.

Sowing

Like all palms, Microcoelum is propagated from seeds. The seed, which germinates irregularly, can be bought in mid-winter. Soak it for 36 hours in lukewarm water, and then sow it out in small fibre pots which can be placed as a single unit in another pot. (Commercial growers use this method, the so-called multi-pot plate). The seeds germinate in a mixture of equal parts of peat dust and river sand.

When the seedlings have one, fair-sized seed leaf, place them, pot and all, into a special, deeper than normal, 3½-in/8-cm pot. The growing time from seed to Palm is about a year. Three plantlets may also be planted together in one large pot. A 'clump' of three little Palms is then obtained from a single pot.

Not too much water

The most serious problem with this Palm arises from its sensitivity to excessive water. It should therefore be grown in a highly porous mixture. A fibrous RHP potting soil is excellent.

During the growing season, keep the Palm moderately moist and feed it weekly. The Palm takes a rest in the winter, when feeding should cease; keep the soil very dry in order to prevent root rot. The roots of the plant are very sensitive to an excess of water.

Place the Palm in slight shade, never in direct sunlight. Repot it annually.

Treatment table

	sowing	growth	rest
pot	frame	3 in/8 cm	—
soil	peat dust and sand 1:1	fibrous RHP	—
feeding	—	1½ tsp compound fertilizer per pt water/3g per litre	none .
watering	moist	moderate	dry
temperature	86° F/30° C	72-77° F/ 22-25°C	60° F/15° C
rel. humidity	95%	90%	60-70%
light	light	slight shade	light

special features Soak seeds for 36 hours in water at 86° F/30° C. The maximum temperature in the sun is 95° F/35° C. The winter temperature should be 60-64° F/ 16-18° C

Microlepia

Difficult in the winter

Microlepia is a splendid Fern with decorative, light-green leaves which does excellently in a slightly shaded position in the house in the summer. In the winter, however, it is difficult, because it then needs more light than we are usually able to give it.

The name Microlepia comes from the Greek words, *mikro* and *lepia*, and means 'small-scale'. Small scaly membranes cover its spores.

Microlepia is indigenous to all tropical regions of the world. The Ferns were cultivated in England in 1876.

Spores

Microlepia can be propagated by dividing it in two when repotting, but plants obtained in this way are somewhat poor specimens. Like most Ferns, it is best propagated by means of spores (see page 168 for propagation by spores). Sow these out in sterile, not-too-acid soil. They will germinate there, forming first of all a green mossy layer, the prothallium. Fertilization takes place in this layer. About three months after the sowing, plant pieces of the prothallium out separately. As soon as individual Ferns emerge, prick out bunches of them and plant them in 3-in/7-cm pots. Each pot will now contain individual plantlets. Place the Ferns into a somewhat larger pot at the annual repotting.

Plenty of light in the winter

Microlepia requires a somewhat heavier soil than most Ferns. It grows well in a mixture of three parts RHP potting soil to one part clay.

Place the plant in slight shade during the growing season in the summer. Water it generously then and feed it weekly.

Feed it once a month in the winter months and above all ensure that it has as light a position as possible. This is no difficulty in a greenhouse or hothouse.

Keep the potting soil moderately moist during the rest period. Repot Microlepia annually in the spring, before the plant has started growing.

Microlepia speluncae

Microlepia speluncae
Although this magnificent Fern grows in the wild in fairly dark places — *spelunca* means 'cave' — it must nevertheless be grown in as light a position as possible in the winter.

Treatment table

	sowing (spores)	growth	rest
pot	frame	3-4 in/8-10 cm	—
soil	frozen peat	RHP and clay 3:1	—
feeding	—	1½ tsp compound fertilizer per pt water/3 g per litre	1½ tsp compound fertilizer per pt water/ 3 g per litre
watering	moist	generously	moderately
temperature	68° F/20° C	64-68° F/ 18-20° C	>60° F/ 15° C
rel. humidity	90%	80%	80%
light	light	slight shade	strong
special features	Feed once a month in autumn and winter. The maximum summer temperature should be 77° F/25° C, with a relative humidity of 80%. The final pot should be 5 in/12-13 cm.		

Mikania ternata

Many relatives

Although Mikania has been known as a houseplant for a very long time, it has only recently become popular.

With its typical leaf shape, its hanging tendrils and purplish-haired leaves, it makes a decorative foliage plant in a box and does particularly well in combination with other plants.

Mikania is named after the 18th-century Czech professor, Joseph Gottfried Mikan.

In 1766 Mikan drew up a list of all the plants which were known at that time; he also made a list of 1,700 errors which Wildenow had made in his edition of the *Species Plantarum* by Linnaeus. As a monument to his work, a recently discovered plant, Mikania, was named after him. Mikania is a member of the Compositae family. The genus contains about 120 species, all of which grow in Brazil.

A quick grower

Mikania can be propagated from seed, but in practice, cuttings are always used.

Take an intermediate cutting with two leaves (see page 169 for cuttings). The tip of the tendrils is usually too weak to take a cutting from because it is not fully grown. Treat the cuttings with growth hormone and place them in peat-based potting compost.

They will root in three weeks, when they should be placed in a 3½-in/8-cm pot. If you want large plants, place four or five plants together in a 4-5 in/10-12 cm pot. They will grow very quickly and produce splendid tendrils after only three or four weeks.

Excellent indoors

Mikania is an ornamental plant which performs exceptionally well indoors. It makes no special demands as regards potting soil. It does well in normal RHP potting soil. Keep the potting soil moderately moist the whole time. If the soil is too wet, the hairs lose their colour. It must be watered fairly generously, even in the winter. Feed it once every two to three weeks, depending on the size. In the spring and summer feed it every week.

The colours are at their most beautiful if the plant is shielded from excessive sunlight in the spring and summer. It must get as much light as possible in the autumn and winter. If the lower ends of the tendrils become bare, cut the tendrils right back; the old plant will produce further growth of its own accord.

Repot the plant annually in mid-spring.

Mikania ternata

Mikania ternata (Mikania apifolia)
This ornamental foliage plant, which usually does exceptionally well in the house, has leaves resembling those of celery (*apium*). They are ternate (*ternatus*) and set in whorls of three. The leaves have purplish hairs.

Treatment table

	cutting	growth	rest
pot	frame	3-4½ in/8-11 cm	—
soil	peat-based potting compost	RHP	—
feeding	—	1 tsp compound fertilizer per pt water/2g per litre	1 tsp compound fertilizer per pt water/2g perlitre
watering	moist	moderately	moderately
temperature	68° F/20° C	64-68° F/ 18-20° C	64-68° F/ 18-20° C
rel. humidity	80-90%	60-70%	60%
light	light	light	strong light
growth hormone	1-naphthalena-cetic acid 0.1%	—	—

special features Shield against excessive sunlight.

Monstera/Swiss cheese plant

Strangely shaped leaf

Monstera means 'strange phenomenon' in Latin and the plant certainly deserves this description. When immature, the leaves are cordate, without indentations or slashes. Later, leaves with indentations and a single slash arise. A mature Monstera has leaves with deep indentations and very many gaps. These are the most beautifully shaped leaves. The plant may also flower at this stage, with a spadix about 4 in/10 cm in size and a light-yellow bract.

The plant is incorrectly called Philodendron pertusum. Monstera is a member of the family Araceae.

It is a native of Central America and was cultivated in Germany in 1848.

Sowing, cuttings or ringing

Monstera seed is normally available at the seed merchant's. Sow in a humus-rich mixture. Place the seeds 3/4 in/2 cm apart under double glass. After three months prick out the young plantlets individually, and after another three months plant them in a 4-5-in/10-12-cm final pot. Support the young plants with a stick; they can become fairly large plants after only a year.

Monstera is also easy to take cuttings from. Take intermediate or eye cuttings in late autumn or early winter and place them under double glass or plastic foil (see page169 for cuttings). Place the cuttings in a 4-in/10-cm pot filled with peat-based potting compost. They will root after a few weeks. A month after taking cuttings plant them in a 5-in/12-13-cm final pot, where the young plant will grow out of the leaf axil in roughly the same manner as a seedling.

If you want to grow the plant with mature leaves and gaps, it must be ringed (see page170 for ringing). Make a wound in the stem, wrap it round with porous peat moss and then cover it with plastic. Roots will grow in the wound providing that the area is kept moist. When there are sufficient roots, cut off the new plant section and pot it up in the final pot. The old plant will make new growth again.

Feed frequently

Monstera requires frequent feeding, particularly when it is growing well. A weekly feed is the minimum requirement. Grow the plant in an airy, fibrous, humus-rich soil. Keep the soil moist at all times; water slightly less frequently in a cold period.

The plant requires a shady position. The leaves fade or scorch if there is too much light.

Monstera is a sturdy houseplant with good powers of adaptation. If you treat it well, you will get a very large climber with stems 3 ft/1 m long. Old plants which are in good condition flower frequently. Their stems must be staked. Keep the numerous aerial roots intact; they are an integral part of the plant and in larger areas, for example, create the illusion of a tropical primaeval forest.

Monstera deliciosa

Monstera deliciosa

This is the well-known Swiss cheese plant, whose ripe fruits have a delicious (*deliciosa*) taste.

Monstera deliciosa 'Borsigiana'

This is a smaller-leaved variety. The varieties supplied are usually plants at different stages of leaf development; the shape will be preserved by the taking of cuttings.

Monstera deliciosa 'Variegata'

This Monstera with variegated leaves is grown to only a limited extent.

Monstera obliqua 'Leichtlinii'

Obliqua is Latin for 'diagonal'. The leaves of this variety sit diagonally to the stem. The immature form is always seen; the mature Monstera is not cultivated. The leaf is smaller than that of Monstera deliciosa and has a larger number of small slashes.

Monstera pertusa

This is a strongly-growing Monstera species which is always supplied by commercial growers as a climber. *Pertusa* means 'cut open' and refers to the gaps in the leaves. As with the previous example, only the immature form of this species is cultivated.

Treatment table

	cutting	growth	rest
pot	3½ in/ 9 cm	4½-5½ in/ 11-13 cm	—
soil	peat-based potting compost	fibrous humus-rich	— -
feed	—	1½ tsp compound fertilizer per pt water/3g per litre	none
water	moist	moist	moderately
temperature	72-75° F/ 22-24° C	72° F/ 22° C	> 54° F/ 12° C
rel. humidity	95%	80-90%	80-90%
light	light	shade	light

special features   The plant takes a rest only during a cold period. It is capable of growth at all other times.
Older specimens flower regularly. Place large plants in larger pots (up to 8 in/20 cm).

Inflorescence of Monstera deliciosa

Concealed flowerets

Neoregelia is a Bromeliad whose flowerets remain inside the leaf sheath. The inflorescence is virtually the same as its relative, Cryptanthus. This Bromeliad is nevertheless grown for its flower effect. During the flowering period, the innermost leaves of the sheath acquire splendid, mostly bright-red, colours. Neoregelia is named after E.G. von Regel, who lived from 1815 to 1892 and was director of the Botanical Gardens in Petersburg, now Leningrad.

Seed and suckers

When Neoregelia has finished flowering, it continues to grow via the side-shoots. They then form suckers, which, when developed sufficiently, can grow into mature specimens. Plants from which you wish to take suckers are best grown outdoors when they have finished flowering.

Neoregelia seed can also be purchased, and should be sown in a very humus-rich mixture. The seeds are not covered because they need the light to germinate. After six months, thin the seedlings out separately for the first time. After another six months prick them out again 1 1/4 in/3 cm apart. Six months later set them out 2 in/5 cm apart.

Six months after the first pricking out, pot the plants up into a 2-in/5-cm pot for cuttings and six months later place them in a 4½-in/11-cm final pot.

When the plants are two years old and have at least twelve fully-developed leaves and six terminal leaves, they will flower after treatment with growth regulators.

Water in the sheath

Neoregelia requires a very humus-rich and airy potting soil. Special Bromeliad soil can be bought for this.

Keep this soil moderately moist and make sure that there is always water in the leaf sheath. During the growing season, feed weekly with a mixture of one part nitrogen to two parts potassium.

Do not set the plant in direct sunlight, but grow it in as light a position as possible, particularly in the winter. Neoregelia can be brought to flower throughout the year, if it is treated with acetylene or 2-hydrazinoethanol (see growing instructions for Bromeliads). The plants are treated three times at an interval of 10 to 14 days.

After the treatment the temperature must be kept constantly above 68° F/20° C to prevent malformation of the inflorescence.

Treatment table

	sowing	growth
pot	frame	4½ in/11 cm
soil	Bromeliad	Bromeliad
feeding	—	1 tsp compound fertilizer per pt water/2 g per litre
watering	moist	moderately
temperature	77°F/25°C	68-77°F/20-25°C
rel. humidity	80%	75-80%
light	light	light
flowers	—	all year
growth regulator	—	acetylene or 2-hydrazinoethanol
special features	The light requirement is 6,000 mW per yd²/m². The minimum temperature is 68°F/20°C. The leaf sheath must always contain water.	

Neoregelia carolinae 'Tricolor Perfecta'

Neoregelia carolinae 'Tricolor', 'Tricolor Perfecta' and 'Flandria'

These varieties have white stripes along the length of the leaf. They are propagated by suckers. Green-leaved specimens are obtained from seed.

Neoregelia carolinae 'Meyendorffii'

This Bromeliad is named after the Dutch Princess, Carolina Louise, who lived from 1723 to 1763. The variety 'Meyendorffii', with orange-red inflorescence, is very widely grown.

Neoregelia concentrica

Concentrica means 'with parallel rings'. These can be seen on the splendid, violet-coloured, cordate leaves with which the inflorescence is surrounded. This broad-leaved Neoregelia is grown to only a limited extent and is mostly propagated by suckers.

Neoregelia spectabilis

This curiosity has dull-green leaves with grey bands on the underside. The leaf tip is carmine-red in colour.

Neoregelia carolinae 'Meyendorffii'

Neoregelia carolinae 'Marechalii'

Neoregelia carolinae 'Marechalii'

This variety is purple-red and has very narrow leaves.

Nephrolepsis exaltata 'Teddy Junior'

Nephrolepsis exaltata 'Rooseveltii Plumosa'

Nephrolepsis exaltata 'Maassii'

Tropical fern

Nephrolepsis is a Fern, some species of which come from tropical America, and some, Nephrolepsis cordifolia for example, from an area stretching from tropical Asia to New Zealand.

Nephrolepsis is a splendid foliage plant which is much used for ornamental purposes and in floral arrangements. The cut leaves of many varieties retain their beauty for a very long time. Nephrolepsis is a houseplant which demands a particular type of treatment, although at the beginning it gives the appearance of adapting well to less favourable conditions. In particular the requirements for a moist atmosphere and the correct amount of light cause quite a few problems in the house.

Spores and suckers

Like most Ferns, Nephrolepsis must be propagated by means of spores (see page 168). Sow them in a clean, not-too-acid soil, and the so-called prothallium, the fruiting body, will emerge.

Plant out individual pieces of this mossy layer, in which the actual fertilization takes place, and after about three months, when the little Ferns can be distinguished as separate plantlets, pick them and place them in a 3-in/7-cm pot. As soon as they are large enough, pot them on into a 5-6-in/12-15-cm pot.

The varieties of Nephrolepsis exaltata are mostly propagated by means of suckers, though recently also by experimental tissue growing (see page 170 for vitroculture).

If you want to get plenty of good suckers, plant the Ferns in early to mid-summer in a nursery bed in the greenhouse. In late autumn detach the young plants with their roots from the old plant and pot them up in an 3-in/8-cm pot. If a number of them are placed in a single pot, a fine bushy plant will be formed. The following year, for example in early spring, transfer them into a 5-6-in/12-14-cm pot.

Sufficient moisture and feed

Nephrolepsis grows exceptionally well in a humus-rich RHP soil. A good deal of extra fertilizer must also be added during the growing season, at least 3 fl oz of compound fertilizer solution per pt of pot content/100 ml per litre. Water generously during the growing season, when the potting soil must be moist at all times, especially since this Fern is salt-sensitive.

Although, as a forest-dweller, Nephrolepsis certainly needs light, excessive light causes yellowing of the leaf colour; on the other hand, excessive shade stretches the leaves and makes them thin. The fern has a long life if treated well.

It is important for it to have a spacious pot and be given regular feeding.

Nephrolepsis causes no great problems in the greenhouse or hothouse; splendid specimens can be grown there.

Nephrolepsis exaltata 'Teddy Junior'
A well-known, coarse-growing variety with corrugated and crinkly leaves.

Nephrolepsis exaltata 'Rooseveltii Plumosa'
This double-feathered variety makes long leaves, the leaflets of which are deeply indented at the tip.

Nephrolepsis exaltata 'Whitemanii'
This is a compact-growing variety, the leaves of which hang over slightly. All the leaflets are deeply indented.

Nephrolepsis cordifolia 'Plumosa'
This Nephrolepsis species comes from an area stretching from tropical Asia to New Zealand. *Cordifolia* means 'with heart-shaped leaves'.
The leaflets are still slightly feathered at the tip and the leaf colour is slightly darker than that of Nephrolepsis exaltata. The plant has a somewhat frizzy appearance.

Nephrolepsis exaltata
This tall-growing (*exaltata*) Fern comes from the tropical regions of America. The original species is grown to a limited extent by means of spores.

Nephrolepsis exaltata 'Maassii'
This is a compact growing variety with single-feathered, characteristically wavy leaves which is widely grown.

Treatment table

	suckers	growth	rest
pot	3½ in/8 cm	5-6 in/12-15 cm	—
soil	RHP	RHP	—
feeding	—	1½ tsp compound fertilizer per pt water/3 g per litre	—
watering	generously	generously	moist
temperature	68°F/20°C	68-86°F/20-30°C	> 64°F/18°C
rel. humidity	80%	80%	80%
light	light	slight shade	light

special features Add 3 fl oz compound fertilizer solution per pt pot content/100 ml per litre during the growing season.

Magnificent berries throughout the summer

Nertera is sometimes called Coral moss, but like many popular names, it gives an entirely false idea of this magnificent plant, which bears berries from mid-spring to late summer. It is certainly not a moss, despite its dwarf appearance, nor does it have much in common with a coral, apart perhaps from its colour and its shiny, bead-like berries. Nertera comes from the Greek word *nerteros*, which means 'low on the ground'. The name speaks for itself. The plant comes from the southern hemisphere, from Peru, Chile and New Zealand among other countries.

It is one of the most beautiful berry-bearing pot plants, and does very well indoors. With proper care it will produce an enormous number of berries. But you must ensure good pollination and be able to control leaf growth during the flowering period.

Nertera belongs to the family Rubiaceae.

Sowing is difficult

The seed of Nertera can be removed from the berries and sown. But it is rather uncertain whether a fine specimen will result. Plants grown from seed will flower only after two years and they rarely produce as many berries as the new growths which are obtained by division of the plant material. This is done in the spring by cutting pieces from the outside of the plant and scattering them in a frame with a potting soil mixture or, better still, in the nursery bed of a greenhouse.

These pieces form together a dense lump of plant material. About 10 months later, cut the lump into about 2 in/5 cm squares. From mid-autumn to early winter lay these squares on the potting soil of 3-in/8-cm pots.

In late winter give the plants about twice as much room. The first flowers will appear in early spring and must be pollinated two or three times a week. One way of doing this is to draw a piece of net curtain carefully over the flowering plants. After pollination, the plants must be ventilated regularly in order to prevent the new leaf from growing over the berries. The relative humidity must be low during the growing season.

If the plant is grown in a greenhouse, watch out for grey mould, to which Nertera is very sensitive. The plant can be treated regularly against it with a fungicide such as Benlate or dichloric acid.

Sub-irrigation

The plant must remain dry at all times. Water it sparingly therefore by sub-irrigation. In the winter and spring, water sparingly to prevent the plant from forming too many stems and leaves; later, ensure once again that newly formed leaves are not growing over the berries.

Feed the laid-out plant material weekly. After potting, give it a smaller concentration of compound fertilizer, stopping feeding completely from mid-winter until the time when the berries ripen. If the leaf colour becomes slightly yellow and the berries are in colour, an extra feed of 1 tsp lime-fertilizer compound per pt water/2 g per litre may be added. From early spring onwards shield the berries from excessive light, or they will lose their colour.

If you treat the plant well, it will last for years and reward you every year with a rich crop of splendid berries.

Nertera depressa (N. granadensis)

Nertera depressa (N. granadensis)

The Greek generic name indicates that Nertera is a low-growing plant, but *depressa* also means 'pressed down'.

More than one species of this popular Coral moss is grown.

Treatment table

	cutting	growth	rest
pot	frame	3-3½ in/8-9 cm	—
soil	RHP and sand 1:1	RHP and sand 1:1	—
feeding	1 tsp compound fertilizer per pt water/2 g per litre	½ tsp compound fertilizer per pt water/1 g per litre	—
watering	generously	sparingly	sparingly
temperature	60° F/16° C	60° F/16° C	46° F/8° C
rel. humidity	< 60%	< 60%	< 60%
light	little	moderate	strong (no sunlight)
flowers	—	all year	—
fungicide	—	Benlate or dichloric acid	—
special features	Ensure always that the leaves do not grow over the flowers and berries. Without fungicide there is a risk of grey mould (*botrytis*). Add water by sub-irrigation. Fine-grained clay or synthetic granules may be used instead of sand. Stop feeding from late winter until the berries ripen. If the berries are red and the leaves yellow, add extra feed of 1 tsp of lime-fertilizer compound per pt water/2 g per litre.		

Neoregelia photographed in the wild in Brazil

Nidularium billbergioides 'Citrinum' (Nidularium citrinum)

This Nidularium species flowers with a yellow inflorescence.
It looks like a Guzmania minor, but, like almost all Nidularium species, the leaf edges of this plant are serrated.

Nidularium fulgens (Nidularium pictum)

Fulgens means 'brilliant' and *pictum* means 'painted'. This brilliant Bromeliad has light-green dentate leaves with darker spots and a red inflorescence.

Nidularium innocentii

This is a coarse-growing species with darker, somewhat bronze-coloured leaves and an orange inflorescence.

Nidularium innocentii

Concealed flowerets

Nidularium is one of the plants whose generic name comes, not from Greek, but from Latin. The Latin word *nidulus* means 'little nest', and refers to the flowers of this Bromeliad, which stand like a nest of coloured bracts on a short stem. This Bromeliad is grown for its inflorescence: during the flowering the bracts acquire splendid colours. Nidularium plants sometimes strongly resemble Neoregelias. They can be recognized by the serrated edges of their leaves and the stalked inflorescence, the latter being one of the distinguishing characteristics between Nidularium and Neoregelia. Nidularium grows in the wild in humus-rich soil in tropical eastern Brazil.

Propagate from seed

Although Nidularium, like all Bromeliads, produces suckers after flowering, and these provide the easiest way of propagating the plant, commercial growers propagate it from seed.

If you want to get plenty of suckers, the plant must be planted in a greenhouse. The suckers will then have enough space to make the good growth which will produce handsome plants later.

Scatter Nidularium seed on a very humus-rich mixture. Do not cover because the seeds germinate under the effect of light. After six months, set the little plants out individually and repeat this after another half-year. They should then stand at a distance of about 2 in/5 cm apart.

When they are large enough, place them in a 2-in/5-cm pot and after six months in a 5-in/12-cm final pot. They may flower at this stage, in which case, so long as the plant is two years old and has at least twelve fully-developed leaves and six bracts, they must be treated with growth regulators (see Bromeliads).

Flowering is not limited to one season

Nidularium can be brought to flower the whole year by treating it with growth regulators. Treat the plants three times with acetylene or BOH at an interval of 10 to 14 days. After the treatment, keep the temperature at 68° F/20° C as far as possible, or malformation of the inflorescence may occur. Like all Bromeliads, Nidularium requires a very humus-rich, airy potting soil. A special mixture for Bromeliads can be bought for this. Keep the soil moderately moist and ensure that there is always a certain amount of water in the leaf sheath, from which most Bromeliads obtain their moisture. Feed them weekly during the growing season, preferably with a compound fertilizer solution in the proportions 10:5:20. Large specimens should be given about 1½ fl oz of this solution per pt pot capacity/100 ml per litre. Nidularium cannot tolerate direct sunlight and should be placed in a slightly shaded position in the spring and summer. Grow it in as light a position as possible in winter.

Treatment table

	cutting	growth
pot	frame	5 in/12 cm
soil	Bromeliad	Bromeliad
feeding	—	1 tsp compound fertilizer per pt water/2 g per litre
watering	moist	moderately
temperature	77° F/25° C	68-77° F/20-25° C
rel. humidity	80%	75-80%
light	light	light
flowers	—	all year
growth regulator	—	acetylene or 2-hydrozinoethanol

special features   The leaf sheath must always contain water.
The light requirement is 6,000 mW per yd²/m².
The minimum temperature is 68° F/20° C.
The plant flowers in the spring in the wild.

Odontoglossum

Freakish shapes

Odontoglossum is a magnificent Orchid, all species of which can last for years as houseplants. The name comes from the Greek words *odous* ('tooth') and *glossa* ('tongue'). The beautiful, freakishly shaped and coloured flowers have one or more teeth on the tongue (called 'lip' in the case of orchids). The plant comes from tropical America and grows in high, mountainous regions. It grows there epiphytically, ie on trees or tree trunks. This must be taken fully into account when growing it, particularly as regards the potting soil.

Risk of roots being removed

In the countries where Odontoglossum is native, the plant is not protected. Odontoglossum grows sympodially, ie with a rootstock which grows at the front and dies from the rear. If you want to propagate the plant, remove the pseudobulbs without leaves from the rear end and place them on a medium with a relative humidity of 95%. The dormant buds can then form a new plant.

Special soil mixture

Commercial growers nurture Odontoglossum in a cold greenhouse and provide it with lots of air. The plant is also easy to keep indoors, but the temperature must not be too high and a light, though sun-free, position must be provided. A large, north-facing window is ideal.

The plant requires a so-called epiphytic mixture, for example, equal parts of fir-bark and coarse-fibred peat litter, to every 20 pt/10 l of which should be added 60-r—7/8 tsp/g growth hormone; 2½ tsp/g general purpose fertilizer and ¼ tsp/g iron chelate sequestrene. The soil must not become too acid. A pH of 5.8 is ideal; whenever it falls below 5.5, additional lime must be added to the mixture (see page 168 for acid levels).

Grow the plant in shallow pots filled to a third with potsherds. During the growing season feed every 10 days in the summer and once every 15 to 20 days in the winter.

Keep the soil mixture moderately moist at all times. The plant can flower with more than one peduncle. The plant must be repotted every two years directly after flowering. Odontoglossum does not have a real rest period.

Treatment table

pot	4-5 in/10-12 cm
soil	fir-bark and coarse-fibred peat litter 1:1 (see text)
feeding	½ tsp compound fertilizer per pt water/1 g per litre
watering	moist
temperature	60° F/15° C
rel. humidity	60-70%
light	strong
special features	The pH must remain above 5.5. Feed every 10 days in the summer and every 15-20 days in the winter. Shield from direct sunlight. The temperature after flowering should be 50-54° F/10-12° C.

Odontoglossum grande

Odontoglossum grande

This beautiful Orchid, with large yellow flowers with a freakish red-brown decoration, flowers in the autumn. It comes from Guatemala.

Odontoglossum schlieperianum

This plant flowers in the summer. It comes originally from Costa Rica. Its colour is similar to that of the previous species, but the flowers have a slightly different structure.

Odontoglossum insleayii

Odontoglossum insleayii

This beautiful orchid flowers in the winter. It comes from Mexico. The colours of this plant are also like those of Odontoglossum grande, but the flowers are somewhat smaller.

Pachystachys lutea

Pachystachys lutea
This beautiful plant with yellow, scaly inflorescences is also called Pachystachys lutea 'Albiflora', because of the white flowers that appear in the inflorescence. But this addition to the name is incorrect and superfluous.

Summer flowerer
Pachystachys is a durable houseplant. The name comes from the Greek words, *pachus* for thick and *stachus* for 'spike'. Its beautiful yellow inflorescences are indeed thick compared with its relatives, Beloperone and Aphelandra, which it otherwise resembles very closely. The family is named after Acanthus, a plant with a characteristic leaf shape that grows in Mediterranean countries. In antiquity, an Acanthus leaf was often used as a motif in architecture. The Pachystachys which we know as a houseplant comes from the Nile region of central Sudan.

Cuttings from mother plants
Commercial growers propagate Pachystachys by cuttings taken from so-called mother plants, which are plants grown specially for cuttings and which may not, therefore, flower. They keep these mother plants on a short day, during which time the plant grows vegetatively, ie the stems and leaves grow, but the plant sets no flowers. With a long day, the shoots immediately form flowers and cannot therefore be used as cuttings.

If you want to take cuttings yourself, either do this in the winter months, or darken the plant (short-day treatment) so that you get stems without flowers. Take a head cutting with three leaf pairs or an intermediate cutting with one leaf pair (see page 169 for cuttings). The axillary buds develop irregularly. Place three cuttings in a 4-5-in/10-12-cm pot filled with frozen peat potting soil and they will form roots in three weeks. Two weeks later, remove the tops so that two leaf pairs per stem are left. When the new shoots are 2 in/5 cm long, spray them with inhibitor or growth will be straggly. Repeat the spraying two or three times at intervals of 10 to 14 days. Pachystachys is a quick grower; in the spring the growing time from cutting to flowering is 14 or 15 weeks, in summer 10 or 12 weeks.

Plenty of light
A slight problem with a Pachystachys in the house may be providing it with sufficient light, while at the same time protecting it from strong sunlight. It requires a long day in order to flower.

The plant makes no special demands as regards potting soil. It does exceptionally well in normal RHP potting soil. During the growing season keep this soil fairly moist, reducing watering somewhat thereafter. Feed the plant weekly and repot it annually.

Treatment table

	cutting	growth	rest
pot	4-5 in/10-12 cm	4-5 in/10-12 cm	—
soil	frozen peat	RHP	—
feed	—	1 tsp compound fertilizer per pt water/2 g per litre	1 tsp compound fertilizer per pt water/2 g per litre
water	moist	moist	moderately
temperature	75°F/24°C (soil)	64-72°F/ 18-22°C	64°F/18°C
rel. humidity	90-95%	80%	80%
light	light	light	light
flowers	—	spring to mid-autumn	—
inhibitor	—	Cycocel ½ fl oz and wetter per pt water/5 ml per litre	—

special features   Inhibit 2 or 3 times every 10 to 14 days.
Vegetative growth occurs over short day

Paphiopedilum/Venus' slipper

Goddess of beauty

Paphos, a town on the west coast of Cyprus, was famous in antiquity as a place where Aphrodite, the Greek goddess of beauty and love, was worshipped. The Roman name for this goddess was Venus. *Pedilon* means 'slipper' in Greek. The popular name for this very beautiful Orchid, Venus' Slipper, is thus an exact translation of the botanical name. It is a splendid flower and its shape is that of a shoe.

Venus' Slipper is native to the mountains and humid forests of eastern Asia. The species are all wild.

No propagation

It is a great pity that many plants, including many Orchids, are being removed from their natural habitat. They are imported as mature plants from their natural growing areas, with the risk that the plants are removed without roots.

Warm and moist

The plant is at home on mountains and in forests and must be kept warm and very humid as a houseplant. It must always have a moist soil and the water used must be of the very best quality. Rainwater at room temperature is the best, since Orchids are extremely salt-sensitive. Paphiopedilum requires a terrestrial mixture, ie a coarse-fibred peat litter substrate, as potting soil.

The soil must never be too acid: when the pH falls below 5.5, extra lime must be added to the mixture (see page 168 for acidity level). During the growth period, feed every 10 days, in the winter every 15 to 20 days. In summer grow the plants in a shaded spot; in the winter they must have as much light as possible. Paphiopedilum flowers once per shoot. After the flowering there will appear, depending on the growing power, one or more new shoots which will flower the following year.

The plant grows best in the greenhouse or hothouse, where the temperature and relative humidity can be kept high.

Before the mixture is excessively digested, thus depriving the thick fibrous roots of air, repot the plant. This must take place every two years.

Although Paphiopedilum is grown mainly for its flowers, its beautifully-speckled leaves also have decorative value.

Treatment table

pot	3-3½ in/8-9 cm
soil	terrestrial mixture (see text)
feeding	½ tsp compound fertilizer per pt water/1 g per litre
watering	moist
temperature	64-68° F/18-20° C
rel. humidity	> 90%
light	shade
flowers	summer
special features	Keep the soil of young plants without roots moderately moist. Give the plants full light in the winter. The maximum temperature in the sun is 75° F/ 24° C. The pH must remain above 5.5. Feed every 10 days in the summer and every 15 to 20 days in the winter.

Paphiopedilum hybrid

Paphiopedilum sukhakulii

This orchid comes from an area stretching from Thailand to Cambodia and often grows alongside the two species listed below. It grows in shady forests, usually on the banks of streams, to a height of 3,300 ft/1,000 m. This species was only discovered in 1965 by the collector-exporter, Von Sukhakul. In addition to three species pictured here, which are relatively inexpensive to buy, there are many other species and hybrids which are grown as houseplants.

Paphiopedilum barbatum

This widely-grown pot plant comes from Malacca and requires a great deal of heat.

Paphiopedilum callosum

Paphiopedilum callosum

This beautiful Orchid, which comes from the rain-forests of south-east Asia, was found in 1885 in Thailand. It grows there between rocks to a height of 2,500 ft/750 m.

Passiflora caerulea

Passiflora caerulea

Passiflora racemosa
This is a typical greenhouse plant which flowers profusely outside with bunches of red (*racemosa*) flowers.

Passiflora caerulea
This is the most widely grown of the 400 species of passion flower which are suitable as pot plants. It has dark-blue flowers (*caerulea* means 'blue').
This plant can also be grown outside, in a shaded position, as a profusely flowering climbing shrub.

Passiflora quadrangularis
This plant, with its square (*quadrangularis*) stems, may also be a greenhouse climber. There it will flower profusely, but it will not bear fruit. The fruits are edible.

Passiflora caerulea 'Constance Elliot'
This is a distinctive variety, the flowers of which are white tinted with blue. There are many references in the literature to hybrids and crosses between Passiflora alata and Passiflora racemosa; in practice, Passiflora caerulea is almost the only one grown as a houseplant.

Flower with a story
Passiflora is the Latin for 'passion flower'. With a little bit of imagination, the parts of the flower can be linked with the life of Jesus, as described in the Bible. There are various versions of the same explanation, which runs as follows:
The three styles with thick stigmas are the nails with which Jesus was nailed to the cross. The ovary is the sponge dipped in vinegar. The five stamina are the five wounds and the style is the centre pole of the crucifix. The corona, which is spotted with red in some species, is the blood-stained thorn of crowns and the 10 sepals and petals the 10 disciples who remained after Judas and Peter. The fruit of two species (Passiflora edulis and Passiflora quadrangularis) is edible. The plant is native to South America.

Cuttings in winter
Propagate Passiflora by taking cuttings from autumn to early spring. Take an intermediate cutting with one or two leaves from mature long tendrils. Treat them with growth hormone and place them in 2-in/5-cm pots filled with three parts peat-based potting compost and one part river sand. Place under double glass or plastic sheeting (see page 169 for cuttings).
The cuttings will have very elementary roots in about a month. Keep them resting in winter at a low temperature and in mid-winter repot them, placing one or two in a 4-5-in/10-12-cm final pot. Then raise the temperature and keep the soil moist. The quick-growing tendrils will flower in the summer. Plants which are late will not flower until the following spring. They must overwinter in a cool, dry place and should be given warmth and moisture again in early spring.

Plenty of light
In order to get a good bud formation, the flower needs lots of light, but shield it against direct sunlight.
The plant grows best in three parts RHP soil and one part river sand. During the growing season, keep the soil only moderately moist; the soil must always be on the dry side. Feed the plant weekly during this period. Stop feeding and water sparingly during the rest period. Passiflora can flower from mid-spring to late summer. Plants which flower early have had a good winter rest. Low night temperatures with strong sunlight are prime requirements for bud formation in the spring.
Sometimes the flower is fertilized, and if so it grows into a bright orange fruit the size of a plum. The seeds of the fruit can be sown. The seedlings grow quickly, but usually flower later and only to a moderate extent.
Passiflora is a genuine summer flowerer which requires plenty of light. Many rooms are too dark for it to flower. Repot the plant in early spring and remove the superfluous tendrils as soon as they have finished flowering. The plant can also be grown outside in a shaded sunny spot.

Treatment table

	cutting	growth	rest
pot	4-5 in/10-12 cm	4-5 in/10-12 cm	—
soil	peat-based potting compost and sand 3:1	RHP and sand 3:1	—
feeding	—	1 tsp compound fertilizer per pt water/2 g per litre	none
watering	—	moderately	sparingly
temperature	64-68° F/ 18-20° C	64-68° F/ 18-20° C	40-50° F/ 5-10° C
rel. humidity	80-90%	60-70%	60-70%
light	light	light	light
flowers	—	summer	—

Smell and colour

Pelargonium is a very popular houseplant which is popularly called Geranium. Both names are of Greek origin. *Pelargos* means 'stork' and *geranos* 'crane'. The long beaks of the birds are responsible for the names. The fruits of all geranium-type plants, Geraniaceae, have a long beak shape. Many Pelargoniums, the Lemon Geranium and the Peppermint Geranium, for example, are grown specifically for their smell. These species have small, pale-lilac flowers with purple decoration. Other species have splendid, large flowers with brilliant colours.

There are hundreds of different varieties, many of them grown specially for the garden. Almost all Pelargoniums are natives of South Africa, but they have been grown as garden or houseplants in Europe for a very long time.

Varieties for profuse flowering

A number of crosses of different varieties of Pelargonium zonale hybrids, the so-called F1 hybrids, are propagated by commercial growers from seed. The seed, however, is fairly expensive and most pelargoniums can be propagated from cuttings. Care must be taken to see that the plants from which cuttings are taken are not infected with a virus disease. Such specimens grow and flower less; they also flower later.

Take a shoot cutting about 4 in/10 cm long or an eye cutting from mid-summer to mid-autumn (see page 169 for cuttings). Do not take the cutting with a knife, but break it off, in order to prevent virus infection. Cuttings taken in the autumn should be treated with growth hormone. Let the cutting wound dry out in a cool place first and then place the cuttings in small pots filled with equal parts of peat-based potting compost and river sand. It is best to place the cuttings under mist or under a newspaper, never under double glass or plastic sheeting, which will turn the leaves yellow and make the cuttings rot.

Treatment table

	cutting	growth	rest
pot	2 in/5 cm	4-5 in/10-12 cm	—
soil	peat-based potting compost and sand 1:1	RHP and clay	—
feeding	—	1 tsp compound fertilizer per pt water/2 g per litre	1 tsp compound fertilizer per pt water 2 g per litre
watering	moist	moist	very dry
temperature	68° F/20° C	60° F/ 15-16° C	46-50° F/ 8-10° C
rel. humidity	80-90%	60-70%	60-70%
light	light	sunlight	light
flowers	—	mid-spring to mid-autumn	—
growth inhibitor	—	1/12-1/6 fl oz CycLocel or CCC per pt water/ 5-10 ml per litre and 1/30 fl oz/2 ml wetter	—
special features	Add no feed during the first 5 to 6 weeks after potting, thereafter 1-1½ tsp per pt water/2-3 g per litre during growth. The temperature may rise to an unlimited level in the sun. Pelargonium Grandiflorum hybrids require a different treatment (see text).		

Pelargonium zonale hybrid 'Rubin'

Pelargonium Zonale hybrids

These are crosses of Pelargonium zonale, Pelargonium inquinans and other species. They were first cultivated in 1740. The dwarf varieties are grown as houseplants. Some good varieties are 'Rubin', twin-flowering red, and 'Stadt Bern', dark-leaved and single-flowering red. The following varieties in particular are dwarf: 'Black Vesuvius', dark-leaved, single-fowering orange-red, and 'Dick's Blanchette', twin-flowering white.

The varieties grown from seed are kept compact by the use of growth inhibitors, by spraying during vegetative growth with a solution of 1/20 fl oz Cyclocel or CCC per pt water/3 ml per litre, after the addition of a wetting agent. Spraying must be stopped when the bud appears. Varieties with beautiful leaf colours, such as the silver-variegated, gold-variegated and triple-tone, flower less profusely and are seen to a limited extent only. For planting in gardens, single-flowering F1 varieties are grown mainly from seed.

P. Grandiflorum hybrid 'White Swan'

Pelargonium radens

This is one of the Geranium species which is grown for the smell of its leaves. Other species and varieties are: Pelargonium radens 'Variegatum' (Lemon Geranium), Pelargonium graveolens and Pelargonium graveolens 'Variegatum' (Peppermint Geranium), Pelargonium crispum 'Variegatum', a species with small crossed leaf, and Pelargonium betulinum, which has dark leaves and an aromatic smell.

Pelargonium peltatum hybrid 'Luisenhof'

Pelargonium Peltatum hybrids
These are hanging plants, for a garden or terrace, and are not suitable as houseplants. The only variety seen as a houseplant is 'Elegance', which has beautiful silver-variegated leaves with a purple glow, but which flowers very inconspicuously.

Pelargonium hybrid 'Catford Bell'

Pelargonium Grandiflorum hybrids
These are the so-called French Geraniums. The variety pictured here is a cross of the South African species, Pelargonium grandiflorum, Pelargonium cordatum, Pelargonium angulosum and Pelargonium cucculatum. The first crossings were made in England in about 1800, but afterwards much improvement work was done in France; hence the name, French Geranium.
The most widely grown varieties are 'Nelly', light-pink with red spotting in the heart, 'Grand Slam', orange-red, 'Lavender Grand Slam', dark lilac-coloured, and 'White Swan', white with a red spot in the heart of the flower.
The French Geraniums have a somewhat individual method of cultivation. The required winter temperature is 50-54°

Pelargonium grandiflorum hybrid 'Lavender Grand Slam'

F/10-12° C and in the spring they must be shielded from direct sunlight. They flower only in the spring, though flowering can be advanced by giving them a four-week short-day treatment or a cold regime at 46-54° F/8-12° C in the winter. Afterwards, advance the plants by lighting them for eight hours a night with lamps (15-20 Watt) or with TL 33 (5-7 W per yd²/m²). The temperature should then be 50° F/10° C. If lighting is started in mid-winter flowering plants can be had before the arrival of spring. The plants do not flower during the long day in the summer. Commercial growers usually supply the plants in the early spring.

In the greenhouse, cover the cuttings with paper and keep them fresh by regular spraying. In two to three weeks, the cuttings will have formed scar tissue, at which point they should be potted off into a 3-in/7-cm pot and kept very dry. The plants can be topped heavily from mid-winter onwards and tops used as cuttings. Place the plants into a 4-5-in/10-12-cm final pot from late winter onwards.

Plenty of light and moderately moist
Grow a Pelargonium in as light a position as possible, preferably in direct sunlight. Only the French Geranium should be shielded from the full glare of the sun in the spring. During the growing season, keep the potting soil moderately moist; in the winter keep it fairly dry. Pelargoniums grow best in a consistent RHP potting soil mixed with clay. Five weeks after repotting, give Pelargonium a weekly or two-weekly feed. The plants can be sprayed with inhibitor once every two weeks for compact growth and advanced flowering. Do this for as long as necessary. Pelargoniums are rewarding houseplants which can grow very large. Older plants can be rejuvenated by cutting back in the early spring.

Pellaea

A fern with round leaves

Pellaea is the Greek for 'dark in colour'. These beautiful broad-growing Ferns have round, dark bronze-green leaves. The most widely-grown species comes from New Zealand, where it grows in a cool climate on rocks. It is very suitable for a cold greenhouse.

Propagation by spores

Like most species of Ferns, Pellaea is propagated by spores. Sow these out in a clean, not-too-acid soil; otherwise they will not germinate. When the spores have germinated they form a mossy-green layer, the so-called prothallium, where the actual fertilization takes place. After about three months, plant out the pieces of this prothallium separately and, when clearly distinguishable Fern plantlets emerge after another three months, prick them out separately again. Three months later, place them in a 3-in/7-cm pot. In another six months you will have handsome Ferns.

Cold and dry

Pellaea grows in nature in a rocky area at temperatures of 41-54° F/5-12° C. A moderately moist potting soil is fairly easy to provide in a house, but the low temperature may create a few problems. Fortunately, the plant will tolerate higher temperatures fairly well, but although as a houseplant it does not require an excessively cool position, summer temperatures above 68° F/20° C are not ideal for growth. Pellaea grows exceptionally well in a normal RHP potting soil. Feed it weekly during the growing season. In the dark winter months, reduce the feed to once a month. Pellaea is best grown in a slightly shaded position, but it can tolerate a somewhat darker position.

Pellaea is a durable houseplant and, so long as you do not give it too much warmth and set a good relative humidity, it can last a long time and become very broad. Repot the fern annually into a slightly larger pot.

Treatment table

	cutting	growth	rest
pot	frame	3 in/7 cm and larger	—
soil	see spores (page 169)	RHP	—
feeding	—	1 tsp compound fertilizer per pt water/2 g per litre	1 tsp compound fertilizer per pt water/ 2 g per litre
temperature	68° F/ 20° C	54-60° F/ 12-15° C	41-54° F/ 5-12° C
rel. humidity	90%	70-80%	70-80%
light	light	slight shade	light
special features	The maximum summer temperature is 68° F/20° C. Repot annually into a slightly larger pot size.		

Pellaea rotundifolia

Pellaea rotundifolia
This beautiful Fern with round leaves (*rotundifolia*) comes from New Zealand. It is a plant for a cold greenhouse.

Pellaea viridis

Pellaea viridis (*syn.* Pellaea hastata)
This Fern, which comes from South Africa and Madagascar, is grown to only a limited extent.

Gloriosa

Peperomia

Pepper family

The name Peperomia comes from the Greek words, *peperi* for 'pepper' and *homoios* for 'similar'. Most Peperomia species, however, do not at all resemble the pepper bush (Piper nigrum), which can grown to a height of 6½ ft/2m. Both species, nevertheless, belong to the pepper family, Piperaceae.

Peperomia is a genus with many species, all of which are natives of sub-tropical and tropical South America. Most Peperomia species are grown as foliage plants, since their greenish inflorescences have little decorative value. There are, however, some species, such as Peperomia resedaeflora, with splendid, long, white inflorescences.

Leaf and stem cuttings

Most Peperomias are propagated by taking whole leaf cuttings, though certain species, such as Peperomia argyraea, Peperomia rugosa and Peperomia verschaffeltii, can also be propagated by taking leaf cuttings, as with a leaf Begonia. The species with longer stems are propagated by shoot or head cuttings (see page 169 for cuttings) and also by intermediate cuttings. Place them in two parts peat-based potting compost to one part river sand or perlite. Place the shoot and intermediate cuttings immediately in a 3-4-in/8-10-cm final pot. It is important that the soil in the pot should not be too wet. When the leaf cuttings have roots, prick them out individually once before potting, which can be left until later.

Moderately moist, highly porous soil

Peperomias sometimes grow in nature epiphytically on trees or tree trunks, but more usually on the ground in humus-rich soil. The best potting soil to use is a mixture of two parts RHP potting soil to one part river sand or perlite; it is highly porous and prevents the accumulation of excess water.

During the summer months, when there is plenty of light, the plants must be watered generously, but the soil must never become too wet or the plants will succumb to root rot. Water sparingly in the winter. Feed weekly about once a month after potting up, once every 14 days in the winter.

The plant requires slight shade for good growth, though the variegated varieties and the grey Peperomia incana must get more light for a good leaf colour. The plants will flower with a

Treatment table

	cutting	growth	rest
pot	3-3½ in/8-9 cm	3-3½ in/8-9 cm	—
soil	peat-based potting compost and sand or perlite 2:1	RHP and sand or perlite 2:1	—
feeding	—	1 tsp compound fertilizer per pt water/ 2 g per litre	1 tsp compound fertilizer per pt water/ 2 g per litre
watering	not wet	not wet	sparingly
temperature	70° F/ 21° C	60-77° F/ 15-25° C	60-77° F 15-25° C
rel. humidity	< 70%	< 70%	< 70%
light	slight shade	slight shade	light
flowers	—	day length > 12 hours	—
special features	Give variegated varieties more light. Flowering plants require a relative humidity of 60%.		

Peperomia resedaeflora

Peperomia resedaeflora

This species, which comes from Colombia, is grown for its flowers, whose pleasant scent, as the name implies, is reminiscent of Reseda. It can flower profusely with 3-4-in/8-10-cm-long white inflorescences on stems about 6 in/15 cm long. It is propagated by leaf cuttings.

Peperoma obtusfolia 'Variegata'

Peperomia obtusifolia (Peperomia tithymaloides)

This Peperomia comes from tropical South America. A sturdy species, it contains the varieties 'Variegata (USA)' with a highly distinctive yellow-and-green leaf colour and 'Green Gold', with a marbled pattern. *Obtusifolia* means 'with stumpy leaf'. If the plant gets too little light, the green colour of the leaves is accentuated.

Propagate the plants by head or intermediate cuttings.

Peperomia caperata

day-length of 12 hours. Flowering can be advanced by shortening the day-length in the summer. Flowering plants must have a low relative humidity of about 60%; otherwise the inflorescences will rot. Peperomias are herbaceous houseplants which do well in the house because they like a low relative humidity. Peperomia obtusifolia and all variegated varieties of it are particularly sturdy. But you will always have to adapt the conditions to the variety. Peperomia verschaffeltii, for example, requires a higher temperature and relative humidity than the other species. Grow young specimens of the weaker species every year. The stronger species can last for many years. It is important to use a highly porous potting soil and ensure that it is never wet.

Peperomia glabella 'Aureovariegata'

Peperomia glabella

This plant, which comes from Central America, is most commonly seen in its variegated varieties, especially the gold-variegated 'Aureovariegata'. It has long, creeping stems and is usually grown as a hanging plant. The plant is propagated by head or intermediate cuttings. It is a very quick-growing, sturdy species.

Peperomia incana

This species, which comes from Brazil, has thick, fibrous leaves and stems with grey hairs. It is somewhat like a succulent and is one of the sturdier species. It requires plenty of light and grows well at only 64°F/18°C.

Peperomia caperata

This plant is a native of Brazil and was discovered in 1955. It has deeply grooved, bronze-green leaves and delicate white inflorescences. It will flower after a short-day treatment of 10 hours for seven weeks and thereafter a day-length of 12 hours (or the natural day-length, when it is short enough). The plant is sensitive to bud and leaf eelworm (black discoloration of the leaf). Take whole leaf cuttings of the plant.
The variegated variety, 'tricolor', is a poor grower and must be propagated by shoot cuttings; if leaf cuttings are taken, a green plant is obtained.

Peperomia griseoargentea (Peperomia marmorata)

This plant, with delicate, silver-grey leaves, comes from Brazil. Take whole leaf cuttings from it.

Peperomia argyraea (Peperomia sandersii)

This Peperomia has shield-like leaves with a silver-coloured (*argyraea*) pattern. It is a sturdy species which is propagated by leaf cuttings.

Other species

A few other species are also, though not commonly, grown as foliage plants. They include Peperomia verticillatas, Peperomia clussiifolia, Peperomia maculosa, Peperomia puteolata, Peperomia rubella and Peperomia rugosa. They grow just like the other species.

Peperomia verschaffeltii

Peperomia verschaffeltii

This plant, which comes from tropical Brazil, is a weaker species which requires slightly more heat. The leaves are somewhat larger than those of the other species and they have a delicate pattern of silver-white, longitudinal stripes. Propagate this plant by leaf cuttings.

Philodendron

Foliage plants with diferent shapes

Philodendrons are beautiful foliage plants whose powerful growth makes them particularly suitable for planting in spacious surroundings. Certain species, however, are very sturdy and have great powers of adaptation, so that they do exceptionally well indoors. Very many species are grown, with the most varied leaf shapes and growth habits. Some species are climbers and a few have flowers with decorative value. But Philodendrons are foliage plants first and foremost. *Philodendron* comes from the Greek and means 'tree-loving'. Many species climb on trees in their natural habitat and attach themselves to the bark with their aerial roots. Philodendrons belong to the arum family, Araceae. Most of the varieties which we know as houseplants come from tropical South America, though some species grow in tropical Asia.

Their natural environment is rain forest, with temperatures of 68-80° F/20-27° C and an annual rainfall of 55-66 in/1,400-1,660 mm. The dry period there is from July to December, when the temperature drops to 60-64° F/16-18° C.

Sowing and cuttings

Philodendron seeds, imported from the tropics, quickly lose their germinating power and must therefore be sown immediately. Sow them in humus-rich sowing soil ¾ in/2 cm apart and allow the seeds to germinate under double glass or plastic sheeting. After three months prick out the plantlets separately and three months later space them out in threes in a 4-5-in/11-13-cm pot. About a year later you will have quite large plants.

Cuttings can also be taken from the plant. Take a stem cutting with one leaf (eye-cutting) and place it in a 3-in/7-cm pot filled with peat-based potting compost. Place under double glass or plastic sheeting. The cuttings will quickly root; when the growth is sufficient, place the plants in a larger pot, up to 6 in/15 cm, depending on the species.

Place one cutting of the climbing species with large leaves in a 5-in/13-cm pot and support the plant with an 18-in/45-cm bamboo cane. Place the cuttings of small-leaved species in a 3-4-in/7-10-cm pot and support the plant with a 12-in/30-cm bamboo cane. Large-leaved species can also be grown in bigger pots. Place two or three plants in a 9-in/22-cm pot and support them with a moss stick about 32-in/80-cm high. The growing time is one to two years, depending on the desired plant size.

Plenty of light but no sunlight

A Philodendron must never be exposed to the direct rays of the sun, but should nevertheless have plenty of light; otherwise growth is long and straggly. They are also sensitive to temperatures below 64° F/18° C, but this is usually not a problem indoors. They require an airy, humus-rich mixture and constant watering during the growing season. Keep the soil moderately moist in the winter. Add no feed then, but during the growing season feed every week. Care must be taken to give them a sufficiently large pot. They will grow very large and with proper care their lifespan is almost unlimited. More and more varieties are appearing all the time, chiefly from the United States where much improvement work is going on.

Philodendron is an ideal plant for hydroculture (see page 171).

Philodendron elegans

Philodendron sagittifolium 'Ilsemanii'

Philodendron scandens

Philodendron elegans

This climber, which comes from tropical South America, has deeply parted leaves with sickle-shaped curved leaf lobes. It is propagated by cuttings.

Philodendron sagittifolium 'Ilsemanii'

This species has feeble growth and cordate entire leaves and comes from Brazil. The large leaves are green with white marbling, while the arrow-shaped young leaves (*sagittifolium*) are green with a mingled white and pink pattern. The plant is propagated by cuttings.

Philodendron squamiferum

Squamiferum means 'scale-bearing' and refers to the thick, red, curly hairs with which the leaf stalk of this climber is thickly covered. This Philodendron, with five-lobed leaves, comes from tropical South America and is propagated by cuttings.

Philodendron pedatum (Philodendron laciniatum)

This climbing Philodendron also has a five-lobed leaf, but the green leaf stalk is smooth and hairless.
This plant is also propagated by cuttings.

Philodendron scandens

This climber (*scandens*), which comes from the Antilles, is very often grown as a small plant tied to a stick in a pot. It is a small-leaved species with entire edges. It is propagated by cuttings.

Philodendron micans

This entire species, with delicate, dark bronze-green leaves with a velvety sheen, comes from Colombia. It is a climber and is propagated by cuttings. *Micans* means 'shining' or 'gleaming'.

Philodendron melanochrysum

This climber is the juvenile form of Philodendron andeanum, which is a native of Colombia. *Melanochrysum* means 'dark-gold coloured' and refers to the velvety leaves, which are entire and cordate. The mature form has larger, oblong cordate leaves.

Philodendron erubescens

Philodendron erubescens 'Emerald Queen'

Philodendron panduriforme

This climber from Brazil has distinctively shaped leaves; the bottom ones are oblong, the middle ones violin-shaped (*panduriforme*) and the topmost three-lobed to five-lobed. All the leaves are a shining green. Propagation is by cuttings.

Philodendron erubescens 'Josephine'

Philodendron erubescens

This climber comes from Colombia. It is the most widely grown Philodendron. The leaves have a reddish glow (*erubescens*) and the petioles and stem of the plants are also red. As an older plant it may flower profusely with deep red flowers. Frequently grown varieties are 'Red Emerald' and the green-leaved 'Green Emerald'. Many varieties of this species are grown. It is propagated by cuttings.

Philodendron selloum

This non-climbing species has an entire, sinuate leaf-edge. It comes from the tropics of eastern Asia and is named after Fr. Sello. It is propagated from seed.

Philodendron 'Tuxia'

This is a non-climbing hybrid with large, green, cordate leaves. It is quick-growing and is propagated from seed.

Philodendron bipinnatifidum

Bipinnatifidum means 'resembling a double feather'. The indented leaves of this non-climber have this appearance. The plant comes from Brazil and is propagated from seed.

Philodendron martianum

This non-climbing Philodendron, with thick inflated petioles, comes from Brazil. It is propagated from seed and cuttings. The plant is named after Von Martius, a botanist who lived from 1794 to 1868 and who wrote extensively on plants from Brazil.

Philodendron crassinervium

This climber also comes from Brazil. It grows quickly and has long, very narrow leaves with a distinct, thick midrib (*crassinervium*). It is propagated by cuttings.

Treatment table

	sowing	cutting	growth	rest
pot	frame	3-3½ in/ 7-9 cm	4½-5½ in/ 11-13 cm *	—
soil	humus-rich	humus-rich	humus-rich	—
feeding	—	—	1½ tsp compound fertilizer per pt water/ 3 g per litre	none
watering	moist	moist	generously	moderately
temperature	86° F/ 30° C	77° F/ 25° C	72-86° F 22-30° C (in sun)	64-68° F 18-20° C
rel. humidity	> 95%	> 95%	80-95%	80-95%

127

Phlebodium

Not too dark

·Phlebodium is a fairly durable houseplant, provided you ensure that it is placed in a position neither too dark nor too sunny. The name Phlebodium comes from the Greek word, *phlebion*, which means 'vein'. *Phlebodium* means 'full of veins'. This splendid Fern is very often called Polypodium. This is not correct, although it is certainly a member of the large Fern family, Polypodiaceae. The Phlebodium which we know as a houseplant comes from South America.

Spore plant

Like most Ferns, Phlebodium must be propagated from spores. Its beautiful, orange-coloured spores are clearly visible on the underside of the leaves. Sow them in a clean, not too acid soil and they form a green germinating layer, called the prothallium. After three months place out pieces of this layer, from which the Ferns will grow. Set the plantlets out individually as soon as they are clearly visible and three months later place the little Ferns in a 3-in/7-cm pot.

Never dust

Phlebodium is a distinctive foliage plant with beautiful, blue-ribbed leaves. The colour comes from a thin layer of wax, which the plant needs in order to grow properly. If you dust the plant, you damage this layer and inhibit growth. Phlebodium grows excellently in a normal RHP potting soil. Keep this soil moderately moist throughout the year. Feed the fern weekly in the spring and summer; stop feeding in the winter months. Place the fern in a slightly shaded position, though not too dark. Take care that it does not stand in the sun.

Phlebodium does not grow as compactly as some other ferns.

But though the plant itself remains fairly thin, the leaves become quite large and long.

Phlebodium aureum 'Mandaianum'

Phlebodium aureum 'Mandaianum' (Polypodium glaucum)

This variety, which comes from South America, has gold-coloured (*aureum*) hairs on its leaf buds and irregular, indented leaves. The variety 'Mandaianum' was developed in 1912 in the United States. The leaf lobes are wavy and indented in a somewhat criss-cross fashion.

Treatment table

	sowing	growth	rest
pot	frame	3 in/7 cm and larger	—
soil	see spores (page 168)	RHP	—
feeding	—	1 tsp compound fertilizer per pt water/2g per litre	none
watering	—	moderately	moderately
temperature	68° F/20° C	64-68° F/ 18-20° C	>54° F/ 12° C
rel. humidity	90%	60-70%	60-70%
light	—	slight shade	light

special features   The maximum summer temperature is 86° F/30° C; the relative humidity may then fall slightly.
Do not dust.
Do not place in too dark or too sunny a position.

Phoenix canariensis

Phoenix canariensis

Phoenix dactylifera
This is the genuine Date palm, the fruit branches of which are used in Christmas floral arrangements. This species is not known in the wild.

Phoenix roebelenii
This Palm comes from Laos and is grown as a houseplant to only a limited extent.

Phoenix canariensis
As the name implies, this Palm comes from the Canary Islands. It is a large, decorative foliage plant which can be placed outside in a shaded position in the summer.

A name with many meanings
Phoenix is the Latin spelling of the Greek word, *phoinix*, which has many meanings. It means 'purple-red'; it is a musical instrument; and it is the name of a legendary Egyptian bird which, after living for 500 years, burned itself on a pyre and was then born again out of the ashes. Phoenix was also the brother (sometimes the father) of the beautiful mythical heroine, Europa, and the ancestor of the race of the Phoenicians. From which of these meanings the name of the Date palm is derived is not certain. The fruits of many Phoenix species are bright-red and the Palm can grow to a great age. Phoenix is a large, decorative foliage plant which can be placed outside in a shaded position in the summer. It is a native of the Mediterranean area and the Canary Islands. The larger specimens are the sturdiest.

Sowing from seed
The Phoenix palm can be grown from seed, which should be sown in a sandy, consistent, humus-rich mixture. The seeds of Palms germinate erratically. As soon as a young plant has a seed leaf about 3-in/8-cm in size, plant it in a 3-in/8-cm pot. A year later repot into a 5-in/12-cm pot. The total growing time from seed to small pot plant is two to three years.

Plenty of light
Unlike some of its relatives, the Date palm requires plenty of light. It may be grown outside in direct sunlight, though young plants should be well shielded against the full glare of the sun. The plant grows well in a mixture of two parts RHP potting soil to three parts clay. Keep the soil moist during the growing season and feed weekly at that time. The Palm rests in the winter; it does not grow then and should be given no feed. Water sparingly and keep the potting soil fairly dry.
Phoenix is a quick-growing palm with great powers of adaptation. Older plants may become so large that they are uncontrollable as houseplants. The Palms require spacious pots and older plants are best grown in tubs and placed outside in the summer in a shaded position.
You must make sure that the roots do not grow through the pot. If the pot is then repositioned, the roots break off, harming growth.

Treatment table

	cutting	growth	rest
pot	frame	large pot (tub)	—
soil	sandy, consistent humus-rich	RHP and clay 2:3	—
feeding	—	1½ tsp compound fertilizer per pt water/3g per litre	none
temperature	86° F/30° C	72-77° F/ 22-25° C	frost-free
rel. humidity	95%	70-80%	70-80%
light	plenty	plenty	plenty

special features The temperature may rise to 95° F/35° C in the sun. Shield young plants indoors against direct sunlight.

Pilea

A 'young' houseplant

Pilea cadierei has not been grown for very long as a houseplant. It grows in the wild in Vietnam and was only introduced as a houseplant, in France, in 1938.

It is a quick-growing, herbaceous plant which can last for many years. One of the species, Pilea muscosa ('mossy') is a plant for enthusiasts; it does not grow higher than 5 in/12 cm and has numerous small leaves. This species is sometimes called the Cannon Plant, because the stamens throw their pollen in the air, giving rise to little clouds all over the plant. The plant does this shortly after a spraying, when the relative humidity is high. Pilea belongs to the nettle family, Urticaceae. The name Pilea comes from the Greek word *pilos* (*pileus* in Latin) which means 'felt hat'. One of the lobes of the perianth of the female flowers is cap-shaped.

Easy to take cuttings from

It is not difficult to take cuttings of Pilea. For all varieties, take shoot cuttings and place them in peat-based potting compost. Under double glass or plastic sheeting they will have sufficient roots after two weeks to be potted off into a 3-4-in/8-10-cm final pot. If one cutting is placed in a pot, the plant will have to be topped a few times. If three are placed in one pot, a good compact plant will be obtained without topping.

Plenty of light, but no sunlight

Pileas are sturdy perennial houseplants which should be grown in slight shade. If grown in too dark a position, however, their growth will be stunted and you will not get their beautiful leaf colour. It is essential to shield them against direct sunlight in the summer.

Pileas grow excellently in a normal RHP potting soil. Water them generously and give them a weekly feed during the growing season. In the darker winter months, when they have a rest period, keep the potting soil moderately moist and stop feeding.

Start to water and add feed again towards late winter. Older plants will have a less beautiful appearance because the bottom leaves fall off. The simplest solution is to grow new plants by taking cuttings, though old plants will produce healthy new shoots if cut higher back in the spring.

Treatment table

	cutting	growth	rest
pot	frame	3-3½ in/8-9 cm	—
soil	peat-based potting compost	RHP	—
feeding	—	1½ tsp compound fertilizer per pt water/3g per litre	none
watering	moist	generously	moderately
temperature	64-68° F/ 18-20° C	64° F/18° C	64° F/18° C
rel. humidity	90-95%	70%	70%
light	light	slight shade	light

special features Start adding feed in mid-winter. The plants should receive no direct summer sunlight, but neither should they be placed in a dark position.

Pilea spruceana 'Silver Tree'

Pilea Cadieri
This quick-growing foliage plant is named after R.P. Cadière, a French botanist of this century.

Pilea spruceana 'Silver Tree'
This variety, like the variety 'Bronze Tree' is grown only to a limited extent.

Pilea involucrata 'Norfolk'
This beautiful, large-leaved variety is not commonly grown.

Pilea muscosa
This is a plant for enthusiasts. It is sometimes called the Cannon Plant, because it shoots off its pollen in tiny clouds after it has been sprayed.

Pilea repens

Pilea repens
Repens means 'creeping'. It is a hanging plant with green leaves and is increasingly in demand.

Pisonia umbellifera 'Variegata'

Pisonia umbellifera 'Variegata'
(Heimerliodendron)
This is the variegated variety of Pisonia
which grows in New Zealand, Australia
and Tahiti as the Bird-catcher tree.
The original species, which has green
leaves, is cultivated to only a limited
extent.

Piso's plant
Pisonia is sometimes regarded as a Ficus, but although it
resembles it closely, it is in fact of a completely different
family. It belongs to the Nyctagynaceae, of which
Bougainvillea is also a member.
The green-leaved Pisonia is a large tree in New Zealand,
Australia and Tahiti. It is called the Birdcatcher tree, because
the inside edge of the seed-pods is coated with a gum-like,
adhesive substance. Glue-sticks for catching birds are made
from this substance. Pisonia is named after the 17th-century
Dutch doctor, Willem Piso, who was the founder of tropical
medicine in the Dutch colonies. Pisonia has beautiful,
quick-growing foliage which can develop into a large plant.

Cuttings under mist
Pisonia is propagated in the spring by taking a well-ripened
head-cutting or an intermediate cutting (see page 169). Place
the cuttings in a mixture of equal parts peat dust and river
sand. The cuttings can be placed in a nursery bed or in
3-in/7-cm pots. The cuttings should ideally be placed under
mist, but double glass or plastic sheeting can be used. The
cuttings will have rooted sufficiently after three to four weeks
to be set in a final pot. Set one cutting in a 3½-in/9-cm pot or
three to four in a 5-in/14-cm pot. A handsome plant will then
be obtained. If the plant is topped, it will branch well, but the
shoots will appear high up and the stem remain bare.

Plenty of light and frequent feeding
Pisonia must have a well-lit environment to produce its
beautiful ieaf colour. It cannot, however, tolerate the direct
rays of the sun. It grows well in a mixture of three parts RHP
potting soil to one part river sand. Water generously and feed
weekly during the growing season. Keep the potting soil
moderately moist during the dark winter months; the plant
hardly grows then and requires no feeding. The rest period
runs from mid-autumn to mid-winter. The plant has small,
greenish flowers of no decorative value.
Pisonia is a good houseplant. The finest specimens are
obtained by taking cuttings regularly. The stems of older
plants get rather bare. It is quite possible to grow large, old
plants, but they must be repotted at the start of the growing
season and be given a good feed when they are growing.

Treatment table

	cutting	growth	rest
pot	3 in/7 cm	3½-5½ in/ 9-14 cm	—
soil	peat dust and sand 1:1	RHP and sand 4:1	—
feeding	—	1½ tsp compound fertilizer per pt water/3g per litre	none
watering	moist	generously	moderately
temperature	72° F/22° C	64-68° F/ 18-20° C	64° F/18° C
rel. humidity	95%	70-80%	70-80%
light	plenty	plenty	plenty

special features The maximum temperatue in the sun is 86° F/30° C.
Avoid direct rays of the sun.

Square peg

In the large Fern family, Polypodiaceae, the Hartshorn fern is a bit of a square peg in a round hole. It is the only one with such large and, in particular, broad fronds, and in addition it has spores in an unusual place, namely on the top of the fertile fronds. Moreover, the Fern has two sorts of fronds: the horn-shaped ones, which form spores, and the barren mantle, or niche, fronds which, with older specimens, grow right around the pot. The latter are of great importance to the plant, and must never be divided or broken off. Great care must therefore be exercised when repotting older specimens of the Hartshorn fern. Platycerium is a native of tropical Australia and New Guinea. The plant grows there epiphytically, ie on trees and tree trunks. We must take account of this when cultivating it.

Do not dry spores

To propagate the plant, take the spores from the plant as soon as they are ripe and sow them directly into a clean, but not too acid, soil (see page 168 for spores). The spores must not be allowed to dry out before sowing. When they germinate, they first form a mossy green layer, called the prothallium. Fertilization takes place in this layer. After about three months, set pieces of the prothallium out separately. When little Ferns start to grow from it, set them out again individually. Place them as far apart as possible and three months later put them in 3-in/7-cm pots to make further growth. As soon as they are large enough, give them a new pot every year until the niche leaves have grown right round the pot. Repot them thereafter with care. Repotting should be kept to a minimum; on the other hand, the plant must always have a sufficiently large pot.

Little water and fertilizer, but plenty of light

The Staghorn fern is a plant which likes a well-lit environment and needs little water. Although direct sunlight is not good for it, continue to grow the plant in as brightly-lit a position as possible.

The plant also grows well in slight shade, but then the fronds are less velvety. Feed it only when it is clearly growing, otherwise not at all. It derives its food from the decomposing mantle fronds.

The Hartshorn fern is a sturdy houseplant which lasts a very long time and can grow very large.

You must ensure, above all, that it does not get too much water. Watering once every two weeks is usually quite sufficient. The plant must never be dusted, because dusting can easily damage the felt layer which protects the plant against the low relative humidity in the house.

Platycerium bifurcatum

Platycerium wilhelminae-reginae, spore-bearing plant

Platycerium bifurcatum (Platycerium alcicorne)

This is the most widely grown Hartshorn fern, with double-forked (*bifurcatum*) fronds. *Platycerium* means 'flat horn' and refers to the flat, horn-shaped frond. The species Platycerium veitchii closely resembles this plant.

Other species, in which the fronds are grown together to form a single whole, are less common. They include Platycerium grande, Platycerium willinckii and Platycerium wilhelminae-reginae.

Treatment table

	cutting	growth	rest
pot	frame	3 in/7 cm and larger	—
soil	see spores (page168)	fibrous frozen peat	—
feeding	—	½tsp compound fertilizer per pt water/1g per litre	none
watering	moderately	moderately	dryish
temperature	68° F/20° C	64-68° F/ 18-20° C	60° F/15° C
rel.humidity	90%	70%	70%
light	light	light	light

special features   Feed seldom (once a month).
The maximum temperature is 95° F/35° C.
Avoid direct sunlight.

Primula acaulis hybrid

Primula praenitens 'Dazzler'

Primula malacoides

Primula malacoides

The colour of the original species shows similarities with Malva (mallow). It is therefore called malacoides.

This annual comes from southern China and was introduced into England in 1906. The plant is very salt-sensitive and the leaves suffer from mildew at an excessively high relative humidity. It comes from a slightly warmer region than most Primulas and is therefore somewhat better able to withstand slightly higher temperatures.

This Primula flowers in the colours pink, lilac-pink, carmine-red and white. The white and red varieties are the rarest. One gram of seed contains 1,300 seeds.

Primula Acaulis hybrids (Primula Vulgaris hybrids)

Whereas the generic name of this Primula comes from Latin, the species name comes from Greek. *A-kaulos* means 'without stem'. The main petiole of this Primula is absent. The hybrids are crosses of Primula vulgaris, which is indigenous to Europe, Primula amoena, which comes from the Caucasus and Asia Minor, Primula elatior, which occurs in Europe as far east as Siberia, and Primula juliae, which is also indigenous to the Caucasus and Asia Minor.

This Primula is seen at the florist's by the beginning of winter and is a real harbinger of spring.

Primula elatior (Primula veris)

This Primula flowers chiefly in late winter to mid-spring. Primula Elatior hybrids in various shades of yellow are often seen before Easter.

The hybrids are crosses of Primula elatior and Primula amoena. They are seen in red-brown and yellow shades and also in white. Some Japanese hybrids have blue, purple, orange and salmon-coloured shades. One tsp/g contains 1,100 seeds.

Primula (x) kewensis

This yellow-flowering Primula arose from a double accident in the greenhouses of the famous English botanical gardens at Kew.

It arose from a spontaneous crossing of a Primula floribunda and a Primula verticillata. This hybrid was barren, but by a spontaneous doubling of chromosomes the plant became tetraploid, so that seed was again produced. One gram contains 1,100 seeds.

Primula praenitens (Primula sinensis)

This Chinese primula comes from central China, where it grows on calcareous rocks. *Praenitens* means 'shining' and refers to the rich colour range. This Primula is being increasingly superseded by Primula Acaulis hybrids, which are cheaper to grow. The Chinese primula requires a cool and light position in the room.

One gram of seed contains 1,000 seeds.

Primula obconica

This Primula is a sturdy plant which grows in the wild on limestone rocks in central China. It is propagated from seed, one gram containing 3,000-5,000 seeds. It is a profusely-flowering pot plant with carmine-red, pink, salmon-coloured, light-orange, blue or white flowers. Much improvement work is being done in Germany. The plant is an excellent houseplant with long-lasting flowers. It is grown at a day temperature of 68° F/20° C and a night temperature of 60° F/16° C. It can withstand 77° F/25° C in the sun. The relative humidity must be 70-80%.

Unjustifiably bad reputation

Primulas have a bad reputation with some people, who think that all Primulas will give them a skin rash. This is not true. For one thing, there is only one species which contains a benzine compound in its calyx, peduncles and leaves which can cause an itchy rash. This is Primula obconica. For another, by no means all people are sensitive to this substance. Matters are, therefore, not so bad as they might seem.

Most Primula species come from the cold and temperate zones of Europe and Asia. They are usually unable, therefore, to tolerate the high temperatures which prevail in most houses today. They are ideal plants for planting in a cold greenhouse or conservatory, where they provide relief at the end of the winter by their splendid profusion of multi-coloured flowers.

Light germinators

All Primula species can be propagated from seed. In many cases the fertilization of the flowers can be advanced by controlling pollination with a brush. Sow in a frame covered with glass or plastic. Do not cover the seeds with soil, but keep them constantly moist. All Primula seeds germinate under the influence of light.

Most species have to be pricked out one or more times before being placed in a 3½-in/8-9-cm pot. Keep the plants cool, but frost-free, until the flower buds develop. Then raise the temperature to advance the flowering.

Cool, light position

Primulas maintain their form for a long time provided they are not grown in conditions which are too warm. An exception is Primula obconica, which requires a day temperature of 68° F/20° C and a night temperature of about 60°F/16° C. The plants require plenty of light, but must never be allowed to stand directly in the sun. They will also do well in slight shade. Most species grow well in an RHP calceolaria potting soil. They are fairly sensitive to yellowing of the leaf, however, and the pH must never drop below 6 during the growing season. If the soil becomes too acid, increase the lime content. Keep the potting soil moist during the growing season and add some fertilizer weekly.

Commercial growers treat Primula Acaulis hybrids with growth hormone before the flower buds open. They do this once or twice (every 10 to 14 days) in order to keep the flower stalks short and firm. After flowering, these hybrids, which are fairly hardy, can be placed in a shaded spot in the garden. They can be brought in again when the flowers appear.

Treatment table

	seed	growth	rest
pot	frame	3-3½ in/8-9 cm	—
soil	RHP Calceolaria	RHP Calceolaria	—
feeding	—	1 tsp compound fertilizer per pt water/2 g per litre	—
watering	generously	generously	moist
temperature	60-64° F/16-18° C	43-46° F/6-8° C	54-64° F/12-18° C
rel. humidity	95-100%	60-80%	70-80%
light	light	light	light
flowers	—	—	spring
growth hormone, only with Primula Acaulis hybrids	—	Cyclocel or CCC 1/20 fl oz per pt water/3 ml per litre and wetter	—

Ideal for cold greenhouse or conservatory

Pteris is a sturdy and tough Fern with great powers of adaptation, but it is not altogether suitable for indoors, where temperatures are usually too high and relative humidity low. It is, on the other hand, ideal for a cold greenhouse or conservatory. Pteris comes from the Greek word, *pteron*, which means 'wing'. Pteris comes from the island of Crete, among other places, and is indigenous to Greece.

Division and spores

Most Pteris species can be propagated by division, though not many new ferns are thereby obtained. Commercial growers always propagate it by means of spores. Set the spores in a clean soil; make sure that the soil is not too acid, since acidity prevents the spores from germinating (see page 168 for spores).

After germination, a green mossy layer called the prothallium is formed. Fertilization takes place here. After about three months set out small pieces of this germination layer separately and in another three months the first little Ferns will appear. Prick them out and three months later place them in a 3-in/7-cm pot. Give them a slightly larger pot at each repotting, so that the roots have room to grow.

Slight shade

Pteris species do not require a warm room. The ideal growing temperature lies between 50-64° F/10-18° C, though they are quite resistant to higher temperatures. They grow excellently in a normal RHP potting soil. Water the plants generously during the growing season and feed them weekly, particularly in the spring and summer. The plants grow only slowly in the autumn and winter. Feed only once a month then and keep the soil moderately moist.

The variegated varieties require slight shade, but the green-leaved varieties can withstand deep shade.

When the plants are one year old, they form spores on their long, fertile leaves. These special fertile leaves are narrower and much longer than the others. They frequently die when the ripe spores have dropped.

Treatment table

	sowing	growth	rest
pot	frame	3 in/7 cm or larger	—
soil	see spores (page 168)	RHP	—
feeding	—	1 tsp compound fertilizer per pt water/2 g per litre	1 tsp compound fertilizer per pt water/ 2 g per litre
watering	—	generously	moderately
temperature	68° F/ 20° C	50-64° F/ 10-18° C	41° F/ 5° C
rel. humidity	90%	70-80%	70-80%
light	light	slight shade	light
special features	The maximum summer temperature is 86° F/30° C, with a relative humidity of 70-80%. The variegated-leaf varieties need more warmth and light than the green ones for beautiful, variegated colours and good growth.		

Pteris cretica 'Parkeri'

Pteris cretica

This Fern, which comes originally from Crete (*cretica*), is indigenous to the Mediterranean and the sub-tropics and tropics. It is the most widely grown species.

The following varieties are commonly seen: 'Albo Lineata', with a white linear decoration, 'Mayii',.with a grey-white decoration, 'Alexandra', with a white decoration and cockscomb-type leaf tips, 'Wimsettii', a green variety with indented leaves branched at the tips in a comb shape, 'Gauthieri', with green, strongly-indented leaves, 'Major', with strong, broad, green leaves, 'Parkeri', with green, very broad leaves and 'Rivertoniana', with fine, saw-tooth leaf-edges. These varieties are usually seen in shops in small pots of all different shapes and colours.

Pteris cretica 'Alexandra'

Pteris ensiformis 'Evergemiensis'

Pteris longifolia

Pteris longifolia (Pteris vittata)

This Pteris with long narrow leaves is a special, ornamental Fern. It comes from the sub-tropics and tropics.

Pteris tremula

This species with finely branched leaves comes from Australia and New Zealand. *Tremula* means 'trembling'. The plant grows strongly in a large pot.

Pteris ensiformis 'Evergemiensis'

The leaves of this variety are sword-shaped (*ensiformis*) and have a broader and whiter midrib than the original species, which comes from tropical Australia, Asia and Polynesia.

Pteris multifida 'Ouvrardii'

This multi-part (*multifida*) species comes from eastern Asia. The leaves are about ½ in/1 cm wide; they narrow towards the tip and at the outside end broaden into a comb shape.

Pteris quadriaurita 'Argyraea'

The leaves of this Fern have four 'ears' (*quadriaurita*) and a broad, silver-coloured (*argyraea*) centre stripe. The plant comes from the tropics and requires more warmth than other species. The growing temperature is 64-68° F/18-20° C. It is a splendid fern from which to grow large plants.

Rechsteineria cardinalis (Gesneria or Corytholomia)

Rechsteineria cardinalis (Generia or Corytholomia)

This splendid flowering plant is sometimes called Stick of Sealing wax because of its scarlet-red (*cardinalis*) flowers. It flowers throughout the summer and can be saved by preserving the dry tubers. The variety with white flowers is seen occasionally but the demand for it is small.

A white-flowering variety of Rechsteineria cardinalis

Sticks of sealing wax

Rechsteineria is a summer-flowering, tuberous plant which can be saved by means of tubers. The plant has splendid, oblong, red flowers, which look like old-fashioned sticks of sealing wax. The generic name, Rechsteineria, comes from a 19th-century Swiss pastor. The plant is sometimes also called Gesneria. This is incorrect, although it is certainly related to the Gesneriaceae, a family which is named after the 16th-century Swiss doctor and botanist, Conrad Gesner. The plant was described for the first time in Germany in 1850 and almost certainly comes originally from Brazil.

Tubers and seeds

If you want to save Rechsteineria, you must preserve the tubers in dry peat dust at 60°F/15°C in the autumn, when the plant has died. In mid-winter place the tubers in a 3-4-in/8-10-cm pot and in late spring or early summer the first flowers will appear. Sowing is the best method of propagating the plant. 30,000 seeds weigh one gram. Sow in late autumn. In the winter the seedlings must be given light from high-pressure mercury or sodium lamps or with TL 33. The required radiation energy is 6,000-10,000 mW per yd^2/m^2. In late winter set the plantlets out separately and in early to mid-spring plant them in a 3-4-in/8-10-cm pot. As spring advances support the shoots with wire pins or split bamboo canes. They will flower in mid-summer, later than plants which are grown via tubers.

No cold water on the leaves

Take particular care during growing that the irrigation water is at room temperature and that no cold irrigation water gets on to the leaves. This will cause ring-shaped patches of dead tissue.

Rechsteineria requires a humus-rich potting soil and is best grown in normal RHP potting soil.

Keep the soil moist during the growing season and feed the plants weeky at that time. Cease watering in the autumn when the plant dies. The tubers are best kept in the dry soil in the pot (at room temperature). In the winter grow the plants in as light a position as possible; in the summer months, however, they will tolerate no sunlight at all. The plants flower from late spring to early autumn. Rechsteineria is an excellent houseplant for the summer months. It requires plenty of warmth and it likes the somewhat reduced light of a normal room.

Treatment table

	sowing	growth	rest
pot	frame	3-3½ in/8-9 cm	none
soil	RHP	RHP	RHP dry
feeding	—	½ tsp compound fertilizer per pt water/1 g per litre	—
watering	—	generously	dry
temperature	72°F/22°C	60-64°F/16-18°C	60-68°F/15-20°C
rel. humidity	95%	80%	dry
light	light	light	—
flowers	—	late spring to early autumn	—

special features No (cold) water should touch the leaves. The maximum temperature in the sun is 72°F/22°C. Shield very strongly against sunlight in the spring and summer.

Rhaphidophora

Climber or hanging plant

Rhaphidophora, with its delicately-coloured leaves, is in origin a climber and needs to be supported or trained, though it also serves as a beautiful hanging plant. It is called Scindapsus by some growers. The name Rhaphidophora comes from the Greek words, *rhaphis* and *phoros*, and means 'needle-bearer'. There are crystal needles in the fruits of the plant. Rhaphodophora, which belongs to the arum family, Araceae, comes from the tropical primieval forest of the Solomon Islands, which lie to the east of New Guinea in the Pacific.

Roots already in the stem

If you take cuttings from the plant, you will find that they form roots very quickly. Embryonic roots are, in fact, already present in the stem and develop into aerial roots. Take intermediate or eye-cuttings (see page 169 for cuttings) from young shoots. If placed in peat-based potting compost, they can be set in a 3-4-in/8-10-cm final pot after only two weeks. Large, handsome specimens can also be grown by planting four or five rooted cuttings in a 6-8-in/16-20-cm pot. The tendrils can then be run along bamboo canes tied together overhead in a pyramid shape.
The growing time for cuttings in a small pot, which should be supported by a bamboo stick or wire pin, is six to seven months.

Think about root rot

Although the plant needs regular and generous watering, the soil must never become really wet, lest the roots suffer from lack of oxygen and start to rot.
Grow Rhaphidophora in a porous, fibre-rich RHP potting soil such as Bromeliad soil. Feed weekly during the growing season and once every three weeks in the dark autumn and winter months.
Give the plant a very light position, but in the winter shield it from strong sunlight. The plant will not flower indoors where it will remain immature. In the greenhouse it can become very large and will then produce very large flowers; fruit formation, however, is rare. Rhaphidophora is an excellent houseplant, and its long shoots do exceptionally well as a trained plant, provided it is repotted each year. Indoors the leaves remain somewhat small because of the low relative humidity. The plant will not tolerate low temperatures and is ideal as wall cover in a greenhouse.

Rhaphidophora aurea

Rhaphidophora aurea
This beautiful hanging plant is sometimes called Scindapsus aureus. The *'aureus'* is correct, because the plant has splendid gold-coloured leaves.

Rhaphidophora aurea 'Marble Queen'
This variety has light-yellow leaves with a little green and because it has little chlorophyll is slow to grow.

Treatment table

	cutting	growth	rest
pot	frame	3-3½ in/8-9 cm	—
soil	peat-based potting compost	airy RHP	—
feeding	—	1 tsp compound fertilizer per pt water/2 g per litre	1 tsp compound fertilizer per pt water/2 g per litre
watering	moist	moist	moderately
temperature	68-72°F/20-22°C	64-68°F/18-20°C	64-68°F/18-20°C
rel. humidity	90-95%	70-80%	70-80%
light	light	moderate	light

special features — Four or five plants may be grown in a 6-8-in/16-20-cm pot. The maximum temperature in the summer is 86°F/30°C.
The potting soil must never be wet.
Feed every three weeks in winter. With insufficient light the leaf turns predominantly green.

Rhipsalidopsis gaertnerii

A spring flowerer

Rhipsalidopsis is a well-known Crab cactus which flowers in the spring. Because it is usually sold at Easter, it is sometimes called Easter Crab Cactus. Rhipsalidopsis comes from the Greek words, *rhips* and *opsis*, and means 'resembling a wickerwork of twigs'. Some species, indeed, produce a very tangled growth, giving the appearance that the limbs are intertwined.

Rhipsalidopsis comes from southern Brazil, where it grows both epiphytically and in the humus-rich soil of the tropical rain-forest.

Cuttings and grafting

Propagate the Crab cactus by taking cuttings from well-ripened limbs or by using the limbs which break off when you tie up the plant for the winter. Take young ripened shoots from the top of the plant in order to avoid the risk of fusarium (a mould which causes root or stem rot). The cuttings are never cut off, but always broken off. Place them in a mixture of four parts peat litter to one part river sand. Protect the cuttings against drying out by covering them with paper. After three weeks they will have grown enough roots to be planted, two together, in a 4-5-in/8-10-cm pot. Larger plants will be obtained if they are first put in a 3-in/7-cm pot and then repotted in a 4-5-in/10-12-cm pot. If cuttings are taken in late winter, they must be potted up by mid-spring at the latest; otherwise there will be insufficient renewed growth for the winter.

The Crab cactus is often grafted by commercial growers on to the rootstock of Pereskia aculeata, Selenicereus grandiflorus or S. kamatus. The grafted specimens often last longer than those obtained from cuttings.

Lots of nitrogen

The Crab cactus requires plenty of nitrogen during the growing season. Add nitrogen-rich fertilizer weekly therefore, discontinuing in late summer and not starting again until after the flowering in the spring, when the plants will start growing again. Vegetative growth, or the growth of stems, must stop by mid-spring, by which time the shoots should have ripened. Grow the Crab cactus in a humus-rich RHP potting soil, which can be mixed with plastic granules to prevent excess water. Keep the potting soil moderately moist during the whole of the growing season. The soil must never be completely dry. The plant should stand in as light a position as possible during the dark months. In the summer place it in slight shade and ensure that it is shielded against strong sunlight. The plant forms flower buds during the short-day at a temperature of 68-72° F/20-22° C. Vegetative growth, particularly of autumn cuttings, can be promoted by long-day treatment in the winter (lighting with 2,000-3,000 mW per yd^2/m^2 in order to get a 14- to 15-hour day by nightly interruption).

Crab cacti are ideal houseplants which can be enjoyed for many years. They can grow into very large plants, provided that you ensure that they grow well at the right time.

Rhipsalidopsis gaertnerii

This widely grown Easter Crab cactus with orange flowers is usually seen as a houseplant.

Rhipsalidopsis rosea

This is a small-flowered species which flowers very profusely in the spring with a mass of pale-pink flowers. The species is grown only to a limited extent because the flowers are small.

Rhipsalidopsis (x) graeserii

This is a hybrid with orange-red to lilac-pink flowers. A large number of varieties of this cross between Rhipsalidopsis gaertnerii and Rhipsalidopsis rosea are seen. They are sometimes difficult to distinguish from Zygocactus hybrids.

Treatment table

	cutting	growth	winter
pot	frame	3-3½ in/8-9 cm	—
soil	peat litter and sand 4:1	RHP and friable styrene granules 4:1	—
feeding	—	1½ tsp compound fertilizer per pt water/ 3 g per litre (nitrogen-rich)	none
watering	moist	moderately	moderately
temperature	72-75° F/ 22-24° C	68-73° F/ 20-23° C	68-72° F/ 20-22° C
rel. humidity	90-95%	85-90%	85%
light	slight shade	slight shade	light
flowers	—	spring to early summer	—
special features	The soil must never be too wet or too dry. The long-day treatment for vegetative growth is 14-15 hours; the short-day treatment is 8-9 hours.		

Popular winter flowerer

The Rhododendrons which we know as houseplants are also commonly known in the trade by their simple name, Azaleas. The Greek words, *rhodon* and *dendron*, when joined together, mean 'red tree'.

The name, Azalea, is a riddle because it is the feminine of the Greek word, *azaleos*, which means 'arid' or 'dry'. And our Azalea, with its splendid flowers and fresh leaves, is anything but arid or dry; nor does it grow in an arid cimate. Azalea belongs to the family Ericaceae and is thus related to our heather bush and Dopheide (Erica).

The pot-plant Azaleas are crosses of far Eastern Rhododendron species such as Rhododendron simsii, Rhododendron indicum, Rhododendron vittatum and Rhododendron tamurae.

The Rhododendron is the most popular flowering pot plant for the winter months. Azaleas are fully in flower from mid-autumn to mid-spring.

Grafted Azaleas

The longest-lasting Azaleas are grafted specimens and the most commonly used rootstock is Rhododendron concinnum, a quick-growing variety which flowers profusely with large mauve flowers. All varieties can be grown on this rootstock and thus acquire a long life-span.

Grafting is possible throughout the year. A good method is whip-and-tongue grafting (see page 170 for grafting), but cleft grafting and side grafting also give good results. Position the graft about 4 in/10 cm up the rootstock, laying it and the rootstock together in a slanting position in the nursery bed under double glass. Graft and rootstock will coalesce in five to six weeks. Azaleas on a rootstock can always be recognized in a shop by their short stem: Azaleas grown from cuttings branch directly above the soil.

Cuttings and saving

If you want to propagate an Azalea, a grafted one is better value than one grown from a cutting. Propagation by cuttings, nevertheless, occurs on a great scale; some plants are even topped chemically. After being sprayed with a chemical plant growth regulator such as Caplets, the growth point burns off, and the side-shoots start to grow. If you want to grow Azaleas for yourself, it is best to take cuttings in the spring from the leaf shoots which come below the flower buds. These are herbaceous cuttings which root quickly, but they immediately become soft if the correct relative humidity is not maintained. After treatment with a growth hormone, place the cuttings in a mixture of peat dust with 1 tsp lime-fertilizer compound per pt/2 g per litre. Three parts peat dust to one part river sand can also be used. If the cuttings, which should stand ¾ in/1.5 cm in the soil, are placed under double glass or plastic sheeting, they must touch the glass or sheeting. The leaf then comes into contact with the condensed water and the cuttings do not become soft. Mist propagation is ideal (see page 169 for cuttings). The cuttings will have roots after six to eight weeks. The cutting medium may be used more than once. The cuttings are pricked out a few times. From mid-spring onwards, when no more night frosts can be expected, set the plantlets outside in a 5-in/12-cm layer of soil. The soil mustbe highly porous to prevent excess water. Water generously and feed regularly. The tops should be removed regularly, about every three months, to get a well-branched plant. In the autumn, before the night frosts come, pot the plants and set them in a greenhouse or in a cool, light position. Make sure that the pot ball always remains moist.

Rhododendron Simsii hybrid 'Paul Schäme

Rhododendron simsii hybrid 'Jan Bier'

Rhododendron Simsii hybrid 'Paul Schäme'

This salmon-coloured variety flowers somewhat late and there is a pink-and-white mutation which is induced to flower specially for Christmas.

Rhododendron Simsii hybrid (Azalea indica) 'Mad Patrick'

This is one of the hundreds of varieties of this Azalea species. 'Mad Patrick' is pink. It is an early-flowering variety which is difficult to grow, but it is, along with its mutants in varying colours, the most beautiful Azalea for Christmas.

The Simsii hybrids are crosses of Rhododendron indicum, Rhododendron simsii, Rhododendron tamurae and Rhododendron vittatum. The crosses were made in the last century in England, Belgium and Denmark.

Rhododendron Simsii hybrid 'Ambrosiana' and 'Helmut Vogel'

These are double-flowered, red varieties which can flower early and are widely grown for their rapid growth. The medium-early, red-flowering 'Reinhold Ambrosius' is also a rapid grower.

Rhododendron Simsii hybrid 'Glaser' varieties

These are profusely-flowering, single-flowered Azaleas in orange, pink and red shades.

Rhododendron Simsii hybrid 'Violacea'

This is a distinctive, late-flowering, bright-purple variety. It is difficult to grow, but several new varieties, such as 'Friedheim Scherrer', 'King Fisher' and 'Rosalie', are making progress.

Rhododendron kiusianum var. japonicum (Azalea japonica)

This group includes small-leaved Azaleas which flower profusely with a mass of small flowers. They are sometimes called 'Kurume hybrids'. They grow somewhat more slowly than the Rhododendron Simsii hybrids and they are propagated by cuttings.

Rhododendron kiusianum var. japonicum 'Kirin'

This pale-pink variety is the most widely grown, together with the salmon-pink mutant form Kirin, 'Rex'. They flower mostly in winter, after Christmas. Christmas flowering is possible, but difficult.

Rhododendron Kaempferii hybrids

These include some large-flowered, almost deciduous, varieties, such as the white 'Palestrina' and the pale-pink 'Schubert'.
Rhododendron malvaticum is one of the ancestors of these hybrids.
They are suitable only for late flowering, though they can be advanced at 60-64° F/15-18° C. The hybrids, including the Vuykiana hybrids, are propagated by cuttings. These arose from large-flowered Japanese Azaleas crossed with hybrids of Rhododendron molle, a deciduous Azalea species.
Hybrids of Japanese Azaleas with Rhododendron Simsii hybrids are still grown. Knowledge of the origin of many hybrids still awaits research.

When the buds reach maturity, bring the plant into a heated room. Spray regularly for a good relative humidity until the flowers open. The small suckers, the so-called thieves, should be removed. To get a well-branched plant, both the cuttings and the mature plants should be topped regularly. If topping is left until too late in the spring, too few flower buds will appear. Top in late winter for early flowering, in late spring for late flowering.

If you have bought an Azalea and want it to flower the following year, set the plant after flowering in a cool, but frost-free place and ensure that the root ball remains moist. The plant can be pruned in spring to preserve its shape. Towards the end of spring place it in the garden and treat it exactly as stated for cuttings. The plant can be left in the pot. In this way you can enjoy your Azala for a long time. The grafted specimens can last for decades, the ones grown from cuttings about four years.

No ideal soil any more

The ideal Azalea soil was previously moss-rich, coniferous litter, but it is no longer available. Azaleas should now, therefore, be grown in frozen peat or a mixture of frozen peat and peat litter. Mix this soil with 1 tsp lime-fertilizer compound and 2½ tsp of other compound fertilizer per pt/2 g and 5 g per litre; the fertilizer should have nitrogen-phosphorus-potassium proportions of 3:2:1. Feed twice a week during high summer and spray the leaves with clean water after feeding. Discontinue feeding in the autumn. Azalea requires frequent watering, but it must not stand in water. The plant makes high demands as regards irrigation water, rainwater being best. Tap water is often unsuitable because of its high acidity and hardness. Grow Azaleas with as much light as possible, but shield them against direct sunlight in order to prevent an increase in temperature. Azalea is a problem-free houseplant, but you must water it regularly and ensure that the root ball never stands in water. The length of flowering is limited by the room temperature. At 50° F/10° C the plant is sure to flower for eight to ten weeks, whereas in a warm living room at 72° F/22° C flowering will be no longer than four weeks.

Treatment table

	cutting	growth	rest
pot	frame	3½-5 in/9-13 cm	—
soil	see text	see text	—
feeding	—	basic feed see text 1 tsp compound fertilizer per pt water/ 2 g per litre	—
watering	moist	moist	moist
temperature	68-72° F/ 20-22° C	68-72° F/ 20-22° C	40-50° F/ 5-10° C
rel. humidity	100%	70-80%	70%
light	plenty	plenty	plenty
flowers	—	mid-autumn to mid-spring	—
growth hormone	1-napthalena-cetic acid 0.1%	—	—

special features For winter growth the plants should have a temperature of 60° F/15° C and a relative humidity of 80%. But setting should be at 75° F/24° C, bud formation (3 to 4 weeks) at 64-68° F/18-20° C, and bud growth at 40-50° F/5-10° C (6 weeks). The N.P.K. proportions should be 3:1:2.

Climbing houseplant

This strong-growing, climbing shrub is excellent for keeping in the house. Rhoicissus is derived from a Greek plant name and 'cissus' comes from the Greek word, *kissus*, which means 'ivy'. Rhoicissus belongs to a family of well-known climbers, the Vitaceae, which includes the vine. Rhoicissus comes from Natal and was cultivated in England in 1887.

Cuttings in the light

Rhoicissus can be easily propagated by taking an intermediate cutting with two leaves from the long branches (see page 169 for cuttings). The cutting must not have any tendrils in the leaf axils; if it does no buds, which are needed for developing into a new plant, will appear there. Take cuttings in the early summer, when they can get lots of light. Cuttings must not be taken in the darker winter months. For good rooting, treat the cuttings with growth hormone, then place them in peat-based potting compost under double glass, plastic foil or mist. They will have roots in a month. Plant them then in a 3½-in/7-8-cm pot. Four to six months later repot them into a 5-in/12-cm pot. For large, strong plants, set four to five cuttings in one pot. Train the long tendrils along bamboo sticks.

Feed generously

Rhoicissus is one of the sturdier houseplants, provided that it is repotted annually and given adequate feed for good growth. Feed weekly during the growing season, twice a month in the winter with a somewhat lower compound fertilizer concentration. Rhoicissus makes no special demands as regards potting soil. The RHP potting soils are very suitable.

Water generously during the growing season and keep the potting soil moderately moist. The plant grows best in full light, but will not tolerate direct sunlight. Rhoicissus also holds its own well in a slightly shady position. The plant drops its leaves at the end of the rest period. Keep the potting soil very dry until the new leaves appear, then add more water.

Treatment table

	cutting	growth	rest
pot	frame	5 in/12-13 cm	—
soil	peat-based potting compost	RHP	—
feeding	—	1½ tsp compound fertilizer per pt water/ 3 g per litre	1 tsp compound fertilizer per pt water/ 2g per litre
watering	moist	generously	moderately
temperature	68° F/ 20° C	68-86° F/ 20-30° C	> 60° F/ 15° C
rel. humidity	85%	70-75%	70-75%
light	light	light	light
growth hormone	1-naphthalenacetic acid 0.2%	—	—

special features The concentration of growth hormone depends on the hardness of the cutting. Shield from direct sunlight. The quickest growth is at 75° F/24° C.

Rhoicissus rhomboidea 'Ellen Danica'

Rhoicissus capensis

Rhoicissus capensis

This is a strong-growing, climbing shrub, with beautiful, large leaves. It is called 'capensis' because it comes from the Cape, ie South Africa.

Rhoicissus rhomboidea (Cissus rhombifolia)

This is the most widely grown species. A well-known variety is 'Ellen Danica', with decorative, somewhat indented, leaves. *Rhomboidea* means 'lozenge-shaped' and refers to the shape of the leaves (*rhombifolia*).

Rochea coccinea

Rochea coccinea (Crassula coccinea)
This splendid succulent can flower annually with splendid red blooms. The plant also gets its generic name from this,because coccinea means carmine-red in Latin.

Flowering succulent

Rochea belongs to the succulent family Crassulaceae. Treatment is similar on the whole to that of other succulents. Although a native of South Africa, Rochea grows in cold regions there because it does not like high temperatures. Rochea is named after the doctor and botanist Francois de la Roche who lived around 1800. Because it grows in winter, it was ascribed all sorts of magic powers in earlier times. Rochea is a beautiful pot plant which can flower annually provided you observe the rules, in particular as to the low temperature it likes.

Sandy mixture

Rochea can be propagated by means of shoot cuttings (see cuttings page 169). Select non-flowering side shoots for this. If you plant them in mid-spring in a frame filled with equal parts frozen peat and river sand and cover the frame with paper, they will root quickly. Pot the rooted cuttings off into a 3 in/7 cm pot after a month. To encourage the growth of side shoots, remove the tops two or three times after this during the growing season. The latest time for topping is mid-summer, otherwise there will be insufficient shoot growth for flowering. The tops which are removed can also be re-used as cuttings. Place four to five of these cuttings in a 3½ in/9 cm pot. Pot off the early cuttings from the 3 in/7 cm pot into a 4 in/10 cm pot in mid-summer. It is also possible to start two or three rooted cuttings straightaway in the 4 in/10 cm pot. In the winter keep the plant cool, light and dry, like all succulents. In the spring increase the temperature and, as soon as the buds are visible, add more water. The growing time of Rochea is about a year.

Cold treatment is necessary

Rochea is an exceptionally strong-flowering houseplant. If you want it to flower every year, cold treatment in the winter is necessary.
Grow Rochea in a mixture of three parts frozen peat potting soil and one part river sand. During the growing period in the summer and during flowering in the spring, keep the potting soil moderately moist. Water sparingly in the winter when the plant has to form flower buds. Take care, however, that the plants do not dry up. Feed weekly during the growing period. Do not fertilize additionally in the bud-forming period and during flowering. Grow the plants in as light a position as possible, shading them slightly against the full glare of the sun in summer. The first plants flower in late spring; most flower in mid-summer and the last ones only a little later. After flowering, cut the old plant back and repot it. With a little trouble you can grow fine big specimens.

Treatment table

	cutting	growth	rest
pot	frame	3½-^ in/9-10 cm	—
soil	sandy	frozen peat and sand 3:1	—
feeding	—	1 tsp compound fertilizer per pt water/2 g per litre water	none
watering	moderately	moderately	sparingly
temperature	50-54°F/ 10-12°C	approx 60°F/ 16°C	38-46°F/ 4-8°C
rel. humidity	approx. 70%	60%	50%
light	normal	normal	normal
flowers	—	late spring- mid-summer	—

special features The plant can also be placed outside in the summer. Maximum temperature in sun: 77°F/25°C.

Ideal houseplant

The African violet grows best at a temperature of 72° F/22° C; it makes no requirements as to sunlight and no extreme demands as regards relative humidity. The plant is therefore very suitable for a normal room, where it will flower for many months, including the winter months.

Saintpaulia was named in 1893 after the discoverer of the plant, Baron Walter von Saint-Paul Illaire of Berlin, who worked for a German company in east Africa. Until 1910, he was governor of the district of Tanga.

In this region Saintpaulia grows in shaded spots, on humus-rich mould, in the tropical rain-forests of the coast. There is an annual rainfall of 60-100 in/1,500-2,500 mm and the temperature does not fall below 64° F/18° C even in the coolest months. The maximum temperature is 73° F/23° C. The African violet belongs to the family Gesneriaceae, which includes a number of well-known houseplants such as Aeschynanthus, Rechsteineria and Sinningia (Gloxinia).

Sowing and leaf cuttings

It is possible to grow Saintpaulia from seed, but such plants are of poorer quality than the cutting varieties. There are 30,000 seeds to the gram. Sow from mid-summer to late winter. Four to six weeks after sowing thin out the seedlings and eight to ten weeks later pot them up in a 3-in/7-8-cm pot. The plants will flower nine to eleven months after sowing. When taking cuttings, select an undamaged leaf from the heart of the plant about 1½ in/4 cm in diameter. Leave a piece of stalk about 1 in/2-3 cm long on the leaf. It is best to cut a number of leaves together and place them in two rows in a frame back to back, so that a sort of tunnel is created. Roots will grow on the leaf stalk four weeks after taking the cuttings and two weeks later the first young shoots will emerge from so-called adventitious (accidental) buds. The taking of cuttings is not limited to a particular season. The cutting medium used is peat-based potting compost or a mixture of two parts peat dust to one part river sand. About eight weeks after taking cuttings, prick out the leaf with the suckers. This can be done in two ways. With the so-called Beidermayer variety, sort out all the plantlets individually and set them out one by one. With the Busch variety, leave all the plantlets from one cutting together and prick them out in bunches. Pot up the Beidermayer plants after eight to ten weeks in a 3½-in/8-9-cm pot. Place the Busch type in a 4-5-in/10-12-cm pot. To get a good plant shape, set the plants very deep in a plastic pot, in which the plants will grow more quickly than in an earthenware pot, where the soil temperature is lower. The water evaporates in the earthenware pot and the heat of evaporation is withdrawn from the potting soil. If the pots are placed close together, the leaves will grow vertically. Water generously directly after the potting; the plant comes from a rainy area. The pot must have a wide brim. The pots can be set out separately in five weeks. The growing time is 10 to 16 weeks, depending on the variety and the season.

No cold irrigation water

The African violet does not like the cold and the irrigation water must be at room temperature in order to prevent leaf spot. Spray gently over the leaves, making sure that the water is at room temperature. Always water generously. Start feeding weekly about six weeks after the potting up. Shield the plants from the sun in the spring and summer. In the winter grow the plants in as light a position as possible.

In the summer it is essential not to give them too much light, but too little light causes poor, flabby growth.

The temperature must never rise above 77° F/25° C. Higher temperatures produce misshapen flowers.

Saintpaulia lonantha hybrids

Saintpaulia lonantha hybrids

These hybrids are crosses of Saintpaulia ionantha and Saintpaulia confusa. The latter is a species which was discovered in 1895 in the same regions of Africa as Saintpaulia ionantha. Saintpaulia ionantha was first grown as a pure species. The flat-lying leaves made the plant difficult to pack and to transport. The crosses with Saintpaulia confusa improved this. The first crosses with Saintpaulia confusa were made in the United States in 1930. Saintpaulia confusa contributed longer peduncles and more upstanding leaves. Saintpaulia ionantha has leaves which lie flat on the ground and a short peduncle.

Saintpaulia lonantha hybrids 'Rhapsody' and 'Ballet'

These are the most important groups of varieties which are grown in shades of blue, mauve, pink and purple. There are also two-tone varieties, eg, white with blue edge. In the United States, where this plant is very popular and where more

than 1,500 varieties are registered, many double-flowered varieties are grown.

Treatment table

	cutting	growth	rest
pot	frame	3-3½ in/8-9 cm or 4-4½ in/ 10-11 cm	—
soil	peat-based potting compost	RHP peat litter soil	—
feeding	—	½ tsp compound fertilizer per pt water/ 1 g per litre	½ tsp compound fertilizer per pt water/ 1 g per litre
watering	moist	generously	generously
temperature	68-72° F/ 20-22° C	68-73° F/ 20-23° C	68° F/ 20° C
rel. humidity	90-95%	80%	80%
light	light	slight shade	plenty

Sansevieria trifasciata 'Laurentii'

Sansevieria trifasciata

This Sansevieria is propagated by leaf cuttings. *Trifasciata* means 'with three stripes' and these are found on the leaf decoration.

Sansevieria trifasciata 'Laurentii'

This variety is the most widely grown and is always propagated by means of suckers.
The variety does not regain its colours after the taking of leaf cuttings. The leavs are then like Sansevieria trifasciata, ie without yellow leaf-edge.

Sansevieria trifasciata 'Hahnii'

This is a compact-growing variety with green leaves.

Sansevieria trifasciata 'Silver Hahnii' and 'Golden Hahnii'

These are also compact-growing varieties with silver-green and yellow-edged leaves respectively. They are propagated by means of suckers.
The following varieties are grown to a limited extent:
Sansevieria metallica,
Sansevieria guineensis,
Sansevieria grandis,
Sansevieria cylindrica.

Sansevieria trifasciata 'Hahnii'

Sansevieria trifasciata 'Golden Hahnii'

Sansevieria cylindrica

Durable houseplant

Sansevierias are among the most durable of all houseplants and are able to survive under the most testing conditions. Really beautiful specimens, flowering profusely every year, can be grown, but only if the rules are adhered to. The plant is named after Raimondo Sangro, an 18th-century scholar from Naples, who was the ruler of Sanseviero. Sansevieria belongs to the lily family, Liliaceae, and comes from tropical west Africa. It grows in Zaire, among other countries, at an average temperature of 75° F/24° C. Rainfall is almost nil for about five months, the natural rest period of the plant.

Leaf cuttings and suckers

Sansevieria can be propagated by cutting a fully-grown leaf into 2-3-in/5-7-cm pieces and placing them vertically in a highly porous mixture. Four to five suckers will grow out of adventitious buds at the base of these cuttings. These suckers are always green-coloured, even when a leaf with a yellow edge is taken as cutting. When these are fully-grown, pot them up, together with the cuttings, in a single pot. The pot size is limited by the number of shoots and the size of the shoots. The plant can also be propagated by cutting off the suckers as close as possible to the mother plant and placing them in a pot.
If you want a large number of suckers for further growing, it is best to grow the plant outside, either on the propagating table of a greenhouse or in a spacious frame. When there is a sufficient number of fully-grown suckers, dig up the whole plant, cut off the suckers and plant out the mother plant again.

Lots of warmth and little humidity

Keep the soil moderately moist during the growing season; after this the soil should remain fairly dry. During the winter rest the plants and keep at a low temperature and a low relative humidity. Grow Sansevieria in a mixture of three parts RHP potting soil to one part river sand. Add no fertilizer during the first few months after potting nor during the rest period. The plants require lots of light. With the exception of the 'Hahnii' varieties, they will flower profusely, with long branches full of mall, white, pleasant-smelling flowerets. Each shoot flowers only once, but new shoots will flower the next year when they are fully-grown. When repotting the plant, which should be done annually, remove the older, less beautiful shoots. Always choose a large enough pot; otherwise the rhizomes will force theplant out of it. Provided that you take good care of them, Sansevierias have an unlimited life-span.

Treatment table

	cutting	growth	rest
pot	frame	5 in/12-13 cm	—
soil	RHP and sand 3:1	RHP and sand 3:1	—
feeding	—	1½ tsp compound fertilizer per pt water/ 3 g per litre	none
watering	moderately	moderately	fairly dry
temperature	68-86° F/ 20-30° C	68-86° F/ 20-30° C	> 50° F/ 10° C
rel. humidity	< 60%	< 60%	50-60%
light	plenty	plenty	plenty

special features When the plant stands in the cold in the winter, the potting soil must be dry.
Shield against the direct rays of the sun.

Two species

Two species of Saxifraga are known as houseplants. Each needs its own method of treatment.
Saxifraga cotyledon 'Pyramidalis' is a large hardy plant which is a native of the Alps and the Pyrenees; the other species, Saxifraga stolonifera, is a hanging foliage plant which is a native of eastern Asia. It was first cultivated in the Netherlands in 1771. The name Saxifraga comes from the Latin words, *saxum* for 'rock' and *frangere* for 'to break'.

Rosettes and suckers

When Saxifraga cotyledon flowers, it also forms individual rosettes from which new plants can be grown. Break these off the flowering plant in mid-spring and place them in the ground outside. Next spring, place the biggest of these in a 4-5-in/10-12-cm pot and move this outside. The spring after, the plant can be brought inside; it will then flower with a large, pyramid-shaped cluster of white, pleasant-smelling flowers which can grow as long as 1½ ft/.5 m. The rosettes flower only once; young rosettes are then formed next to the peduncle and can be used in turn for propagation purposes. Saxifraga stolonifera is sometimes called 'Mother of a thousand'
It forms very long suckers with young plantlets at one end. As a hanging plant, therefore, it looks like a mother with lots of small children. If you want the young plantlets to make good growth, the plant must be placed in a wide frame or outside on the propagating table of a greenhouse.
Spread the plantlets out as far as possible; they will form roots and grow independently. When they are large enough, pot them up in a 3½-in/8-9-cm pot.

Indoor and outdoor plant

As soon as Saxifrage flowers, bring it inside for its decorative value. It does excellently in an RHP potting soil, which should be kept moderately moist. This soil is also suitable for the mother plant, which remains indoors.
Feed the latter weekly in the growing season, not at all in the winter months. Place the pot in a lightly shaded position and ensure that it does not get too much light. Give the variegated variety 'Tricolor' slightly more warmth and light. The mother plant flowers with a mass of white flowerets, which appear on older plants. The variety 'Tricolor' hardly ever flowers.
The outdoor plant flowers chiefly in mid-spring. Flowering can be advanced by lighting the plant with 400 mW per yd²/m² for four hours per night in late winter in the cold greenhouse. Repeat in early spring for three hours per night. The plants will sometimes flower spontaneously in the autumn. Repot the plants annually and the mother plant will grow very large, with a vast number of tendrils with young plantlets.

Saxifraga stolonifera

Saxifraga stolonifera

This is the mother plant which comes from eastern Asia.
Stolonifera means 'bearing suckers'. The weaker variety 'Tricolor' was first cultivated in 1863 in England.
The original species can be grown outside in the garden as ground cover. In a severe winter, however, the plant may be killed by frost. The plants flower very profusely in the ground outside.

Saxifraga cotyledon 'Pyramidalis'

This Saxifrage is a sturdy, hardy plant which comes from the Alps and the Pyrenees.
Cotyledon means 'shell' or 'navel' and refers to the leaf shape. Grow the plant outside for a good part of the year. It must be kept sufficiently cold for good flower initiation. The plant normally flowers in the long-day period. Flowering can be advanced by lighting with TL 33, 80 Watt per yd²/m² for four hours a night in late winter.

Saxifraga cotyledon

Treatment table Saxifraga cotyledon

	rosette	growth	rest
pot	outside	5-5½ in/10-11 cm	—
soil	RHP	RHP	—
feeding	—	1 tsp compound fertilizer per pt water/ 2 g per litre	none
watering	—	moderately	moderately
temperature	—	54-60° F/ 12-15° C	41° F/ 5° C
rel. humidity	—	70%	70%
light	sunlight	plenty	plenty
flowers	—	late spring	—
special features	They often flower poorly after a mild winter (outdoors). The maximum temperature is 77° F/25° C.		

Treatment table Saxifrage stolonifera

	suckers	growth	rest
pot	frame	3-3½ in/8-9 cm	—
soil	RHP	RHP	—
feeding	—	1 tsp compound fertilizer per pt water/ 2 g per litre	none
watering	—	moderately	moderately
temperature	54-60° F/ 12-15° C	54-60° F/ 12-15° C	54-60° F/ 12-15° C
rel. humidity	70%	70%	70%
light	little	little	plenty
special features	Grow the variety 'Tricolor' at a temperature of 64-68° F/18-20° C in slight shade. Place larger plants in a 5-6-in/11-13-cm pot.		

Scindapsus pictus 'Argyraeus'

Scindapsus pictus 'Argyraeus'
This variety, the most widely grown, is a juvenile form which never flowers. The variety was first cultivated in England in 1875.
Argyraeus and *pictus* mean 'silver-coloured' and 'decorated', respectively; the plant has a distinctive silver-coloured leaf decoration.
The original species, Scindapsus pictus, grows more quickly; it has larger leaves, but the silver-coloured decoration is less distinctive.

Climbing or hanging
Scindapsus is a splendid houseplant which can be grown either as a climber or as a hanging plant. Scindapsus pictus, especially the variety 'Argyraeus', is most common as a houseplant. Previously many more plants were called Scindapsus; sometimes you will even hear growers refer incorrectly to Rhaphidophora as Scindapsus. The plant comes from tropical south-east Asia. The variety 'Argyraeus' remains in its juvenile form and never flowers. It was first cultivated in England and has a distinct, silver-coloured leaf decoration. Scindapsus belongs to the family Araceae. Scindapsus is an old Greek plant name and means 'similar to ivy'. Scindapsus can cling to a surface with its aerial roots just as an ivy can with its tendrils.

Easy to take cuttings from
Because the long tendrils of Scindapsus already have embryonic roots (the aerial roots), taking cuttings from the plant is very easy. Intermediate or eye cuttings can be taken from the shoots (see page 169 for cuttings). In peat-based potting compost, under double glass or plastic foil, they will have enough roots to be potted up after only 10 to 12 days. The shoots can also be laid out on peat dust. They then form roots and the rooted cuttings can be cut off later. Pot the rooted cuttings up in a 3-in/7-8-cm final pot. They can remain in this small pot for about a year because growth is very slow and they will not become large quickly. Tie the shoot to a split bamboo stick or to a wire pin 10-12 in/25-30 cm long.

High temperature
Scindapsus does not grow quickly, but the best results will be obtained if it is grown at a very high temperature. It is a beautifully coloured climbing or hanging plant which really requires some care in the house. It is an ideal plant for the greenhouse or hothouse.
Grow Scindapsus in a moist, humus-rich RHP potting soil. Water it generously during the summer months when temperatures are high.
Keep the potting soil moderately moist in the darker months. Feed weekly during the growing season; twice a month is sufficient in the winter. Place the plant in a slightly shaded position and above all not in the sun.
Repot Scindapsus annually.

Treatment table

	cutting	growth	rest
pot	frame	3 in/7-8 cm	—
soil	peat-based potting compost	RHP moist and humid	—
feeding	—	1 tsp compound fertilizer per pt water/ 2 g per litre	1 tsp compound fertilizer per pt water/ 2 g per litre
temperature	77° F/ 25° C	72-86° F/ 22-30° C	> 68° F/ 20° C
rel. humidity	90%	80%	80%
light	plenty	slight shade	light

special features Add extra fertilizer in the winter months (depending on the rapidity of growth).

A useful family

Scirpus is the Latin for 'rush'. The Rush belongs to the large Sedge family, Cyperaceae, which was extremely useful to man in the past.

Scoenoplectus lacustris, the Bulrush, from which floor and chair coverings used to be made, is well known. Also a member of this family is *Cyperus papyrus*, which the Egyptians used for paper-making 6,000 years ago. The plant previously had a name unsavoury to modern ears: Woman's hair with nits. The fine, green stems were the hair and the white spikelets the nits of the head-louse. The Rush which we know as a houseplant is a marsh plant from Indonesia, where it has been cultivated for a very long time. It is an ornamental plant with filiform stems approximately 12 in/30 cm long, which first grow upright and then assume a drooping position.

Only one pot needed

Scirpus can be potted off twice a year. A good time for doing this is mid- to late spring. If you wish to propagate it, divide the roots with a knife during potting, placing the pieces immediately into a 3-3½-in/8-9-cm final pot. The plants can be divided at any time of year, but spring is the best growing period. Decent plantlets will then be obtained in two to three months. If you buy *Scirpus* from a nursery, it is best to place it in a larger pot immediately, since in most cases the roots will already have outgrown the existing one. You can give the plant a slightly raised position by laying a ring of clay or loam around it.

Ideal for those who like aquariums and terrariums

Scirpus is an ornamental plant which is eminently suitable as a houseplant if you remember that it is a marsh plant in the wild. The best results are obtained by keeping it permanently in a dish filled with water. It is therefore popular with terrarium enthusiasts, who can grow it 'at the water's edge'. It is also an ideal hydro-plant. *Scirpus* grows exceptionally well in humus-rich RHP pot soil. During the growing season give the plant extra fertilizer weekly. It is tolerant of sunlight and should simply be shielded against excessively fierce sun in the summer. The grass-like inflorescence grows on each stem. When the stems have finished flowering, they turn yellow and wither. They should then be removed, since they make the plant unsightly.

Treatment table

pot	3-3½ in/8-9 cm
soil	humus-rich RHP potting soil
feeding	1 tsp compound fertilizer per pt water/2 g per litre
watering	keep well moistened
temperature	68° F/20° C
rel. humidity	as high as possible
light	strong sunlight
special features	Shield against fierce sunlight. The plant has no rest period. The minimum winter temperature is 41° F/5° C. Place larger specimens in a 5-6-in/12-15-cm pot.

Scirpus cernuus (Scirpus gracilis or Isolepis gracilis)

This decorative (*gracilis*) plant is a marsh plant in the wild and therefore requires frequent watering. *Cernuus* means 'nodding' and refers to the habit of the stems. The plant needs rejuvenating regularly. The old leaves turn yellow and make the plant unsightly.

Scirpus cernus

Reverse: *Selaginella martensii 'Watsoniana'*; Centre: *Selaginella kraussiana 'Aurea'*, Front: *Selaginella apoda*

Selaginella martensii 'Watsoniana'

This Selaginella, which is a native of Mexico, is the most common variety. It has silver-white, overhanging tips. The genus Selaginella contains hundreds of species of which only a limited number are cultivated. This species was first cultivated in Belgium in 1866.

Selaginella kraussiana (Selaginella denticulata) 'Aurea' and 'Variegata'

This species, which comes from South Africa, is the least widely cultivated. 'Aurea' has yellow-golden tips, 'Variegata' silver-white ones.

Selaginella apoda

This species is also a native of South Africa. It is a small plant with a maximum height of 2 in/5 cm; *apoda* means 'without paws'. It is spherical-shaped and grows like a moss.

A poor houseplant

Selaginella is a moss-type plant requiring a relatively high degree of humidity. It is therefore difficult to keep indoors for long periods. The plant has splendid ramified leaves and is very well suited for growing in bottles, where the humidity can be controlled.

The name *Selaginella* is of Celtic origin and means 'little wolf's paw'. The real Wolf's Paw (*Kycopodium*) is not a sporophyte like Selaginella and is not related to it. Selaginella comes from the cool rain-forests of America and South Africa. The plant carries the spores in leaves shaped specially for the purpose. In the cultivated state the leaves do not appear, and spores are therefore never found on this plant. The plants are much used for floral decoration at Christmas time.

Cover cuttings

Despite being a sporophyte, it cannot therefore be propagated by means of spores, but only by cuttings. Take fully-grown branches in early or mid-spring and plant them directly in a 3-3½-in/7-8-cm final pot filled with a light, humus-rich mixture. The cuttings require a relatively high degree of humidity. They should therefore be well covered. Place the pots close to each other at first, giving them more room later. They will have become pretty plants by the autumn and should be fully grown by Christmas.

Water frequently and keep shaded

Selaginella is really a forest plant which needs little sunlight, and it should therefore be grown in the shade and screened well. This also prevents an increase in temperature. The plants are cultivated in a mixture of three parts humus-rich RHP potting soil and one part river sand. Water the plants generously at all times, so that the soil and the surroundings remain permanently moist. Give no fertilizer for the first six weeks after potting, then add some up to mid-autumn. Starve them of fertilizer during the winter. Selaginella has a short life as a houseplant, but in the greenhouse, for example along the edge of the pathways beneath the propagating table, they do really well. In a bottle the plant tolerates temperatures up to 68° F/20° C, provided that the required humidity is maintained.

Treatment table

	cutting	growth
pot	3-3½ in/7-8 cm	3-3½ in/7-8 cm
soil	RHP and sand 3:1	RHP and sand 3:1
feeding	none	1 tsp compound fertilizer per pt water/2 g per litre
watering	generously	generously
temperature	60-64° F/16-18° C	40-50° F/10-15° C
rel. humidity	95%	85-90%
light	weak	shade
special features	The plant is suitable for growing in bottles. Add no fertilizer during the winter. The maximum temperature is 68° F/20° C.	

Selaginella apoda

Annual pot plant

Senecio is an annual flowering pot plant which flowers in the period from mid-winter to mid-spring. The demand for it is decreasing, because room temperatures are at present too high and it is less durable as a result.

Senecio belongs to one of the largest plant families, the composite flowers, or Compositae. A number of very common plants are members of this family. The Senecio varieties which we know as houseplants are crosses of species which are indigenous to the Canary Islands, where there is an annual rainfall of 24 in/600 mm and the plants grow to a height of 1,500-5,000 ft/450-1,500m. There are also many succulent species of Senecio.

Sowing

Senecio is an annual which is propagated from seed. The small-flowered varieties have 5,500 seeds in one gram, the large-flowered ones 3,500. Sow from early summer to late autumn, depending on the desired flowering time and the size of the plant you want to grow.

Sow as thinly as possible in boxes protected against excessive light and cover with a glass. Ventilate well for a good climate. The seeds will germinate in a week. Three weeks after sowing, set the young plantlets out individually about 2 in/5 cm apart and eight to ten weeks later pot them up in 3-4-in/8-10-cm final pot. If you want large plants, sow early and pot them first in a 3-in/7-cm pot and three months later in a 5-in/12-13-cm final pot.

If you want to obtain seed, select the finest specimens and place them together by colour in order to avoid undesirable cross-pollination. Pick the fluffy seed quickly; otherwise there is the risk of it being blown away. It is ripe about three weeks after pollination.

Think about the temperature

Senecio, with its splendid, glossy, velvet flowers, must be grown in conditions as cool as possible. If the plant becomes too warm, it will weaken and growth will be straggly. Place it in a light position, but shield it against strong sunlight. Use special calceolaria soil as sowing and potting soil and keep this soil moderately moist in order to prevent weak and flabby growth. The largest leaves can be removed. Do not feed the plants. Senecio can flower from early winter onwards; most specimens flower in the period from mid-winter to mid-spring. After flowering the plant dies. Commercial growers spray the plant a few times with inhibitor, to inhibit luxuriant growth, up to the time the first flower buds are visible.

Senecio cruentus hybrid 'Nana Multiflora

Senecio Cruentus hybrids

These annual hybrids are crosses between Senecio cruentus and Senecio maderensis, which come from Madeira and the Canary Islands, among other places. The plants are grown in many shades of blue, mauve, violet, purple, terra-cotta and creamy-white. The flowers are either single-coloured or have a white ring in the centre. The 'Nana Multiflora' varieties with small flowers are the most common.

Senecio Cruentus hybrids 'Grandiflora'

Plants of this variety have larger flowers, but the umbel is usually smaller than that of the 'Multiflora' varieties. The plant also grows taller and has a larger leaf.

Treatment table

	cutting	growth
pot	box	3½ in/4 cm or 5 in/12-13 cm
soil	Calceolaria	Calceolaria
feeding	—	none
watering	moist	1 tsp compound fertilizer per pt water/2 g per litre
temperature	64-68° F/ 18-20° C	54-60° F/ 12-15° C
rel. humidity	90-95%	90-95%
light	light	light
flowers	—	mid-winter to mid-spring
inhibitor	—	1 fl oz chlormequat per pt water/50 ml per litre
special features	Grow in as much light as possible in the winter. Shield in the summer against strong sunlight. Feed as required. The winter temperature should be 40-50° F/5-10° C. The night temperature for sowing should be 60-64° F/16-18° C.	

Senecio citriformis

Senecio herreianus

Sinningia hybrids

Sinningia hybrids

The hybrids are crosses of Sinningia specosia and Sinningia reginae, both of which come from Brazil. Early-flowering Sinningias are varieties of 'Anja Egels' (red) and 'Schweizerland' (red-white). The varieties 'Gierths Rote' (red) and 'Gierths Blaue' (blue) are fairly early flowerers. Sinningias are grown in the colours red, purple, pink, violet, white and red-white.
Coarse-leaved varieties, such as 'Kaiser Wilhelm' (blue and white) and 'Kaiser Friedrich' (red and white), are grown from tubers.

Treatment table

	sowing	growth	tuber
pot	frame	4½-5 in/ 11-12 cm	—
soil	Calceolaria and peat dust 1:1 with 1½ tsp lime-fertilizer compound per pt water/ 3 g per litre	frozen peat RHP	dry peat dust
feeding	—	1 tsp compound fertilizer per pt water/ 2 g per litre	none
watering	moist	moderately moist	dry
temperature	72° F/22° C	64-68° F/ 18-20° C	60-64° F/ 16-18° C
rel. humidity	95%	75%	dry
light	light	shady	—
flowers	—	late spring to early autumn	

A profusely-flowering plant

Sinningia or, as the plant is more popularly called, Gloxinia, is a useful flowering pot plant. It is a tuberous plant of which the old-fashioned, coarse-leaved varieties can still be saved. With the modern seed varieties this is very difficult, because they hardly ever form tubers.
The plant is named after Wilhelm Sinning, a 19th-century horticulturist at the botanical college in Bonn. The Sinningias which we know as pot plants are crosses of species which are natives of the tropical, humid forests of Brazil. The plants were introduced to Europe for the first time in England in 1815. The first improvement work was also carried out there. The new varieties came later from Germany and Switzerland. The plant belongs to the family Gesneriaceae. Sinningia is a beautiful pot plant, with its large, velvety flowers, which appear mainly in the spring and summer.

Sowing and saving

Seed the plants from mid-autumn to late winter in a mixture of equal parts RHP calceolaria soil and peat dust, to which is added 1½ tsp lime-fertilizer compound per pt/3 g per litre. The seeds are very small. One gram contains 25,000-30,000 seeds. You must therefore sow very thinly. Sow from mid-autumn to the beginning of summer. Do not cover the seeds with soil, but place a glass over the seed box to prevent drying out. The seed will germinate in about 14 days.
Five to seven weeks after sowing, set the plantlets out about 2 in/5 cm apart and five to seven weeks later prick them out once again. Then place the little plants immediately in the 4-5-in/10-12-cm final pot. In the winter months prolong the day to 14 hours by lighting with 6,000-10,000 mW per yd²/m². Place the plants very shallow in the pots and compress the soil only slightly for good growth.
When flower buds appear on the sturdy plants, remove the centre leaves so that the flowers develop well. The growing time is five to seven months, depending on the variety.
Old-fashioned varieties, grown as tubers from seed as happens especially in Belgium, can also be saved. After flowering, allow the plant to grow on into the autumn. Then preserve the tubers in dry peat dust. From early winter onwards place the tubers in moist peat dust at 72° F/22° C at a mutual distance of 4-6 in/10-15 cm. When they get going, pot them up, clod and all, in 5-in/13-cm pots.

Not an easy plant

Sinningia is a splendid houseplant which requires careful treatment. It must get sufficient warmth, not too much light, and regular, careful watering.
During the growing season keep the soil moderately moist but above all not wet. From early spring onwards, give it shade and shield it from excessive light. The plant grows excellently in a frozen peat RHP soil. The first plants flower from early spring onwards and continue to flower in great profusion until mid-autumn. Most specimens flower best in late spring and early summer.

Mock Orange fruits

Solanum is derived from the Latin verb *solare*, which means 'to soothe' or 'to calm'. This name is connected with some species of this plant family which were used as tranquillizers and pain-killers in Holland at one time. Most members of the nightshade family are annuals or biennials; the Solanum which we keep as a houseplant is a semi-shrub with large, orange-coloured fruits. It can last for 20 years in some cases. The plant is a native of South America and was cultivated for the first time in England in 1596. The plant has now run wild throughout the tropics. It can bear berries for almost the whole year, except for the early spring.

'Green' and 'white' varieties

The decorative value of Solanum comes from its berries, from which the plant gets its name, Mock Orange tree. There are white varieties, the berries of which first become white, and green varieties, which first have green berries. The berries later become permanently orange. The white varieties are the first sown; they also turn orange earlier than the green ones. Sow the plants from late winter to the beginning of spring at 68° F-20° C in a moisture-retaining, nutritious soil. You can obtain the seed yourself in the autumn from the ripe fruits. There are 450 seeds to the gram. A month later set the plantlets out individually at intervals of about 1 in/2.5 cm. The plants can be potted throughout the spring. Some people set the plantlets first in a pot for cuttings, but it is simpler to plant them directly in a 4-in/10-cm final pot. At the beginning of summer, after the night frosts are over, plunge the plants outside in the ground. If the plant's roots grow through the hole in the pot, the main roots must be broken off. The potting soil must be moist. The plant flowers from late spring to late summer, depending on the growing time; the berries turn completely orange after 10-12 weeks. They are not edible.

Think about the roots

Care must always be taken that the roots do not grow too deeply into the soil. If they do, when you attempt later to free the plant, it will lose its leaves. If the deep-growing roots are broken off, this will not happen. Grow the plant, if possible, in an RHP potting soil; this is not a hard and fast rule, however, and any moisture-retaining, nutritious soil may be used. During the growing season keep the soil very moist, but as the berries ripen water sparingly. Feed weekly until the fruits turn their natural colour. Give the plants as light a position as possible for good growth, profuse flowering and healthy fruit-setting.

Commercial growers spray the plant with inhibitor every 10 days in late summer to early autumn to get compact growth. Growth regulators based on ethylene are also sometimes used to get the berries to turn orange earlier and more uniformly. When the berries are finished, cut the plant back to a length of about 6 in/15 cm. Keep the plant cool and the soil dry.

In early spring pot them on into a larger pot and give them sufficient water and fertilizer again for growth. They can be placed outside again in late spring or early summer. In this way large plants can be grown and they will flower for years in your house with splendid miniature mock oranges.

Solanum pseudocapsicum (Solanum capsicastrum)

This plant, with its beautiful orange fruits, somewhat resembles its relative the Spanish pepper (Capsicum). Hence the name Pseudocapsicum. The berries are sprayed to encourage them to turn orange with the ethylene-containing agent ethephon 48% in a solution of 1/30 fl oz per pt water/2 ml per litre.
The soil must be moist for good cell tension in the plant and the temperature must be higher than 60° F/16° C to prevent leaf drop.

Solanum pseudocapsicum

Treatment table

	sowing	growth	rest
pot	box	3½-4 in/ 9-10 cm	—
soil	moisture-retaining, nutritious	RHP	—
feeding	—	1tsp compound fertilizer per pt water/ 2 g per litre	none
watering	moist	moist	dry
temperature	68° F/20° C	60-63° F/ 15-17° C	40-50° F/ 5-10° C
rel. humidity	90%	60-70%	60% or lower
light	light	light	light
inhibitor	—	Cycocel or CCC 1/16-1/8 fl oz per pt water/4-8 ml per litre	—
special features	Grow young plants at a temperature of 63° F/17° C (up to 86° F/30° C in the sun). Discontinue feeding when the fruits turn orange.		

Sparmannia africana

A large foliage plant

The Lime is a magnificent tree, with beautiful leaves and a lovely-smelling blossom from which bees make a delicious, fresh-tasting honey.

Sparmannia is a beautiful plant with large leaves. In the spring and summer a full-grown plant produces a large number of sizeable flowers in long stalked clusters in which the flower buds point downwards. The corolla is white.

In the wild the Indoor lime grows in South Africa as a large bush. It was introduced as a houseplant in 1790. Sparmannia is named after the Swedish naturalist, A. Sparman, who among other things travelled to the Cape in South Africa. Sparmannia belongs to the lime (linden) family, Tiliaceae.

Cuttings from side-shoots

The Indoor lime is propagated by means of cuttings. Take side-shoots from the branches which have flowered from early spring to late summer. These cuttings grow more compactly and flower more profusely than cuttings from branches which have not yet flowered, which grow very luxuriantly and make few or no flowers. Place the cuttings under double glass or plastic sheeting in two parts peat-based potting compost to one part river sand. The cuttings will develop sufficient roots in four weeks to pot them up in a 3-in/7-cm pot for cuttings.

After two months repot the plants in a 5-in-12-cm final pot. If you do not top, you will have a beautiful plant after six to eight weeks. Topping will produce a branched plant. The growing time is about four to five months.

Pruning and topping

The Indoor lime is a beautiful, large foliage plant which lasts a long time. Prune when necessary in the early spring, making sure to leave the well-ripened shoots which have formed the previous year; the plant will flower on these. Grow the plant in three parts RHP potting soil, one part clay and one part river sand. Water generously and feed weekly during the summer growing season. Keep the potting soil moderately moist and discontinue feeding in the dark winter months. Set the plants in a light position for sturdy growth; in the spring and summer, however, they will not tolerate direct sunlight. The plant is also content with less light, though growth is then somewhat flabby and weak. If the relative humidity in the room is too low, the plant may be attacked by red spider mite. Combat this by spraying the underside of the leaves heavily with cold water.

Sparmannia africana, inflorescence

Sparmannia africana

This is the splendid Indoor lime (linden), with its large, delicate leaves and its brilliant flowers. As the species name indicates, the plant comes from Africa. The double-flowered variety 'Plena' is occasionally seen. The variegated variety 'Variegata' is making some headway at the present time. Compactly growing plants sold under the name 'Nana' are also occasionally seen. It is not a separate variety; its compact growth has arisen through the choice of cutting.

Flowering Sparmannia africana

Treatment table

	cutting	growth	rest
pot	frame	5 in/12 cm	—
soil	peat-based potting compost and sand, 2:1	RHP, clay and sand, 3:1:1	—
feeding	—	1½ tsp compound fertilizer per pt water/3g per litre	none
watering	moist	generously	moderately
temperature	64° F/18° C	60-64° F/ 16-18° C	50° F/10° C
rel. humidity	90-95%	60-70%	60-70%
light	light	light	light
flowers	—	spring and summer—	
special features	The maximum temperature in the sun is 77° F/25° C. Shield well against sunlight.		

Pot plant and cut flowers

Spathiphyllum is a beautiful, profusely-flowering pot plant which is not yet common as a houseplant. In view of its need for humidity, the plant can also be regarded as a marsh plant. The name Spathiphyllum is derived from *spatha* and *phyllum*, which mean 'spathe' and 'leaf'. The white spathes of the plant are leaf-like. The species name comes from a German horticulturist, Gustav Wallis, who became the agent for a German firm in Brazil in 1856. In 1858 he started working for the famous Belgian firm, Linden, and took a collecting tour through South America, from the mouth to the source of the Amazon. In 1870 he started working for the English firm, Veitch & Sons, on behalf of which he brought back to Europe from Colombia a rich collection of plants, including Spathiphyllum. In 1875 he returned to South America, where he died of dysentery in 1878 in Ecuador.
Spathiphyllum belongs to the family Araceae. The plant shows a clear resemblance to the white Anthurium and the splendid flowers are also sold as cut flowers.

Sowing and division

The original botanical species of Spathiphyllum can be propagated from seed, in the manner described for Anthurium.
This method is generally used by commercial growers. It is easier, however to propagate the plants by division in early to mid-spring. The plant forms numerous side-shoots. When you repot the plant, pull it apart, roots and all. Do not select pieces which are too small, because the plant must quickly reach full-size again to provide good decorative value. After division, set the plants in a 5-in/10-cm final pot. If you want large plants, larger sections must be placed in a large pot.

Plenty of water

This plant is to be regarded somewhat as a marsh plant and therefore watered generously throughout the year. Feed it weekly during the spring and summer growing season. It grows well in a humus-rich, coarse-fibred, highly porous soil. The so-called Anthurium soil is particularly suitable for Spathiphyllum. The plant must be shielded against the sun; it even prefers a slightly shaded position. Grow it in as light a position as possible in the winter, but start to shield it from the sun as spring approaches.
Spathiphyllum keeps well in the house, but reaches its full potential in the greenhouse. It flowers for almost the whole year. The main flowering occurs in the spring and the flowers remain on the plant for many months.

Spathiphyllum wallisii

Spathiphyllum 'Mauna Loa'

Spathiphyllum wallisii

This is a beautiful, profusely-flowering houseplant which must be treated as a marsh plant.
Numerous tetraploid hybrids of this plant are grown by name in the United States. One of the best-known is the variety 'Mauna Loa', with its profuse flowering and large, brilliant white flowers. This variety is grown for cut flowers.

Spathiphyllum patinii

This Spathiphyllum has a narrow, more pendulous, spathe. The species is grown to only a limited extent.

Treatment table

	growth	rest
pot	4½ in/11 cm	—
soil	Anthurium soil	—
feeding	1 tsp compound fertilizer per pt water/2 g per litre	—
watering	generously	generously
temperature	68-86° F/ 20-30° C (sun)	60-64° F/ 16-18° C
rel. humidity	85-95%	85-95%
light	slight shade	light
flowers	all year	—

special features Start shielding against direct sunlight in late winter.

Treatment table

	cutting	growth	rest
pot	frame or pot	4-4½ in/ 10-11 cm	—
soil	peat litter and sand 5:1	RHP	—
feeding	—	1½ tsp compound fertilizer per pt water/ 3 g per litre	none
watering	moist	generously	sparingly
temperature	73° F/ 23° C	68-104° F/ 20-40° C (in sun)	46-50° F/ 8-10° C
rel. humidity	95%	70-80%	60-70%
light	light	sun	sun
flowers	—	all year	—
growth hormone	1-naphthalena-cetic acid 0.2% (hard cuttings)	—	—

special features Treat soft cuttings with 3-indoleacetic acid 0.5% or BT 0.1%. Maintain the correct relative humidity by constant spraying.

Stephanotis floribunda

No separate varieties of this exuberantly flowering (*floribunda*) plant are grown by name. Many profusely-flowering breeders' varieties are currently coming from Denmark. Stephanotis is sometimes called Bride's Flower. The splendid, white-scented flowers are often seen worked into brides' bouquets, diadems and wreaths.

Profuse flowering and lovely scent

The name Stephanotis comes from the Greek words *stephanos* for 'crown' and *our* for 'ear'. It is given to the plant because of the five tips of the auricles in the staminal crown, which are set like a crown. Stephanotis belongs to the family Asclepiadaceae. It is a left-spiralling climber which is a native of Madagascar. The plant was introduced into England as a cultivated plant in 1839. Stephanotis is a profusely-flowering houseplant which can grow extremely well in the house and which produces lovely, scented flowers for a large part of the year.

Not to be placed on its head

Stephanotis is propagated by taking an intermediate cutting from profusely-flowering plants. Take a piece of stem measuring 1¼ in/3 cm below the leaves and ¼ in/.5 cm above the leaves. Because the plant spirals in this way, care must be taken that the cutting is not placed on its head in the cutting medium. After taking the cuttings, soak them thoroughly in water and then treat them with growth hormone. Cuttings are best taken from mid-winter to mid-spring. In the summer the cuttings are too soft. Under plastic sheeting the cuttings will have roots in a month. Six weeks after taking the cuttings, place them in a 3-in/7-cm pot.
Commercial growers sort the cuttings into those 'with blind eye' and those 'with eye' (where the axillary bud has already started). Three to four weeks after potting, they train the growing tendrils along strings overhead. The fastest-growing specimens are then placed in a 4-5-in/10-12-cm final pot. When the flower buds are well formed, the strings are untied and the tendril is run with string along a wire bow in the pot. The plants which are potted up in early spring will flower in mid-autumn. The relative humidity must remain high to prevent the buds from dropping. Commercial growers supply the plants when the flower buds are coloured white.

Dryness and cold produce strong flower clusters

To enable plants with strong flower-clusters to be grown, specimens for flowering must be placed in a cool spot (46-50° F/8-10° C) in late autumn and the potting soil kept dry. After this rest period, which must last three months, the plants will flower at 60° F/15° C. Grow Stephanotis in a nutritious RHP potting soil. Water generously during the growing season and give it a good feed every two weeks. Fully-grown specimens can also be brought to flower by keeping the potting soil fairly dry at 60° F/15° C and maintaining a relative humidity of 60-70%. The correct humidity must be maintained during the growing season in order to prevent the buds from dropping. Grow plants for flowering in the full sun, but maintain the correct humidity. The sun ensures flower initiation on the young branches. These young branches will appear in the spring in a light position with a high temperature and humidity. After the cold treatment the plants will flower in late spring or early summer and they may continue to flower throughout the year. Commercial growers induce winter flowering by prolonging the day to fourteen hours for six to eight weeks and providing lighting of 800-1,200 mW per yd²/m² with TL 33 as a nightly interruption. Stephanotis is an ideal climber for the conservatory or greenhouse.

Profuse summer-flowerer

Streptocarpus is one of the Gesneriaceae. The genus Streptocarpus has about 1,300 species, which are natives of such countries as South Africa, Zaire, Angola, Madagascar, China, Thailand and Sumatra. Numerous crosses are developed in England from blue and red-flowering species from South Africa.

Streptocarpus is a profusely-flowering pot plant which lasts well in the house. The flowers stand proudly above the leaves on decorative stalks. It is a genuine summer-flowerer, whose splendid colours can be enjoyed for many months. Its durability as a cut flower is also good.

Easy leaf cuttings

Only the somewhat rare 'Wiesmoor' variety is propagated from seed, in a manner similar to that for Sinningia (Gloxinia). There are 51,000 seeds to the gram. All other Streptocarpus varieties are propagated by leaf cuttings. This can be done throughout the year. Take a leaf from which the midrib has been removed and place it almost vertical with the wound tissue in peat-based potting compost, making sure to treat the wound tissue first with growth hormone and a fungicide. The young plantlets will now emerge from adventitious (accidental) buds on the wound tissue. Under plastic sheeting, the cuttings will root after four weeks and the young plantlets will develop three weeks later. Three months after taking cuttings, prick out the young plantlets about 2 in/5 cm apart, grading them by size. Another three to four months later place them in the 4-5-in/10-12-cm plastic final pot. The plant should flower four months after this. For spring flowering, take cuttings in the summer months. For late flowering in early autumn, the plant must be potted up in late spring; take cuttings therefore in late autumn. The growing time is just under a year.

Humidity and light

Grow Streptocarpus in a humus-rich RHP potting soil and keep the soil moist during the whole of the growing season. Feed the plants weekly. If the sun is strong, set them in a slightly shaded position, but grow them on in as much light as possible.

Although the most profuse flowering occurs in the summer months, the plant can continue to flower throughout the year. Streptocarpus is a houseplant which can last a long time. Repot it once a year and feed it regularly. The temperature, the light and the relative humidity must also meet the plant's requirements.

Treatment table

	cutting	growth
pot	frame	4-4½ in/10-11 cm
soil	peat-based potting compost	humus-rich RHP
feeding	—	1 tsp compound fertilizer per pt water/2 g per litre
watering	moist	moist
temperature	68-72° F/ 20-22° C	64-68° F/18-20° C
rel. humidity	90-95%	80%
light	light	light
flowers	—	spring and summer
growth hormone	1-naphthalena-cetic acid 0.2%	—
fungicide	captan	
special features	The plant has no rest period. The maximum temperature in the sun is 77° F/25° C. Shield slightly in direct sunlight.	

154

Streptocarpus hybrid 'Wiesmoor'

Constant Nymph'

Streptocarpus hybrid 'Constant Nymph'

This variety arose in 1946. It is a profusely-flowering variety from which mutations have arisen spontaneously through radiation. It commonly has brilliant blue colours, though there is also a white-flowerd variety. 'Constant Nymph' and the mutants from it can also be used as 'father plants', but the plant cannot form any seed itself. The pistil is sterile. The anthers grow together and have to be opened with a pair of scissors to get at the pollen. There are new varieties in England in many shades of white, pink, red, purple and blue.

Streptocarpus hybrid 'Wiesmoor'

Stromanthe amabilis

Confusing relatives

Stromanthe belongs to the family Marantaceae, which as houseplants often have brilliantly decorated leaves. This results in some confusion with foliage plants such as Maranta, Calathea and, above all, Ctenanthe. The difference between Stromanthe and Ctenanthe consists, among other things, in the leaf structure. Stromanthe has a thicker leaf with a more solid feel than that of Ctenanthe. Stromanthe is also slightly more tolerant of a lower relative humidity in the room. It is a quick-growing foliage plant, and although it is grown for the decorative value of its leaves, there is one species, Stromanthe sanguinea, which bears magnificent flowers. It does not, however, flower profusely or regularly. The name Stromanthe comes from the Greek words, *strooma* and *anthos*, which mean 'bed' and 'flower' respectively. This refers to the shape of the inflorescence of the first described species, Stromanthe sanguinea. Stromanthe comes from Brazil.

Not difficult to take cuttings from

Stromanthe is a plant which can be propagated by means of shoot cuttings. Treat the cuttings with growth hormone and then place them in peat-based potting compost under double glass or plastic foil. The cuttings will have grown sufficient roots in two to three weeks to be potted up in a 3½-in/8-9-cm pot. Two months later repot them into a 5-6-in/11-13-cm final pot, where they should be left until they are fully-grown in about a year.

Quick grower

Stromanthe is a fast-growing foliage plant which is particularly suitable for mixed planting in large boxes, where its delicately patterned leaves have a highly decorative effect. Nor does the plant cause any problems when grown in the greenhouse. It should be potted in an airy, fibrous, highly-porous potting soil. The so-called Bromeliad soil is highly suitable for Stromanthe.

Water the plant generously during the growing season without allowing the sub-soil to become too wet. Also feed the plant weekly at this time. Water more sparingly in the dark winter months and add fertilizer only once every three weeks, depending on the growing rate. Grow the plants in a shaded position.

Stromanthe amabilis

This is a dwarf foliage plant which comes from Brazil. *Amabilis* means 'lovable'; the plant has a delicately patterned leaf.

Stromanthe sanguinea

This species also comes from Brazil. It grows to a great height and its stems are a deep red colour (*sanguinea* means 'blood-coloured'). Fully-grown specimens can flower in the summer with small white petals surrounded by distinctive bright-red bracts.

Treatment table

	cutting	growth	rest
pot	frame	4½-5 in/11-13 cm—	
soil	peat-based potting compost	Bromeliad soil	—
feeding	—	1 tsp compound fertilizer per pt water/ 2 g per litre	1 tsp compound fertilizer per pt water/2 g per litre
watering	moist	generously	moderately
temperature	68° F/ 20° C	64-68° F/ 18-20° C	64-68° F/ 18-20° C
rel. humidity	95%	80%	
light	slight shade	shade	light
growth hormone	3-indolea-cetic acid 0.1%	—	—
special features	The sub-soil must not become too wet, since the plant is salt-sensitive. The maximum summer temperature is 77° F/25° C. Feed once every three weeks in the winter.		

Succulents

Sun lovers

Succulentus means 'juicy' in Latin and this is the derivation of the name, succulents, by which is meant a large group of Xerophytes and Cacti, most of which grow in hot, dry climates and have fleshy roots. Many succulent plants grow in the dry regions of Africa, Madagascar and Southern Arabia. The Cacti are nearly all indigenous to the Americas. Succulents are characterised by their thick, fleshy stems, in which large amounts of water (sap) can be stored in large, thin-walled cells. The plants have penetrating roots which enable them to suck up groundwater from the depths beneath. They also have a widely-branched, surface root system which can easily absorb water from dew and mist. The stomata lie quite deep in order to limit evaporation. The epidermis is provided with a wax layer, hairs, thorns or a thick layer of epidermal cells. Most succulents are grown for the decorative value of their leaves. But many of them, including the Cacti (which are discussed separately in this book), produce beautiful flowers.

Sowing, cuttings, grafting

Many Cacti and also some other succulents are propagated from seed. Always sow in a lime-rich, very highly porous mixture. Cactus seeds, in particular, germinate very quickly. In the deserts they germinate in the very short time in which rain falls. The sowing soil must therefore never be dry. If you want to take cuttings from a succulent plant, do so by means of full-grown shoots or leaf cuttings. This means that cuttings should be taken during the plant's rest period, when the shoot or leaf is fully-grown. Many succulents, including Crassulaceae, can be propagated by means of leaf cuttings. Always let the wounds dry out first. The cuttings, including those of Cacti, must stand upright during the drying in order to ensure good rooting later around the whole wound. Place succulents in a mixture of equal parts peat dust and river sand. Many Cacti are grafted on to a rootstock to ensure better growth. The following are often used as rootstocks: Peireskia, Peireskiopsis and Trichocereus. Grafted Cacti will usually grow more quickly than specimens grown from seed or cuttings. Sometimes a rootstock is used which, despite its rapid growth, in fact leads to a reduction in the overall life of the grafted Cactus. The red Gymnocalycium mihanovichii 'Friedrichii', for instance, is often seen grafted on to a Myrtillocactus geometrizans. This is a species which requires lots of water and warmth in the winter, while Gymnocalycium actually needs little water and a lower temperature. From a commercial point of view, such a combination is profitable, since the grafted cactus grows more quickly and the plant is sold in the juvenile state. But in fact this Cactus is of no use to anyone, because the life-span is limited.

Lots of sunlight and warmth but little fertilizer

Grow most succulents in the full sun, and with as much warmth as possible, during the spring. It is an advantage if the day and night temperatures differ sharply, since this is what happens in the desert areas which are the plants' natural habitat. Water the plants generously, but only once a week. Feed sparingly, but add a lime-rich mixed feed during the growing season. Too much fertilizer will cause straggly growth.

Add no feed at all during the rest period; keep the soil dry and the temperature as low as possible. The rest period usually runs from mid-autumn to the beginning of spring, depending on the species. Grow the plants in a plastic pot filled with a mixture of three parts RHP frozen peat potting soil, two parts heavy clay and one part river sand. The soil temperature is higher in a plastic pot. If the pH is too low, it can be restored by adding 2½ tsp lime-fertilizer compound per pt of this soil mixture/5 g per litre. Succulents and Cacti can produce

156

A selection of succulents

Sedum stahlii

Ceropegia woodii, lantern plant

Faucaria tigrina

beautiful flowers. Conditions for profuse flowering are low winter temperatures, a low relative humidity and a dry potting soil in the rest period. The plants often fail to flower in the house because the winter temperature is too high. The golden rules for growing good succulents are as much sunlight as possible throughout the year, high daytime and low night temperatures in the summer, sufficient light, a good rest period with low winter temperatures and a good quality potting soil which is kept dry. In the house the lack of sunlight and the excessively high winter temperature cause the most problems.

Family	Genus	Species
Asclepidaceae	Ceropegia	various (Chinese lantern plant)
	Stapelia	various (Carrion flower)
Compositae	Senecio	citriformis (Pea plant)
	Senecio	herreianus
Crassulaceae	Crassula	various
	Echeveria	various
	Kalanchoe	various
	Sedum	various
	Rochea	various
	Cotyledon	various
	Pachyphytum	various
Euphorbiaceae	Euphorbia	trigona
	Euphorbia	obesa
	Euphorbia	grandicornis
Ficoidaceae	Lithops	various (living stone)
	Faucaria	various (Tiger's mouth)
	Aptenia	various
	Lampranthus	various
	Mesembryanthemum	various
	Conophytum	various
	Oscularia	various
Liliaceae (Agavaceae)	Agave	various
	Yucca	various
Liliaceae	Aloë	various
	Gasteria	various
	Haworthia	various
	Sansevieria	various
Cactaceae	(see Cactaceae or discussed separately)	

The garden plant, Yucca flaccida, in flower in the Himalayas

Treatment table

	sowing	cutting	growth	rest
pot	frame	frame	dependent on size	
soil	very highly porous and lime-rich	peat dust and sand 1:1	RHP and clay and sand 3:2:1	
feed	—	—	½ tsp compound fertilizer per pt water/ 1 g per litre potassium-rich	none
water	moist	generously	generously	almost none
temperature	68° F/ 20° C	68° F/ 20° C	105° F/ 40° C	40-60° F/ 5-15° C

Profusely-flowering annual

Thunbergia is a popular pot plant which can brighten up the home from spring right through summer with splendid, mostly golden-yellow, flowers with a black eye. This is the origin of the plant's popular name, Black-eyed Susan. Thunbergia is named after the Swedish doctor and botanist, Carl Peter Thunberg (1743-1828), who was a friend of Linnaeus. He gained fame from his journeys to Japan to collect plants and seeds on behalf of wealthy Amsterdam merchants. A public monument was erected to him in Nagasaki. Thunbergia does not, however, come from Asia, but from South Africa. The plant belongs to the family Acanthaceae.

An easy guest

Thunbergia does not cause any particular difficulties as a houseplant and it is an easy plant to propagate from seed. The seed is coarse: there are only 40 seeds to a gram. Sow in a frame filled with normal potting soil and after about four weeks the seed will germinate. You can also sow straight into the pot. As soon as the plantlets are large enough, set two or three of them together in a 4-in/9-10-cm final pot. Place a split bamboo stick, 16 in/40 cm long in the pot. When the stems start growing, twist them round and round the stick, first upwards, then downwards, then up again, until you get a good compact plant. This twisting must be carried out punctiliously, otherwise the tendrils of different plants will get entangled in one another. The stems, which reach several metres if treated well, can also be trained along a wire. If the plant is sown in early to mid-winter, the growing time is 15 weeks; if sown in early or mid-spring the growing time is only 10 weeks.

Plenty of water and fertilizer, no direct sunlight

Grow Thunbergia in a normal RHP potting soil kept constantly moist. Four weeks after potting start to feed the plant weekly and ensure that it is shielded from excessively strong sunlight. Excessive solar radiation turns the leaf-colour red. Also grow the plant in as light a position as possible. Make sure that the relative humidity does not exceed 75%; otherwise cork will spread over the leaves. If treated well, Thunbergia will flower from mid-spring to late summer. Deadhead regularly to prevent seed formation. In a greenhouse or hothouse it is a beautiful, profusely-flowering climber which reaches a height of several metres. The plant must then be placed in a larger pot or the ground.

Treatment table

	cutting	growth
pot	frame	3½-4 in/9-10 cm
soil	RHP	RHP
feeding	—	1½ tsp compound fertilizer per pt water/3 g per litre
watering	moist	moist
temperature	68° F/20° C	64° F/18° C (night) 86° F/30° C (sun)
rel. humidity	90-95%	70-75%
light	light	light
flowers	—	mid-spring to early autumn
special features	The relative humidity should not rise above 75%; otherwise cork spreads over the leaf. Excessive sunlight discolours the leaf. Deadhead to prolong flowering.	

Thumbergia alata 'Aurantiaca

Thunbergia alata 'Aurantiaca'

This is the most common Black-eyed Susan. It is a variety with golden-yellow flowers and a black eye. *Alata* means 'winged' and refers to the wing-type, broadened leaf stalk.
The variety 'Alba', in creamy-white and black, the single-coloured, golden-yellow 'Lutea' and a single-coloured, creamy-white variety are also seen. But their decorative value is diminished by the absence of the black eye.

Thumbergia grandiflora growing in the wild in Columbia

Tillandsia flabellata

Tillandsia leiboldiana

Tillandsia cyanea
This Tillandsia is grown to only a limited extent. It has dark-blue flowers (*cyanea*) and comes from Ecuador, where it lives epiphytically on trees.

Tillandsia falbellata
Flabellata means 'fan-shaped' and refers to the branched inflorescence of this species, which is a native of Mexico, Guatemala and El Salvador. It grows there in misty wooded regions on mountain slopes at a height of 330-4,300 ft/100-1,300 m; the relative humidity is very high. This species is a good houseplant with great powers of adaptation.

Tillandsia leiboldiana
This plant is a native of America, from southern Mexico to Costa Rica, where it grows epiphytically on trees to a height of 4,300 ft/1,300 m. Like many other Tillandsia species, it was cultivated in the middle of the last century. The plants originating from Costa Rica have bright, violet-coloured flowers, which make a beautiful contrast to the red colour of the bracts. This species should make headway as a houseplant. In addition, the flowers can be used as cut flowers in floral arrangements.

Widespread Bromeliad genus
Tillandsia, which has more than 400 species, is the most widespread genus of the family Bromeliaceae. The species grow over the whole of South and Central America and have spread into the southern United States. They occur in tropical and sub-tropical climates and also in forests and on mountain slopes where the temperature is low. Some species grow in dry regions; others are indigenous to the humid rain forests. Many species live epiphytically, ie on trees and tree trunks. One species, Tillandsia usneoides, the so-called Spanish Moss, a twining plant which can hardly be recognized as a Bromeliad, causes much trouble in South and Central America because it grows on telephone and telegraph lines, which sometimes break under the load. Most of these plants do not survive in houses for very long, because the relative humidity is far too low. Tillandsia is named after the 17th-century Swedish botanist, Tillands.

Fluffy seed
Tillandsia has fluffy seeds which are difficult to distribute. After pollination the seeds ripen in six months. Sow them very close together in a humus-rich mixture. Do not cover them, because they need light to germinate. After four months place clumps of the emerging grassy plantlets out separately and after another three months distribute the clumps so that the plantlets stand separately. Then prick the plantlets out once again. About 18 months after sowing, place them in a 3½-in/9-cm final pot. Plants which are two-and-a-half years old will flower and should be treated with 2-hydrozinoethanol for good flowering (see Bromeliad). When the plants are old enough and fairly large, they may also be treated with acetylene in the light summer months for good flowering, provided that they are old and big enough.

Special feed
Tillandsia requires a special type of feed. In the summer feed it one week with ½ tsp/g of compound fertilizer per 2 pt/1 l of water in the proportions 17:6:18 or 20:5:20. The next week give it a solution of ½ tsp/g of nitrate of potash (13.5:0:45). In the winter give it only ⅛ tsp of this compound fertilizer per pt water/¼ g per litre. Pour the compound fertilizer over the leaves and then spray them down with pure water. Grow Tillandsia in the special Bromeliad soil. Keep this soil moderately moist, but ensure that there is always water in the leaf sheath. Genuine epiphytes require very little water, but care must be taken that the relative humidity does not fall below 80%.
Tillandsia requires slight shade in the summer and full light in the winter. The light requirement is 6,000 mW per yd²/m². Tillandsias make splendid houseplants. If you have an epiphyte, you must always repot it into a highly porous mixture, and since it does not make a great root ball, it must not be placed in a large pot. The soil mixture must not decompose too much, and the plant should therefore be repotted every eight to ten months. Because of their origins in rain and mist forests, they require a high relative humidity for good growth. Care must nevertheless be taken that the potting soil does not become too moist.

Treatment table

	sowing	growth	rest
pot	frame	3½ in/9 cm	—
soil	humus-rich	Bromeliad soil	—
feeding	—	see text	—
watering	moderately	moderately	moderately
temperature	72-75° F/22-24° C	77-86° F/25-30° C	68-72° F/20-22° C
rel. humidity	95%	90%	> 80%
light	light	shade	light
flowering advancement	—	8 fl oz 2-hy in 4 pt water/250 ml in 2 litres	—

special features: The leaf sheath cannot contain much water. Spray the plant therefore with 2-hydrozinoethanol (2pt/1 litre per 5m²). The minimum temperature applies to the night and the maximum temperature to the day.

159

Outdoor flowering

Tolmiea is grown for the decorative value of its leaves and also for its special growth habit, from which the plant gets its popular name. It is a sturdy plant, hardy enough even to be grown outdoors. Tolmiea never flowers as a houseplant, but outside it forms greenish and brown flowers in clusters up to 10 in/25 cm in length. Tolmiea is named after W. Fraser Tolmie, who was a doctor at Fort Vancouver in British Columbia and made a reputation for knowledge of the flora of North America. Tolmiea is a member of the Saxifrage family, Saxifragaceae. It is a native of the west of North America and was first cultivated in England in 1812.

Simple to propagate

The appealing way in which the plant can be propagated makes it popular with many people. A complete young plant appears on full-grown leaves, which can be planted leaf and all in a 3-in/8-cm pot. The young plant will then take root and form leaves on which new young plants will in their turn be able to grow. The growing time from potting to a fair-sized plant with children-on-a-lap of its own is three to four months. This quick propagation has also contributed to the popularity of the plant.

Problem-free houseplant

Tolmiea is a houseplant which causes few problems. The plant has great powers of adaptation and although it really should be grown in as much light as possible, it is content with less light, though in that case it grows less quickly. Nor is the plant fussy about temperature. Room temperature is best, but having it slightly higher or lower does not create difficulties. The plant grows excellently in a mixture of three parts RHP potting soil and one part river sand. Keep this soil permanently moist, but do not water too generously, or growth will be flabby; it will grow ugly, long leaf stalks and fewer young plants will appear on the leaves. Feed weekly in the growing season. If lots of nitrogen-rich fertilizer is added, it will grow handsome, dark-green leaves, but far fewer young plants on the blade. The plant should be shielded against strong sunlight and repotted annually in late winter or early spring.

Tolmiea menziesii

Tolmiea menziesii

Only one species of the genus Tolmiea is grown as a houseplant, namely this Tolmiea menziesii. The species name comes from A. Menzies who lived from 1754 to 1842 and was a gardener at the Botanical Gardens in Edinburgh. As a doctor's assistant he also made a world tour starting from Fort Vancouver in British Columbia, during which he collected many plants.

Treatment table

	young plant	growth	rest
pot	3 in/8 cm	3-5 in/8-12 cm	—
soil	RHP and sand 3:1	RHP and sand 3:1	—
feeding	—	½ tsp compound fertilizer per pt water/ 1 g per litre	none
watering	moderately	moderately	moderately
temperature	64-68° F/ 18-20° C	64-68° F/ 18-20° C	50-54° F/ 10-12° C
rel. humidity	80%	70-80%	60-70%
light	light	light	light

special features Shield against excessive sunlight (indoors). The plant flowers only as a garden plant.

Tradescantia blossfeldiana in flower

Tradescantia albiflora

This beautiful hanging plant comes from Central America. The sap of the plant is colourless and the leaves are green on the underside. *Albiflora* means 'with white flowers'. Some varieties are 'Albivittata', with yellow-striped leaves, and 'Rochfords Silver', with coarse, silver-striped leaves.

Tradescantia fluminensis

This species comes from Brazil. The sap is purple-coloured, as is the underside of the leaves. *Fluminensis* means 'by a river'. The variegated variety 'Variegata' is widely grown.

Better with no flowers

Tradescantia is a splendid hanging plant with beautifully coloured leaves. The plant must be rejuvenated regularly by cuttings and/or topping. You must also ensure that it never flowers. Although the flowers have some decorative value, flowering ages the plant rapidly. Tradescantia is named after the father and son of the same name, John Tradescant, who were both court gardener at the court of King Charles I of England in the middle of the 17th century. The plant belongs to the family Commelinaceae, which is named after the Amsterdam merchant and chemist, J. Commelin (1629-1692), who as a horticulturist in 1682 was charged with supervising the laying-out of the Dutch physic garden 'Artsenijhof' (*Hortus medicus* and now *Hortus botanicus*). Later he entered the service of the Hortus and wrote some botanical works. Tradescantia albiflora, with green translucent leaves, comes from Central America. The other species used as a houseplant is Tradescantia fluminensis, with purplish-green leaves, which is a native of Brazil.

Think about the leaf decoration

Cuttings of Tradescantia should be taken from specimens with the most beautiful leaf decoration. They can be taken throughout the year. Cut the herbaceous cuttings to a length of about 3 in/8 cm. Four to six weeks later place them in a 4-in/10-cm final pot and cover the cuttings with paper to prevent drying out.
The cuttings will root in a week and in six to eight weeks the plant will grow into a real hanging plant. At the beginning, tie the suckers up by placing four 10-in/25-cm sticks or wire pins in a square. Tie round with cotton thread to give support to the stems.

Plenty of water and slight shade

Tradescantia grows well in an RHP potting soil kept constantly moist. Add no feed for the first four weeks, but feed weekly thereafter. The plants must not be grown in conditions of too much warmth, or growth will be flabby. They require slight shade, and will tolerate a comparatively dark position, though lack of light may cause the variegated leaf-colour to fade considerably.

Treatment table

	cutting	growth
pot	3½-4 in/9-10 cm	3½-4 in/9-10 cm
soil	RHP	RHP
feeding	—	1½ tsp compound fertilizer per pt water/3 g per litre
watering	generously	generously
temperature	64° F/18° C	60-64° F/15-18° C
rel. humidity	70-80%	70%
light	slight shade	slight shade

special features The plant has no real rest period. Top frequently to prevent flowering.

Beautiful Bromeliad

Vriesea forms suckers from out of the topmost leaf bud. As soon as a Vriesea splendens, for example, has finished flowering, a new plant grows in the sheath from out of the topmost leaf bud. With most Bromeliads the suckers are formed from out of the bottom-most leaf bud. They then grow downwards on the side of the plant. Vriesea is named after H.W. de Vries, who lived from 1806 to 1862. He was professor of horticulture at Amsterdam and Leiden and founder of the Dutch Botanical Association. The genus Vriesea is a native of Central and South America, in particular Brazil. There are about 150 species, although an accurate figure cannot be given. There are numerous natural crosses. There is some confusion regarding the nomenclature in the horticultural world. This is the result of, among other things, the numerous crosses, the oldest of which are no longer known.

Vrieseas are splendid flowering pot plants and Vriesea splendens is one of the most widely grown flowering Bromeliads. The genus also includes many beautiful foliage plants.

Cross-pollination

Apart from a few hybrids, all species of Vriesea are propagated from seed.

Make sure to obtain the seed of good plants, paying particular attention, with the flowering species, to the colour and shape of the inflorescence and structural compactness. Pollinate by cross-pollination (in the morning!). It is sometimes necessary to open the flowers with a nail in order to pollinate them. The fluffy seed is ripe in three to nine months, depending on the time of year. If you pollinate in early to mid-spring the seed will ripen more quickly than if you pollinate in late summer. Sow as thinly as possible in a humus-rich mixture; the fluffy seed is very difficult to distribute.

Do not cover the seed; the plant needs light to germinate. After three or four months set clumps of germinated seed out separately. Repeat the pricking-out three times at five-monthly intervals. Set the plantlets out individually at the second pricking out. Pot up two-year-old plants in a 4-5-in/10-12-cm final pot. They should flower four to five years after the sowing.

Growth regulators

Vriesea reacts favourably to all growth regulators for flowering treatment. The plants flower about four months after the treatment. In the winter months it is best to use 2-hydrozinoethanol. Pour ½ fl oz/15 ml of this (in a solution of 8 fl oz to 15 pt water/250 ml to 7.5 litres) in the previously emptied leaf sheath. The solution should be left in the sheath for seven days and then replaced with water again.

Use the special Bromeliad soil for growing and keep it moderately moist. As with most Bromeliads, ensure that there is always water in the leaf sheath.

In the summer, feed one week with ¼ tsp of compound fertilizer per pt water/½ g per litre (17:6:18 or 20:5:20), and the next week add a solution of ¼ tsp of nitrate of potash (13.5:0:45) per pt water/½ g per litre. In the winter add ⅛ tsp per pt/¼ g per litre.

The solution can be added to the potting soil or poured into the leaf sheath. Give Vriesea shade in the summer; in the winter grow it in as light a position as possible. If the light intensity is 15,000 lux, shield the plant. The light requirement is 6,000 mW per yd^2/m^2.

The plant must be repotted annually. The pot does not have to be all that large, because the plante are epiphytes and do not form many roots.

Vriesea psittacina

This is a small Vriesea with brightly coloured flowers. (*Psittacina* means 'parrot-coloured'). There are numerous varieties of this species, which comes from Brazil and Paraguay. They are all propagated via suckers. The flowers are also sometimes used as cut flowers.

Vriesea psittacina

Vriesea splendens

Vriesea splendens

This characteristic Bromeliad, which comes from Surinam and Venezuela, was cultivated in 1850.

A common variety, with a beautiful leaf decoration and a splendid inflorescence, is 'Favoriet'.

Vriesea hieroglyphica

This plant also comes from Brazil. It can grow very large, and it has a beautiful, dark, freakish leaf decoration (like hieroglyphics). It is one of the most difficult species to cultivate, because it requires a consistently high degree of humidity (approximately 85%) and makes high demands as regards temperature and light.

Vriesea saundersii

This Vriesea also comes from Brazil. It is a particularly beautiful foliage plant, distinguished by its single grey leaves with small red dots. It flowers after four to five years, when the seed can be obtained. The greenish inflorescence has little decorative value.

Vriesea fenestralis

Vriesea fenestralis

This plant, which is native to Brazil, flowers only after eight to nine years with a large inflorescence of insignificant, yellow-green flowers. The particular appeal of this Vriesea comes from the distinctive window pattern (*fenestralis*) of its beautifully decorated leaves. The decoration is already seen on young specimens.

Vriesea tessellata

This is one of the larger species. Once again, it comes from Brazil. This Vriesea has a beautiful blue-green, mosaic-type (*tessellata*) leaf decoration. The plant flowers only after eight to nine years with insignificant, yellow-green flowers.

Vriesea hybrids

These hybrids form a large group of green-leaved crosses with distinctive red inflorescences. Many flower at the juvenile stage. They rarely have names and are grown by number.

Vriesea Poelmaannii hybrids

This is a green-leaved cross with a branched, red inflorescence.
The ancestors of this beautiful plant are not precisely known, but Vriesea carinata, Vriesea viminalis, Vriesea vigeri and Vriesea barilletii have played a major role in the numerous crosses. These hybrids are now sometimes propagated by tissue-growing in vitroculture.

Treatment table

	sowing	growth	rest
pot	frame	3½ in/9 cm	—
soil	humus-rich	Bromeliad soil	—
feeding	—	see text	—
watering	moderately	moderately	moderately
temperature	72-75° F/ 22-24° C	77-86° F/ 25-30° C	68-72° F/ 20-22° C
rel. humidity	95%	90%	80%
light	light	shade	light
influencing of flowering	—	2-hydrozinoe-thanol (see text)	—

special features The minimum temperature applies to the night and the maximum to the day.
Ensure that there is water in the leaf reservoir.

Zebrina

Tradescantia family

Zebrina is sometimes called Tradescantia, understandably since the two genera belong to the same family, Commelinaceae. They also bear resemblances to one another and their treatment is also identical.

Zebrina has a distinctive, striped decoration on its leaves; hence the name Zebrina ('like a zebra'). Tradescantia has a loose-leaved corolla, whereas Zebrina's corolla grows tightly together; this is the distinguishing characteristic.

Zebrina must also be kept young by constantly taking cuttings and topping. This prevents the plant from flowering and thereby enhances vegetative growth. The plant is a native of Mexico, Central America and the Antilles. It is a splendid hanging plant with leaves which are purple with green and greyish-white stripes on top and a purplish-coloured underside.

The plant was cultivated in England in 1849.

Rapid rooting

Cuttings can be taken from Zebrina throughout the year. Select herbaceous cuttings about 3 in/8 cm long and place four to six of them directly into a 4-in/9-10-cm final pot. Cover the cuttings with paper to keep them drom drying out.

The cuttings will root in a week and in one or two months you will have a fair-sized plant.

Support the first shoots by placing four 10-in/25-cm sticks in a square in the pot. Wire pins can also be used for this. Tie cotton thread round the sticks or pins; the stems will then grow on them and form a beautiful hanging plant.

Plenty of water, little light

Two things which you must pay attention to with Zebrina are the humidity of the potting soil and the light. They grow best in slight shade, although they can also grace a darker position. The strongly variegated specimens must not be grown in too dark a spot, however, because then the leaf colour will fade. Zebrina grows well in a normal RHP potting soil, which should be kept constantly moist. Add no feed for the first four weeks; thereafter feed weekly, depending on the growth.

Treatment table

	cutting	growth
pot	3½-4 in/9-10 cm	3½-4 in/9-10 cm
soil	RHP	RHP
feeding	—	1½ tsp compound fertilizer per pt water/3 g per litre
temperature	64° F/ 18° C	60-64° F/15-18° C
rel. humidity	70-80%	70%
light	slight shade	slight shade
special features	The plant has no real rest period. Top if you want to prevent flowering.	

Zebrina purpusii

This species is a native of Mexico and was first cultivated in Germany in 1920. It is a large variety and the top side of the leaf is variable in colour, ranging from dark green to wine-red, but with no white stripes.

Zebrina purpusii

Zebrina pendula (Tradescantia pendula)

This is a beautiful hanging plant which is somewhat like Tradescantia. The difference consists in the structure of the corolla.

Tradescantia has a loose-leaved corolla, whereas that of Zebrina is tightly grown together. *Pendula* means 'hanging' The variety 'Quadricolor' ('four-coloured') has red, pink and white stripes, mixed with purple, on a green leaf. It was obtained in Germany in 1896.

Zygocactus truncatus

This pure species is still grown sporadically. Many of these Crab cacti, with their beautiful purple-red flowers and distinctive white, projecting stamens, are still seen in houses today. *Truncatus* means 'truncated' and refers to the shape of the leaf.

Zygocactus truncatus hybrids

These are crosses of Zygocactus truncatus with the strong-growing Schlumbergera russelliana. These Schlumbergera plants have good resistance to foot rot. The crosses grow more quickly and produce larger flowers than the original species. There is a wide selection of colours from white to pink, lilac and red shades.

The first cross was made in 1850 in England. In 1870 the cross was repeated in France, and in this century many outstanding varieties have been obtained from German crosses, such as 'Weihnachtsfreude', with bright orange flowers, the carmine-red 'Andenken an R. Zenneck' and the weak-growing, white variety 'Wintermaerchen'. There are about 120 varieties of this cactus. Strong-growing and profusely-flowering varieties have come from the United States in recent years; they have no name but are sold by flower colour.

A winter flowerer

Zygocactus is a well-known Crab cactus which flowers at about Christmas time in the northern hemisphere. It is therefore popularly known as the Christmas crab cactus. Zygocactus means connected with, or allied to, a cactus. This is a somewhat strange name, because it is simply a cactus. At the time it was named, however, none or very few Crab cacti were known, and it was therefore believed to be simply allied to the cactus.

The plant was first described in 1818 and was cultivated as a houseplant in 1821.

It is indigenous to the mountainous rain forests on the eastern coast of Brazil and grows there as an epiphyte, ie on trees or tree trunks or in humus layers on the rocks. The air in the region is so humid that water drips from the trees.

Cuttings and grafting

The Crab cactus is often grafted on to a rootstock of Pereskia aculeata or Eriocereus justbertii.

If you want to propagate a Crab cactus, select well-ripened limbs and do not cut, but break, them off. This is best done in the spring after flowering. Select young ripened shoots from the top of the plant. In this way you reduce the risk of a mould which causes foot rot (*fusarium*).

Place the cuttings in a mixture of three parts peat litter to one part river sand and protect them against drying out by covering them with paper. The cuttings will root in three weeks, when they should be placed, mostly two together, in a 3½-in/8-9-cm pot. (They may first be planted in a 3-in/7-cm pot and later in a 4-5-in/10-12-cm pot. This produces larger specimens.)

Plenty of nitrogen

A Crab cactus requires plenty of nitrogen during the growing season. Give it a nitrogen-rich compound fertilizer every week up to mid-summer. Give it this fertilizer again in mid-winter when it starts to grow again after flowering. Vegetative growth (of the stem) must stop and the shoots must have ripened by late spring.

Grow the Crab cactus in a humus-rich RHP potting soil, which can be mixed with styrene (plastic) granules in the ratio 4:1 to prevent the accumulation of excess water. Keep the potting soil moderately moist throughout the year, but ensure that the soil never becomes dry. In the dark months place the plant in as light a position as possible; in the summer shield it against excessive sunlight.

The plant forms flower buds at a temperature of 50-60° F/10-15° C, irrespective of the day-length. It is not easy to find such a cool place in centrally heated houses, but this difficulty can be overcome by giving the plant a short-day treatment, with a day-length of nine hours, for four to five weeks. The plants will then form flowers at 60-64° F/15-18° C, with a night temperature of 60° F/15° C. The well-known, red-flowering variety 'Weihnachtsfreude' ('Christmas Joy') forms flowers at 68° F/20° C.

Treatment table

	cutting	growth	flower initiation
pot	frame	3-3½ in/8-9 cm	—
soil	peat litter and sand 4:1	RHP and styrene granules 4:1	—
feeding	—	1½ tsp compound fertilizer per pt water/ 3 g per litre	none
watering	moderately	moderately	moderately
temperature	72-75° F/ 22-24° C	64-73° F/ 18-23° C (in sun)	50-60° F/ 10-15° C
rel. humidity	90-95%	80%	70-80%
light	slight shade	slight shade	light
flowers	—	early winter	—
special features	The soil must never be wet, nor completely dry. The flowering time can be delayed by long-day treatment. Flower bud formation is enhanced by short-day treatment at 60-64° F/15-18° C.		

Information

Pots

Earthenware pots.
Red earthenware pots are still widely used at the present time. These pots are sold by sizes, which are given in numbers or in the diameter in in/cm.

There is some variation as regards the in/cm size, depending on the manufacturer. With a standard pot the diameter size practically coincides with the in/cm size.

A good earthenware pot must be porous and able to absorb sufficient water. The earthenware pot vaporizes a lot of water in the room, and the potting soil will therefore oversalt in the top layer.

In addition earthenware pots are more expensive than plastic pots, the difference being particularly noticeable in larger pots.

The plastic pot
Plastic pots are often regarded simply as replacements for earthenware ones. This is incorrect. The plastic pot has several advantages:

a.   The pot requires only 40-50% of the water which would be required for an equivalent earthenware pot.

b.   The soil temperature remains higher because the pot wall does not vaporize any water; the plant therefore grows more quickly.

c.   The roots do not stick to the wall, so that the root ball is not damaged when the plant is knocked out of the pot.

d.   The pot is unbreakable in normal use and is also cheaper.

e.   The weight of the pot is light and the pots require little storage space.

f.   Root penetration through the clod is better on the whole, partly due to the low water vaporization, with the result that oversalting in the top layer does not occur so quickly.

A disadvantage of the pot is its low stability; taller plants fall over more easily.

The pots are sold in in/cm sizes, which indicate the diameter. The height of the pot and the openings in the bottom are different, depending on the make. Buckets are sometimes used for large plants; a number of holes then have to be made in the bottom of them for good drainage. The best results are obtained in dark-coloured buckets; a light-coloured bucket lets light through and algae may then grow in the bucket and inhibit growth.

Fibre pots
For plants which have to spend only a short time in a pot, eg cuttings, fibre pots are available. The pots are made of compressed fibrous material which decomposes in the soil when the plant and the pot are planted together in a frame or in a larger pot. These pots come in various sizes, both round and square.

The so-called 'Jiffy' pots, which are much used for cuttings, consist of compressed slices of organic material in a nylon net. If these dry slices are laid out individually and sprayed, they swell up into standard 3-in/7-cm pots.

The advantage of these fibre pots is that the plant never has to be knocked out of the pot. The pot ball is not damaged.

In addition you are not left with old pots.

Commercial growers also use round paper pots without bottoms, which are supplied in mats stuck together. The mats are pulled apart and the pots filled with soil. When the pots are used for cuttings, the cuttings are repotted, after rooting, together with the paper pot. The pot then decomposes in the soil.

Multi-pots and baskets
Multi-pots are plastic pots which are compressed together and supplied as a unit. Commercial growers use them, for instance, for taking cuttings and for pricking out seedlings. They are cheap because they can always be re-used. Baskets are of compressed plastic. They have many openings through which the roots can grow later. They are used, among other things, for cuttings and can therefore be placed pot and all in a frame or in another pot.

Potting up and repotting

Sizes
When you are potting up young plants, do this in the pot sizes 2-3 in/5-8 cm, depending on the size of the plant. Place fully developed plants which may possibly flower in a final pot of a size ranging from 4 in/10 cm to 5 in/13 cm. For older plants use still larger sizes, with a content of 10-40 pt/5-20 litres or more.

Clod
When potting up young plants, make sure that the potting soil is fairly dry. This promotes rapid growth. Press the soil down slightly after repotting, so that the plant is standing firmly. Select for the repotting, in most cases, a pot which is two or three sizes bigger than the old one.

Remove from the old clod only the topmost layer of soil and the soil which does not contain roots. Leave the clod containing the roots intact.

In order to facilitate watering, do not fill the pot completely. Provide a brim whereby the earth remains a little below the edge of the pot.

Feeding

Plants need nutrients for good growth. The most important are the so-called macro-elements. These are nitrogen, phosphorus, calcium, lime and magnesium. In addition, plants require a large number of other nutrients in very small amounts. These are the so-called trace elements, such as iron, manganese, copper, zinc, boron, and molybdenum.

Normal potting soils contain a basic amount of all these substances, often sufficient for a complete growth cycle. These elements may also be introduced into the soil by means of a general-purpose fertilizer, such as is suitable for growing tomatoes.

Additional feeding
A shortage of certain macro-elements occurs in the soil after four to six weeks and these must be made up by additional feeding. Composite fertilizers are available for this purpose, with high concentrations of nitrogen (N), phosphorus (P), calcium (Ca) and sometimes magnesium (Mg). These artificial fertilizers are available in varying proportions of the nutrients. There are also special fertilizers for Bromeliads. These high-concentration, compound fertilizers contain a minimum of fillers, so that the salt concentration in the potting soil does not increase excessively.

The liquid fertilizers which are often sold to consumers have a low concentration and are rather expensive in relation to their nutritive value. Their only advantage is that, since they contain so few nutritive salts, they do not cause any harm. The most beneficial are the general-purpose artificial fertilizers in larger packs, of about 15lb/7 kg, such as are used for growing tomatoes. Many plant fertilizers with an organic or so-called biological base are commonly available today. Their chief effect is a psychological one for the user; their nutritive value is generally negligible.

How much fertilizer?
Give the plants 1-1½ tsp of the easily soluble fertilizers per pt irrigation water /3g per litre. Feed weekly during the growing season, in exceptional cases twice a week. In the darker winter months, feed once every 14 days or not at all. When feeding, ensure that the potting soil is always moist; otherwise the salt concentration in the soil will become too high.

Add a total of 1½-2 fl oz artificial fertilizer solution to the potting soil per pt pot content/100 ml per litre. In some cases, notably a number of Bromeliads, the artificial fertilizer solution should be sprayed over the whole plant. The plant must not be in flower then; otherwise the flowers and the buds will scorch. Spray the plants down with clean water after the spraying.

RHP potting soil
The RHP potting soils contain on average the following fertilizers per

200 pt/100 l: 700-800 tsp/g Dolokal; 150 tsp/g of an NPK fertilizer, for example in the proportions 16:10:15; 15 tsp/g triple superphosphate and 25 g /tsp Sporumix PG. This Sporumix provides the soil with the required trace elements. This mixture contains 25% magnesium oxide; it also contains small amounts of copper, boron, molybdenum and manganese.

Irrigation water

The best irrigation water for plants contains a minimum of salts. Many plants, for example Orchids and Ferns, are very sensitive to chlorine salts (such as cooking salts); on other plants the total salt concentration has a harmful effect. Salinity can be determined by electrophoresis. Normally, rainwater contains the smallest amounts of dissolved salts and is, therefore, ideal irrigation water. Depending on local circumstances, however, rainwater may be somewhat acid, if, for example, it has been contaminated by sulphur dioxide in the atmosphere. Sulphur dioxide combines with water to make sulphuric acid, which can lead to an excessive drop in the acid level (see page 168), particularly in humus-rich potting soils. In that case spray about 200 tsp/g per yd²/m² of a lime-fertilizer compound over the potting soil. In this way lime in the soil is washed away. For one square metre of plants in a greenhouse, 1,400-2,600 pt/700-1,300 of water are required. The rain falls mainly in the autumn and winter. If you have a greenhouse, you must possess a tank with a capacity of 300 pt/150 l per square metre of greenhouse.

Spring water

Spring water can make good irrigation water. Often, however, it contains a large amount of iron, so that spraying with it turns everything brown in the course of time. Spring water may also contain salts harmful to plants. You must therefore have it tested annually by one of the soil research laboratories.

Tap water

Tap water can sometimes make good irrigation water, but often it is too hard and for warm dry periods, when plants consume a great deal of water, it may contain too many chlorine salts. Nor should irrigation water contain fluorine. Even so tap water is frequently the least bad alternative for supplementing rainwater, though the latter should be used as far as possible. It is possible, technically, to clean bad water, for example by means of reverse osmosis or by demineralization, decarbonization, iron removal and filtering.

Watering

Sprinkler system

In addition to normal watering with a can or, if the tap water is good, with a hose, a sprinkler system can be used in greenhouses or hothouses. The water is then sprayed over the plants via plastic pipes with spray nozzles. Although this 'sprinkling' is a natural form of watering, it sometimes creates problems with flowering plants. It must in any case always be ensured that the plants are dry at nightfall.

Volmatic

Use is also made in gardening of a system in which the plant is watered via thin hoses per individual pot. The so-called Volmatic system is sometimes difficult to operate for a collection of plants requiring different amounts of water.

Sub-irrigation

A much-used system is so-called 'sub-irrigation', in which a layer of river sand, or a so-called irrigation mat of compressed textile waste, is placed on a water-tight, horizontal sub-soil. The plants can take up water through the irrigated sand or mat. A disadvantage of this system is the oversalting of the top layer caused by the constantly rising flow of water. With this system the pot has to be watered generously at least once every two weeks, so that the dissolved salts are flushed out of the soil.

Rinse thoroughly

Instead of rinsing frequently in small amounts, it is better to rinse thoroughly on a single occasion after a longer interval. The water must not remain too long in the topmost layer of the pot, since this leads to oversalting.

Selection

Mass selection

In order to maintain the quality of a plant, selection is necessary. The quality of plant varieties can decline through virus diseases, mutations, or degeneration due to inbreeding.
With plants which are propagated from seed, the grower can apply mass selection, propagating the plants via some of the best individual plants from a restricted group. He grows the offspring *en masse* and does not know which were the mother or father plants. This method, in the most favourable cases, maintains the quality of a group of plants.

Single plant selection

Another method is single-plant selection, growing each offspring on separately from the parent plants. It is then possible to know which combination produced the best offspring.
With plants grown from seed single-plant selection is not simple, but the results are excellent. With plants which are propagated vegetatively, eg by cuttings, things are easier. The grower has simply to select from the external appearance of the plants. With a few exceptions (eg the variegated Sansevieria) the hereditary properties cause no problems. Commercial growers have then to apply single-plant selection and breed and classify the offspring by the parent plants.

Hybrid varieties

F1 hybrids

With many flowers grown from seed the range consists of hybrid varieties. They are sometimes called F1 hybrids or Heterosis Hybrids and are the result of much improvement work. They are distinguished by uniformity, growing power, profuseness of flowering and other favourable properties. The hybrids arise by first making specific parent lines 'pure' (homozygotic) by inbreeding. But since inbreeding causes degeneration, inbred lines, as little related as possible, are later crossed again. The offspring are then F1 hybrids, which surpass all ancestors. This improvement is the result of a remarkable phenomenon, the so-called 'heterosis effect', which unfortunately cannot yet be explained. The hybrids are not further cross-bred, for the properties of the ancestors would then be dissipated. Plants which are further cross-bred are called 'heterozygotic'. They are sometimes sterile, like Begonia Semperflorens hybrids; and sometimes they diverge, with the result that they show too much variation.

Expensive

In order to get a variety back, the cross with the specific parents must always be repeated. This improvement work requires a great deal of time. The seed of hybrid varieties is also very expensive, sometimes 100 times more expensive than that of non-hybrid varieties. Not every cross yields a good variety. Two parent lines are always grown, whereas there is only one group of plants which produces seed. The improvement is labour-intensive, because the stamens have to be removed from the seed plants (emasculation) and the pollination of the flowers has to be carried out by hand.

Propagation

Various methods

Plants can be propagated in various ways. They can be propagated by sexual or generative multiplication. The plants are then grown from seed. They can also be propagated non-sexually or

Information

vegetatively. Sections of the parent plant are then used to grow plants. The taking of cuttings and grafting, for example, are methods of vegetative propagation. Ferns and other spore plants are propagated by means of their spores. This is, in fact, another instance of sexual propagation, but the fertilization takes place not on the plant, but on the ground on a mossy layer called the prothallium.

Sexual or generative reproduction

This is a quick and generally not very expensive method of propagation, achieved by taking a large number of offspring from parent plants which are free from disease. It is not even an expensive method. Not even from the F1 hybrids, since much less disease is encountered with this method than with vegetative reproduction. The disadvantages of vegetative reproduction, too, are that one starts with a small plant and that natural variation makes it impossible to produce completely uniform plants. The F1 hybrids, on the other hand, yield completely uniform offspring.

Sowing soil

The ideal sowing soil consists of peat dust, river sand, lime and the required nutrient elements in small quantities. Young seedlings have small food requirements. The top layer of the sowing soil must be fine, especially for seeds with a small grain size. With a Begonia, for example, there are 50,000 - 70,000 seeds to the gram. They are therefore very small. The sowing soil must always remain sufficiently moist after the sowing. It is best to sow in a box of foam plastic (styropur), in which the soil dries out relatively slowly. Sow small amounts of seeds in pots.

Disinfecting

Before sowing disinfect the seeds with a 'mild' anti-mould agent (fungicide) in powder form. Captan, Zineb, Benlate or another agent can be used for this. The powder which does not stick to the seed must be screened out. If the seed is not disinfected, a fungicide can also be added to the irrigation water with which the sowing soil is moistened.

The sowing

Fine-grained seeds are usually 'broadcast'. This requires a strict routine. Usually too much seed gets into a box, which prevents the young plants from developing properly. Quite small plants then have to be set out individually. Sufficient space must therefore always be allowed for when sowing. A normal seed box will contain, depending on the plant, 250-1,000 seeds. Fine seeds can be mixed with powdered chalk to obtain more sowing volume. You can also practise sowing beforehand with some fine sand. Sowing on lines is simpler than sowing broadcast. The main thing is to leave sufficient space so that the seedlings can develop properly.

Covering

Do not cover fine seeds with earth. Cover coarser seeds with a layer of soil the thickness of the grain size. Some seeds must not be covered. These are the 'light germinators', which include, as indicated in the text of the book, the Primulas and Bromeliads. Coarser seeds, such as those of Cyclamen and Anthurium, should be placed at a regular distance, about ¾ in/2 cm, from each other in the sowing soil and covered with a layer of fine, sifted soil the thickness of the grain size. For sowing on a large scale, finer seeds are sometimes wrapped beforehand with a thin layer, so that they become bigger and uniform. This wrapped seed is known as 'pill seed' and can be sown mechanically. Cover seed boxes or pots with a glass or sheet of plastic sheeting to prevent drying out of the sowing soil. You will then not have to water the seeds before they have germinated.

Water, light and frost

Water carefully to make sure that the seeds are not washed away nor the young seedlings knocked over. As soon as the seeds have germinated, provide sufficient light in order to get sturdy young plants. The relative humidity must be high for good germination, in most cases 95% or higher. In addition each plant has an optimum germination temperature, which is given in this book for all seed plants. Under the most favourable circumstances the percentage of the seeds which germinate varies from 50% to 80%, but this high rate is difficult to achieve in practice.

Propagation from spores

Many Ferns are propagated by means of spores. The mature Fern plant forms spores by non-sexual means. The placing of the spores on the underside of the leaf determines the plant genus to which the Ferns belong. Some Ferns have both fertile leaves, on which the spores sit, and sterile (barren) leaves.

Sowing soil

Cut off the leaves from the parent plant when the spores are ripe, before they are due to fall. Then dry the leaf and wipe or brush the spores off. Sow the spores out in a humus-rich mixture. The soil must be clean and have a pH of about 6 (see page   for acid level). If the soil is too acid, the spores will not germinate. Place the humus-rich mixture, usually an RHP potting soil based on frozen peat, in a new styrofoam box. Sow ½-1 tsp/g of spores per box. The spores are light in weight and can remain suspended in the air for a long time. Different Fern species must therefore not be sown quickly one after the other in the same space — preferably not more than one species per day. The spores of Adiantum, in particular, spread easily. Keep the seed box in a seed bed at a soil temperature of 68° F/20° C and a relative humidity of approximately 90%.
The sowing soil must not dry out. Check this daily and water if necessary with good irrigation water at greenhouse temperature. Ferns are extremely salt-sensitive and they are also sensitive to many pesticides.

Prothallium

The spores will germinate in six to eight weeks. They then form a green mossy layer, called the prothallium. Female sex-organs (archegonia) and male sex-organs (antheridia) grow on the underside of the prothallium. The new Fern plant arises from the fertilization of these organs and the leaves of the Fern emerge.

Pricking out of Ferns

Two to three months after sowing the spores, place out individually pieces of the prothallium about ½ in²/1.5 cm² in size. During the pricking out set 270 pieces in a box. The young plants of most Ferns are grown from these pieces of prothallium.
With Asplenum nidus and the Harthorn fern, the clumps of the plants which have grown from the prothallium are distributed and pricked out again a number of times, until such time as a single plant is obtained. One seed box may well produce 15,000 to 20,000 plants. If the prothallium is not divided, about 1,500 plantlets are produced. Prick the plantlets out in frozen peat potting soil and grow them on at a temperature of 64-68° F/18-20° C and a relative humidity of 80-90%. Two to three months later they can be pricked out again, or they can be left for three to four months and then planted in a pot for cuttings. The temperature should then be adjusted according to the species of the fern. About six or seven months after potting up the fern will have grown into a handsome plant. Commercial growers accelerate growth by increasing the carbon dioxide content of the air to 0.15% (normally it is 0.03%). This is called CO_2 feeding.

Non-sexual or vegetative propagation

If plants do not form seed, or do not come back as pure plants from the seed, apply non-sexual propagation. The advantages are that the plant remains a genuine variety and is very large from the beginning. On the other hand, it is an expensive method. In addition, all diseases, such as viral infections, are transferred from the parent plant to the young plant; so are any parasites present, such as red spider mite or aphid. The principle of this method of propagation is that you always start with a section of the plant, for example a leaf, a bud or a shoot. Vegetative propagation also occurs in nature, by tubers, bulbs and rootstocks and by division or suckers.

Bulbs and tubers

With perennial bulbs, those of Hippeastrum for example, propagation is a lengthy business. In order to stimulate the formation of young bulbs, these bulbs receive special treatments. One treatment is called 'crossing-out', in which the receptacle is hollowed out, thus destroying the main bud. The side-buds then grow up into young bulbs. The bulbs may also be divided into small pieces, a process called 'scaling'. Little bulbs then appear on the edges of the scales (ie a form of leaf cutting).

Tubers usually form during the growing season, one strong new tuber and several smaller ones (cormlets).

Tubers of Cyclamen, tuberous Begonias and some other tuberous plants do not form young tubers, because the tuber grows out of the bottom part of the stem of a seedling. This stem section is called the 'hypocotyl axis' and it forms no side-buds, only terminal buds.

Cuttings

A cutting is a cut-off or broken-off part of a plant which has the ability to form roots. Growth hormones, which are called auxins, stimulate the formation of roots. There are various forms of cutting, some of which have to be used specifically for specific plants. The best type, or types, of cutting for each individual plant is given in the text of this book.

Shoot cutting

A shoot cutting is also called a tip or head cutting. And if part of the mother plant, or 'heel', remains attached to the cutting, the term 'heel cutting' is often used.

Many plants, such as Azaleas and Chrysanthemums, are propagated by means of shoot cuttings. Break the cutting off or cut it off with a sharp knife in order to keep the wound tissue as undamaged as possible. If a knife can transfer virus diseases, as it can, for example, with Geraniums, it is better to break the cutting off with your hands. The length of the cutting, the time for taking cuttings, and the cutting temperature for each plant are given in the text. The best soil in which to place the cutting, the so-called cutting medium, is also given there.

Intermediate cutting

An intermediate cutting is a section of stem without top, with two or more leaves. These intermediate cuttings are taken from plants with long stems, such as Cissus and Hedera. A large number of cuttings can often be cut from a single mother plant by means of intermediate cuttings.

Eye cutting

An eye cutting is a cutting of a small stem section with a single leaf and a bud in the leaf axil, which grows up into a new plant.

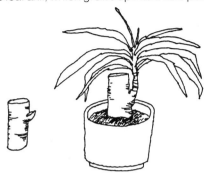

Stem cutting

The difference between an intermediate cutting and a stem cutting is that a stem cutting has no leaves; instead it has dormant buds on a piece of stem.

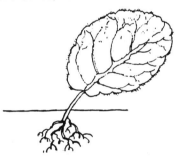

Leaf cutting

Leaf cuttings are taken from plants on which the leaf has the ability to form roots and accidental buds (adventitious buds). Sometimes a whole leaf cutting can be taken, as in the case of Saintpaulia. The leaf stalk then forms roots and the young plants will grow on the leaf stalk. With other plants, such as leaf Begonias, take pieces of leaf about ¾in²/2 cm². Roots, and later young plants, will then grow on the wounds of the nerves.

Root cutting

Some succulents, such as Papavers, are propagated by means of root cuttings. This method is not used for houseplants.

Layering

Layering is a propagation method which is much used with trees and shrubs, including a fruit tree which is also grown as a houseplant, Citrus varieties or Ornamental Chinese Orange. The method is also

Information

easy to use with other plants. Take a somewhat longer stem and fix it halfway into the ground. Bend the tip up into a vertical position as far as possible. In the course of time, depending on the plant, the stem will form roots in the ground. When there are sufficient of them, the new plant can be detached from the mother plant. Layering is a good method for an enthusiast who wants to propagate an individual plant which is difficult to propagate by other means.

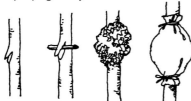

Ringing

Ringing is a method of propagation, and it is also a way of getting the top section of a plant which has grown too high to root. After this the plant is cut off below the rooting point.

With ringing, make some incisions in the bark of the stem at the desired point. The incisions must in no circumstances completely circle the stem, because then the sap stream in the plant will be interrupted. The incisions result in congealed cuts. Place on the wound a sizeable piece of moist peat moss. Wrap plastic sheeting round this peat moss to prevent drying out and tie the whole up firmly. Roots will now grow on the wound. When sufficient roots have formed, cut the new plant off from the bottom part of the stem. The old stem will continue to grow and can again provide a fine plant. Ringing is a form of plant rejuvenation and is also a way of shortening a plant which is too high.

Limiting vaporization

Cuttings vaporize water, but they have no roots for absorbing sufficient water again from the cutting medium. In order to limit the vaporization and thereby prevent drying out, cover the cuttings with glass, plastic sheeting or paper. These methods are not always fully effective and they take up time. For the amateur this is not so important, but for the enthusiast with a large greenhouse or hothouse filled with many plants, mist propagation is a better method. One requires for this a special spraying system by which very finely atomized water is distributed over the cuttings. The mist-spraying nozzles must not let through more than 2pt/1 litre of water per minute. The mist is automatically controlled by electric pulses via a sensor. If the leaf dries out too much, the sprinkler comes on; if the leaf and the sensor have become wet, the sprinkler is turned off. It is also possible to control the sprinkler with a meter or a time-switch. The advantages of mist propagation are obvious. The leaf never becomes flabby, because it is covered with a thin layer of water and therefore cannot dry out. The tissue temperatue of the leaf falls as heat is lost by the evaporation of the water and the respiration is thereby reduced, so that the cutting uses less stand-by food and is stronger. The cuttings can normally stand in the full daylight and thereby become more vigorous.

Mould-attack (mold) is completely absent because the mould (mold) spores are washed from the leaf. More cuttings are saved and the method is less time-consuming than with other methods. With mist propagation water of exceptional quality is required.

Grafting takes place non-sexually

Use grafting or propagation by means of rootstock with plants which cannot be propagated by other means. Grafting can also be used for better growth, especially for Roses, or for better cropping, as with fruit trees. Graft and rootstock must be related; otherwise the tissues will reject each other.

Rootstocks are plants with a root which is simple and cheap to grow from seed. Often they are botanical (natural) species, such as Rosa canina, the Dog Rose which normally grows in the wild.

Sometimes the plants which are used as rootstocks are propagated by means of cuttings. This is the case, for example, with Azalea and

some Cacti. With grafting, make a cut in the rootstock and the graft of the plant you want to grow, so that the cambium layers of rootstock and graft can come into contact with each other. The cambium is a layer of growth situated between the bark and the inner tissue of a stem. From this layer there is formed one edge with new stem tissue and an outer edge with new bark tissue. If the two cambium layers of related plants come into contact with each other, there arises a new common cambium tissue which is of irregular structure.

Grafting with cut-off twig

Grafting plants the rootstock and the graft of which are equally thick is called 'whip-and-tongue' grafting. For this type of grafting, the graft and the rootstock are cut off cleanly in the same direction. Place them against each other and fix them together by tying or another form of fixing, taking care not to damage the bark. Whip-and-tongue grafting is much used with Azaleas and Cacti.

Side-setting and cleft-grafting

Azaleas can also be grafted by means of 'side-setting'. With this grafting method the top of the rootstock is retained. An incision is made in the bark at the side.

Pare the graft cleanly and tie it on to the cambium tissue in the incision made in the bark. If, with Cacti, the rootstock is thicker than the graft, use cleft-grafting. With this method, the graft is pared cleanly on two sides. The rootstock is split and the graft slid into the opering in such a way that the cambium layers of graft and rootstock fit closely against each other, so that they can grow together.

Vitroculture

New development

Vitroculture is the growing of plants in propagating tubes, on a nutrient medium which corresponds to the food contained in the plant cell. It is a new development in the propagation of plants and in the combating of certain virus diseases, especially those afflicting Chrysanthemums, Carnations and Freesias.

Vitroculture is used for the propagation of Gerberas, Freesias, Anthuriums, Bromeliaceae and other plants. With vitroculture a young plant is grown from a small piece of a mother plant, whether a piece of leaf stalk, a leaf, a part of the receptacle, a bud or a piece of rootstock (rhizome). The piece of plant is placed in a test-tube on a nutrient medium. And with the aid of certain hormones and growth promoting substances a young plant is produced.

For the growing of virus-free plants, individual cells of the growing point (meristem) of a plant are used. With Orchids the meristem does not directly form a plant, but makes a lump of tissue (protocorm). This protocorm can be divided about once a month. In theory it is possible to grow from one growing point more than 1,000,000 young plants in a year. In practice this does not happen. As a rule, 500 to 1,000 offspring are grown from one growing point, in order to prevent mutations.

Growth regulators

Growing, flowering and inhibiting

In the 1930s Professor Went discovered a substance in the tips of germinating oat plants which stimulated the rooting of plants. Since then scientists have discovered increasing numbers of substances which influence the life processes of plants.

They are called growth regulators and are added in small quantities. Their effect can be compared with that of hormones. In most cases the substances are of vegetable origin. The use of growth regulators is increasing, because more and more is being learnt of their effects. There are regulators which stimulate growth and there are inhibitors.

Growth hormones

These substances act in very low concentrations, for example 0.1%. There are three effective growth hormones, from which a choice has to be made for each species of plant:

Indolebutyric acid,
Indoleacetic acid is the weakest growth hormone,
Naphthylacetic acid is the strongest growth hormone.

Root formation on cuttings

For the taking of cuttings, a layer of growth hormone is placed in a dish and the cuttings with the wound tissue are dipped in the powder. Then the excess powder is scraped off and the cuttings are placed in the soil. The concentration of growth hormone depends, among other things, on the hardness of the cutting. Soft herbaceous cuttings receive a lower concentration than harder woody ones. For cuttings of woody plants, the growth hormone tablets are dissolved in water. The cuttings absorb the growth hormone into the wound tissue. Conifers are also dipped in a growth hormone solution of this kind. The powder method is the best and most simple method for flower-growing.

Prevention of bud-drop

Pot plants such as Bougainvillea can, with a change of climate, form crack tissue and then reject their flowers. If they are moved, for example from the greenhouse into the house, they drop their flowers and buds. To prevent this, you can dip the whole plant in a growth hormone based on naphthylacetic acid. The solution must be allowed to dry on the plant as rapidly as possible.

Advancing flowering

In order to advance the flowering of Bromeliads and to spread it over the whole year, these plants are treated with ethylene-based substances. How this works is described in this book under the treatment of Bromeliads.

Inhibitors

Substances such as Alar, Cyclocel, CCC, chlormequat and Fosfon D (used only with Chrysanthemums) have the ability to inhibit the upward growth of plants. The cell tension decreases, the plant stays more compact, the leaves turn dark-green in colour and the plant switches from vegetative growth (stalks and leaves) to generative growth (flowers). The substance, therefore, not only has an inhibiting effect on the upward growth, but a stimulating one on flower initiation. This last effect is very important with Azaleas and Seringias. The agent Fosfon D is sometimes mixed with the potting soil of pot Chrysanthemums. The other agents are sprayed over the leaves. During and after spraying the relative humidity must be high in order to prevent leaf discoloration.

Hydroculture (hydroponics)

Growing in water

The principle of hydroculture is that the plant does not grow in earth, but in water in which the nutritive salts are dissolved. Plants require less tending when grown in hydroculture. Hydroculture has therefore made great strides in the growing of plants in buildings. A special pot or box with an inner pot, the so-called culture pot, is required. Most boxes are made of plastic and they are often expensive.

Special fertilizers

A special fertilizer is required for hydroculture. Many liquid, low-concentration fertilizers are available, though they are very expensive. Nor are the so-called ion-exchangers (a sort of battery with nutrients) cheap. The best fertilizer to use is Solufeed, which is formulated specially for this purpose. Use a solution of 1 tsp per pt water/2 g per litre. Good water, above all low in salt, must be used. The pot should contain 2 in/5 cm of water for good growth and this level must be maintained as far as possible by re-filling. Depending on the evaporation rate, do this once a week or once every two to three weeks. The nutrient solution must be renewed every two to three months in order to prevent oversalting. For reading the water level you need a water-level gauge, usually a plastic tube 1 in/2.5 cm in diameter, in which a float indicates the water level. To enable the correct level to be read off, you must ensure that the bottom edge of the meter is level with the bottom edge of the inner pot. Use as

substrate fired and expanded clay or synthetic granules which also provide a good supply of oxygen, and allow the roots to breathe.

Different roots

The roots of hydroplants are different in structure from those of plants which grow in the ground. You must therefore choose for hydroculture plants which are grown as hydroplants. If you use another plant, the plant has to form new roots which can grow in water. The old roots will be redundant, leading to delayed growth. *Any* plant can be used for hydroculture, provided it is cultivated as a hydroplant.

Plants with a short flowering time, such as Cyclamens, will not often be seen as hydroplants. But in technical terms there is no reason why they should not be. In general the plants used for hydroculture are those which keep their decorative value for a long time, foliage plants such as Ficus benjamina.

Climate

Light

The climate in the greenhouse or in the house determines to a considerable degree the rate of growth of plants. The climate is determined by a number of closely interrelated factors. The most important is the light, for the simple reason that light is the form of energy which enables the leaves of the plant to convert carbon dioxide from the air into structural elements and oxygen by the process of photosynthesis. Light comes directly from the sun and if the sunlight becomes stronger, the temperature rises. The heat requirement of a plant is therefore dependent on the amount of light which shines on it. Light is therefore *the* critical factor for plants. The amount of light or radiation energy is expressed and measured in joules per cm². This amount can vary greatly according to the season. For example, the radiation energy in late summer may be some 2,200 joules per cm², on a dark day in late winter only 107. Only part of this energy reaches the plant. In a greenhouse at least 30% is lost through the glass and the structure of the greenhouse. In the house this loss is even greater.

Part of the energy is used by the plants for the vaporizing of water via the leaves, whereby the tissue temperature falls. The remainder is used by the chlorophyll of the plant for photosynthesis.

Temperature

The temperature which is suitable for a plant is not therefore a set value: with more light the temperature may be higher than with a small amount of light. High temperatures with little light — for example, in winter — produce weak, flabby growth.

Relative humidity

The relative humidity (RH) of the air gives the percentage of water which is present in the air for a particular temperature. Every plant needs a particular relative humidity for good growth. Each growing stage also requires a particular RH. A non-rooted cutting, for example, or germinating seed requires an RH of 95%, whereas a plant whose seed is ripening will prefer one of 50%.

If the temperature falls, the RH rises. This can be illustrated by the case of grass, which is wet on a summer morning when the temperature is low, and dry when the temperature rises. In the late summer and autumn some difficulties may arise in greenhouses when the RH rises too much while the temperature stays low. Flowers can spoil then. In sunlight in the winter, a low RH can also occasionally cause problems, while in the house a low RH always has a harmful effect.

Humidity of the soil

The humidity of the soil has a great influence on the humidity of the air and thus on the RH. The moisture which evaporates in the soil withdraws heat from the soil, with the result that the temperature falls. During hot weather, therefore, spray the soil and the paths in the greenhouse in order to lower the temperature and increase the humidity.

Information

Ventilation

When the temperature in the greenhouse rises too high, you can ventilate. This ventilation has in turn an effect on the RH and the humidity of the soil. In order to prevent a build-up of mould, care must be exercised in ventilating. You must always ventilate in good time, before the temperature has risen too high, ie as soon as you suspect that it will shortly be necessary, and in this you must be guided mainly by the sun.

Carbon dioxide (CO_2) is an essential component of the air for plants. During photosynthesis, which is sometimes called carbon dioxide assimilation, the green leaf obtains oxygen and sugars (carbohydrates) from CO_2 under the influence of light as an energy source.

The air normally contains 0.03% CO_2. For stronger growth you can raise this percentage to 0.15-0.30%.

About an hour before it becomes light, start to add CO_2 to the air and finish at 11 or 12 am. In sunny weather you can stop slightly later. CO_2 can be added from cylinders, though this is not suitable for small areas.

In large greenhouses the CO_2 content is increased by the burning of natural gas or propane gas or by a central system from the heater. CO_2 can also be obtained by burning petroleum. A disadvantage of this is the rather unpleasant smell; it is better to use methylated spirit. Growth can be greatly improved by adding CO_2 to the air. The amount used varies per plant. The best results are obtained during vegetative growth.

CO_2, in the concentration used, is harmless to human beings and animals.

Heating

Heating, of course, plays a major part in controlling the temperature of a greenhouse. Strong radiant heat must be avoided: heating by a stove, in particular, causes quite a few problems. Heating is very expensive in a small greenhouse. In a normal greenhouse about 100-250 ft^3/30-85 m^3 of natural gas are required per yd^2/m^2 greenhouse area per year. The amount depends, of course, on the temperature desired. The smaller the greenhouse, the greater the required amount of natural gas per yd^2/m^2 surface area. One cubic metre of natural gas corresponds to 0.93 litres of petroleum or 0.82 kilo of fuel oil. For soil heating you can make use of a special plastic coil. The water temperature in the coil must not be higher than 104° F/40° C; higher temperatures will damage the roots and the plant. Soil heating has a higher yield than pipe heating overhead or along the walls. The pipes lose a great deal of heat through radiation on to the cold walls.

Screening

Sometimes the amount of light (radiation energy) is too great for certain plants. Screening is then needed in greenhouses. In the house the choice of position of the plant is a useful means of control. Screening from the light is provided in order to prevent excessively high temperatures and a drop in RH. The evaporation is then not too strong and the plant does not scorch. There are plants which require less light because they grow in the wild in a shady spot. Most Ferns, for example, come originally from a forest environment. Screening removes 50-65% of the strongest daylight. It is best to screen with plastic sheets which do not remove more than 65% of the light. In addition to acting as a screen, plastic exercises a useful role in winter by limiting the radiation of heat. If you apply the screen in the evening and remove it again in the morning, you wil make savings of 25-30% on fuel.

Growers sometimes have curtains of screenig material which are operated automatically by means of a light meter or, in the winter months, by a time-switch.

You can also screen in a greenhouse by painting lime or silicate-containing agents on to the glass. One kilo of these agents can screen 30-40 yd^2/m^2 of glass. A modern agent which remains opaque while dry, but becomes translucent when wet allows more light through in dark rainy weather.

Colours of the light

Light normally appears to our eyes as white, but it is actually composed of all the colours of the rainbow: red, orange, yellow, green, blue and violet. Light is a sort of wave movement and each separate colour has its own wavelength, which is expressed in nanometres (a nanometre is a millionth of a millimetre). Red light has the biggest wavelength: 780 nm (nanometres). Violet has the smallest: 380 nm. Yellow-green colours, around 555 nm, are the easiest for our eyes to observe.

Effect of the colours

Red light has a 'stretching' effect on plants. This light is important for photosynthesis, because carbon dioxide is converted to oxygen and carbon compounds, from which fats and proteins are produced in the plant, together with mineral substances which are absorbed by the roots. Red light sometimes also has a great influence on flowering, for example with Carnations. Green and blue light give a more compact growth and have an influence on the shape of the plant. The plant needs all the visible colours of light, ie those with a wavelength of 380-780 nm, for balanced growth.

Photoperiodicity

Day-length

In the wild every plant is exposed to daylight for a certain number of hours a day. The number of hours is determined by the season and the distance of the region where the plant grows from the equator. This time is called the day-length and it is critical for the formation of growth regulators in the plant. The *amount* of light is less important than the *period* (length of time) for which the plant is exposed to it. The growth regulators in a plant determine whether a plant will set flowers or remain growing vegetatively (forming stems and leaves). Because houseplants come from different parts of the world, they are classified by groups according to the influence of the day-length.

Short-day

There are short-day plants which set flowers with a day-length of less than 12 hours. These are plants which by nature flower in the autumn or winter, such as the Chrysanthemum, the Christmas Star and Kalanchöe. In practice, commercial growers bring these plants into flower at whatever time they wish, by giving them a short-day treatment artificially, ie shortening the day to 8 or 10 hours. The period of this treatment varies according to the plant. With Chrysanthemums, for example, the variety 'Dramatic' flowers after eight weeks of short-day treatment, whereas the variety 'Japannerin' needs 14 weeks. For this artificial short-day commercial growers darken the room in which the plants are growing with black plastic foil .02 mm thick. The maximum light transmission is 0.1%. They usually darken from five o'clock in the afternoon to seven or eight o'clock the following morning. This darkening can be operated by a time-switch.

Long-day

There are plants which set flowers with a day-length of more than 12 hours. These are long-day plants which flower naturally in the summer, for example the Star of Bethlehem. For the flowering of these plants commercial growers lengthen the day to 14 or 15 hours. By artificial long-day treatment the flowering of plants which flower in the summer can be advanced into the spring. This long-day treatment can also be given to short-day plants to get them to grow vegetatively.

Assimilation lighting

This is a strong lighting with a high installed power which greatly promotes photosynthesis, or carbon dioxide assimilation. This lighting is used only when a large number of plants can be given light together per surface unit. This is the case, for example, with seedlings and cuttings, and with the advancing of lilies; otherwise the costs are too high.

The amount of light energy required varies according to the plant. A Chrysanthemum, for example, requires a radiation energy of only

3,500 mW, while a Sinningia (Gloxinia) requires 10,000 mW. (A tomato requires as much as 45,000 mW for good growth.) These powers are all per square metre. Lamps with a high rating are used — high-pressure mercury, mercury iodide or sodium lamps with a rating of 375 to 400 Watt. These lamps, with their attached pre-switching units, are very expensive. It is therefore important that as much light as possible is trained on the plants. Lamps with a built-in reflector are therefore often used. This is indicated by an R in the lamp specification.

Hanging height
The hanging height is determined by the desired power per square metre. If the lamp is hung twice as high, the lamp will light four times the surface area and the light intensity will then become four times less. Lamps which transmit a large amount of heat in addition to light must not be hung too high. Incandescent lamps, for example, must always remain at a distance of 3-3½ ft/1-1.2 m from the plant. A TL tube, on the other hand, can safely be suspended 20 in/50 cm above the plant.

Indifferent plants
There are plants, such as the Rose and the Cyclamen, on whom the day-length has no effect, neither on their growth nor on their flowering. These are indifferent or daylight-neutral plants. Many of them come from regions near the equator, where the day-length is almost constant at 12 hours.

Long-day treatment
The best results are obtained if the plant is given light as a nightly interruption. Start, for example, in the evening just on 11 o'clock, not when it gets dark, and continue for so long as is necessary to achieve the desired day-length. In early autumn this may be only one hour a night; in winter it may be as much as eight hours.
In order to economize on electricity, cyclical lighting is used in commercial plant growing. The required number of hours of lighting are not provided continuously, but only for a certain period, or cycle. Thus Chrysanthemums get a lighting cycle of 6 minutes light during the first 30 minutes (the percentage lighting time is then 20%), after which they get 24 minutes of no light followed by another 6 minutes of light. The grower then refers to 'lighting with frequency 2', ie with two periods of lighting per hour. The results from this abbreviated lighting are exactly the same as those achieved by continuous lighting. If incandescent lamps are used, the required radiation level for a long-day treatment is low (7-20 Watt installed power per square metre). With short-day plants, such as Begonias or Chrysanthemums, which are given light for vegetative growth, incandescent lamps are suitable. For long-day plants which are lighted for advancing flowering, TL33 lamps are often used. These lamps give a beautiful compact growth. Incandescent lamps give lots of red light and no blue light. Plants under incandescent lamps, therefore, do not stretch.

Radiation strength
The strength of the light is often stated by the installed power in Watt per yd²/m². When, for example, incandescent lamps are used for the lighting of winter-flowering Begonias, a power of 7 Watt per yd²/m² is required. If TL 33 is used, a power of 3 Watt per yd²/m² is quite sufficient. This method is quite usable in practice if you know both the energy required for the plant and the lamp specification. The light intensity is also given in lux. A lux is one lumen of luminous flux distributed uniformly over one square metre. But a 'lumen' is used for the light which is visible to our eyes, and the plant also reacts to light which is invisible to us, such as infra-red light.
The quantity of lumens can vary greatly. For example, the light intensity in the direct sun on a summer day may well be 100,000 lumens, while in the shade it is only 10,000 lumens.
The best method is to give the radiation energy in milliwatt per square yard/metre (mW per yd²/m²). This is the amount of energy which the plant receives from the band with a wavelength of 380-750 nanometres. The radiation requirement varies greatly according to

the plant and the effect sought. A Chrysanthemum requires for vegetative growth during the long-day treatment only 300 mW per yd²/m², but for assimilation lighting, ie for strong growth, 3,500 mW per yd²/m²; for strong growth a Gloxinia needs as much as 10,000 mW per yd²/m². The energy requirement for many plants is known. When it is, it is given for each plant in the text of this book.

Incandescent lamps
The choice of lamp is determined by the purpose of the lighting. For plants which do not stretch too much, the incandescent lamp can be highly suitable. It is true that it has a low light output (only 7% of the absorbed electricity is converted into light, the remaining 93% into heat), but the bulb is cheap and it is available with a built-in reflector. The lamp is not suitable for assimilation lighting, however, owing to its low output. A large part of the light of the incandescent lamp is red and contains no blue light, so that it has a powerful stretching effect. For houseplants the hanging height is 3-3½ ft/1-1.2 m above the plant.

TL tube
The TL tube or fluorescent lamp does not, thanks to the predominant blue colour, give a beautiful effect. The Number 33, which is usually used in commercial flower growing, gives a particularly chilly, blueish light. For use in the house it is therefore better to use softer lighting. The TL tube has a high light output. Number 33, for example, the one with the highest output, gives 23% light. For plant irradiation, 40W and 65W lamps are mainly used. With the TL 33, 27 Watt per yd²/m² must be installed for a radiation strength of 3,000 mW per yd²/m².

Combined lighting
A good lighting system for houseplants is a combination of incandescent lamps and TL lamps in one fitting. The incandescent lamps then give you 100 Watt per yd²/m² and the TL tubes 40 Watt per yd²/m² If you light with this lamp combination for 12 to 16 hours, the plants remain in good condition without daylight.

160 WL lamp
The 160 WL lamp is a mixed lamp with a built-in reflector specially made for the lighting of houseplants. A special round cylindrical cap is made for this lamp, type MDK 051. The hanging height is 3 ft/1m above the plants. Under this lamp the plants show their beautiful colours and they remain in good condition. The light intensity is 700 lux measured on the plant.

Great power
For assimilation lighting lamps with a high power are used (375-400 Watt), because it is not easy for incandescent lamps and TL tubes to deliver so much power per square metre. The light output varies from 11% for the high-pressure mercury lamp to 27% for the high-pressure sodium lamp. The installed power is dependent on the required radiation strength. This strength can be controlled by the hanging height and the distance of the lamps. The super-high-pressure mercury lamp, with a power of 400 Watt, delivers 3,000 mW per yd²/m². If you light with this lamp combination for 12 to 16 hours,

Growing activities

Topping
When topping a plant, take a tip of the plant so that the plant will branch and become bigger. The topping time usually has an

Information

influence on the flowering. A small growing point is usually topped, whereby the plant develops better and more uniformly. Topping must not be carried out in the darker months, when plants do not grow so well and the quality of the side-shoots is not so good.

With some plants the effects of topping can be achieved simply by setting a large number of plants in one pot.

Pinching out
Pinching out is the removal of superfluous side-shoots or buds. With Azalea flower buds, for instance, the young leaf shoots must be pinched out.

Redundant leaf shoots must not be removed when they are still young, because then they will start growing again before the flower is mature. Flower buds are also sometimes removed from the leaf axils. The main flower bud will then be bigger. Remove superfluous shoots as well. This is called shoot selection.

Supporting or tying-up
Train plants with climbing or twisting stems along wire bows or plastic frames. This is done, for example, with Stephanotis and Hoya. By so doing you are helping the plant, whose stems and tendrils would otherwise become entangled.

Thunbergia (Black-eyed Susan) is particularly prone to this. Support plants which have hanging or insufficiently strong stems with wire pins. In some cases tie the stems to the pins. This applies particularly to Begonias. A cotton framework is sometimes wound round the pins, notably with Star of Bethlehem.

Plant protection

Diseases and pests
Houseplants are susceptible to many diseases and pests. You must be in a position to prevent attacks by the latter as far as possible by ensuring the best possible growing conditions and by growing varieties which have a sturdy resistance to a particular disease. With houseplants one cannot count upon the natural balance, which has already been disturbed by man.

Biological control of diseases and pests may be better from a moral point of view, but at the moment these methods offer only limited possibilities. In some cases, therefore, you will have to have recourse to chemical pesticides. But these chemical controls must be restricted to urgent cases, when no other solution is possible.

Safety
All chemical agents are toxic and must be handled with the greatest care. The use of them is governed by law. They must be kept in a locked cupboard bearing the word 'Poison' and marked with a skull-and-crossbones. Leaky packaging material must not be discarded. Where necessary, suitable clothing, rubber gloves and a gas-mask, must be worn. When working with pesticides, you must not smoke, eat or drink.

After working with pesticides, you must take a shower, using plenty of soap and water. If there are any symptoms of poisoning, consult a doctor immediately and show him the original packaging, which will give the name of the poison, and enable him to prescribe the antidote. Once again: use pesticides only when it is absolutely necessary. In many countries, additional safety precautions apply;

consult the agricultural authorities if in doubt.

Pesticides
Aphids can often be successfully washed from the plant by spraying strongly with water. Scale insects can be washed from the plant with a small brush. For this, use a solution of 2 fl oz methylated spirit per pt water/100 ml per litre.

Prevent red spider mite and other mites by maintaining a sufficiently high relative humidity. Infection by mites can be combated by spraying the underside of the leaves with a strong jet of water and dislodging the parasites. Many pesticides are applied in aerosol form. Certain agents are available as fumigants in powder or tablet form. The use of these is very simple. Some agents are also available as dusting powder, which is also simple to use, so long as you possess a good duster.

Sprayed substances usually work best and are the least expensive. The agent is dissolved in water and the solution is finely spread over the whole plant. But take the necessary precautions.

Nomenclature

Three names
Popular names are often confusing and sometimes give a wrong impression of the plant. For instance, the Mock Orange is a member of the potato family and not a citrus fruit. It is therefore best to use the scientific names, which can cause no misunderstandings about which plant is meant. There are, of course, exceptions. There are plants which are so well known by their popular names that even the experts use them. Apart from the 'trade', hardly anyone says Pelargonium instead of Geranium or Rhododendron instead of Azalea.

There is also more than one Children-on-Mother's-Lap plant, although this plant is also incorrectly called Brother Plant. The scientific name is therefore always better.

The scientific name usually consists of two, sometimes three, parts, the first part usually being of Greek or Latin origin and the second part of Latin origin. The generic name is the first name of a plant. It is usually a substantive noun and is always written with a capital letter. The species name is the second name of a plant. This is often an adjective and is written with a small letter. The species name of a hybrid is an exception here, since this is written with a capital letter, for example Begonia Semperflorens Hybrid.

The variety name, also sometimes called culture variety (CV), is the third name of the plant. By no means every plant has one. Older variety names are often of Latin origin and refer to a property of the plant, for example, Variegata (variegated) or Pendula (hanging). The third name is always written with a capital letter, whether it is a Latin name or not. The name is written between quotation marks, as in Cyclamen persicum 'Beacon-light'.

'Botanical varieties' are also known. These are forms of plants occurring in the wild which differ from the original species. These variety names are written with a small letter. A red-flowering Water lily, for example, of which the original species has white flowers, is called Nymphea odorata var. rubra.

One advantage of using scientific names is that one knows immediately that certain plants are related. Plants with certain properties regarding flower shape are combined into families in plant classification, the science of which is called taxonomy. The naming of plants is based on the binary nomenclature which Linnaeus invented in the 18th century.

While every effort has been made to ensure that the chemical compounds mentioned in this book are readily available, legislation in some localities may prohibit the use of certain chemicals or limit it to professional horticulturists. If in doubt, consult your local agricultural research station, or an agrochemicals manufacturer, who can suggest suitable substitutes.

Index